COOK'S
FREESTYLE
CUISINE

EDITED BY JUDITH HILL
AND JUDITH SUTTON

ILLUSTRATIONS BY STEPHEN KELEMEN

Simon and Schuster · *New York*

Published by Simon and Schuster
A Division of Simon & Schuster, Inc.
Simon & Schuster Building
Rockefeller Center
1230 Avenue of the Americas
New York, New York 10020

SIMON AND SCHUSTER and colophon are registered trademarks of Simon & Schuster, Inc.

Designed by Irving Perkins Associates, Inc.
Manufactured in the United States of America

1 3 5 7 9 10 8 6 4 2

Library of Congress Cataloging in Publication Data
Cook's freestyle cuisine.

Includes index.
1. Cookery.   2. Menus.   I. Hill, Judith.
II. Sutton, Judith.   III. Cook's magazine.   IV. Title: Freestyle cuisine.
TX715.C7856 1986   641.5   86-17824
ISBN: 0-671-62007-X

COOK'S Magazine gratefully acknowledges use of Paul Prudhomme's
Oyster and Artichoke Soup recipe. Copyright © 1985 by Paul Prudhomme.

ACKNOWLEDGMENTS

As many people are responsible for this book as work on *COOK'S* magazine—and more. We gratefully acknowledge the many recipe contributors who are mentioned either in headnotes to the recipes themselves or in the credits at the back of the book. They are all important contributors to the magazine as well as to this book. Several members of staff developed recipes for the book, too, as well as helping in many other ways, including most especially *COOK'S* food editor Pamela Parseghian, along with her staff, assistant food editors Melanie Barnard and Brooke Dojny and recipe tester Amy Manny, and also our director of food styling, Beverly Cox.

We thank co-editor Judith Sutton for heroic work on a tight schedule and both Sheila Lowenstein and Mary Caldwell for constant editorial support. Special appreciation goes to Donna Schaefer, copy editor and chief right-hand person. Thanks also to Shirley Lantz, who pulled the recipes together from their original form.

Barbara Ensrud contributed wine recommendations, and art director Sara Barbaris was responsible for all the beautiful photographs, along with our photographers listed in the credits at the end of the book. This cookbook is clearly a *COOK'S* magazine "family project," and we all extend thanks to Carole Lalli, our editor at Simon & Schuster, for helping to make it possible.

—Christopher Kimball, Publisher
Judith Hill, Editor-in-Chief

Contents

Introduction

Freestyle Cuisine—Interchangeable Courses Explained

Our dining style is loosening up. The once hard-and-fast progression from soup to nuts is no longer de rigueur. Soup isn't just for starters; salad needn't be a luncheon-only item. Contemporary meals more and more frequently include several dishes of equal importance that can be switched from course to course at the discretion of the cook or the diner.

Many restaurants are de-emphasizing their main courses and supplementing previously thin appetizer offerings so that the distinction between the two is becoming fuzzier—sometimes even vanishing completely. Because restaurants are the pioneers in this new style of eating, many of the recipes in this book come from professional chefs, but that doesn't mean the dishes are difficult to make—quite the contrary. In fact, the proportion of quick dishes—salads, pastas, stir-fries, sandwiches—is higher here than in any other cookbook we've seen other than those written specifically as quick-and-easy collections. This is because the new interchangeable courses are a response to public demand for simple, lighter food that can be put together in a variety of ways and still be as satisfying as the more complex traditional menus— menus that simply no longer suit our harried but less physically active lives.

At many new restaurants, it's quite acceptable to order simply a salad followed by a soup or just an hors d'oeuvre and a dessert. Variety and satisfaction without overfill are the obvious rewards of this style—a "modular" system with interchangeable courses. The elaborate French-restaurant *dégustation* menu offering sample-size portions of many specialties is the clear forerunner of this eating style, now scaled down for everyday practicality.

We propose to bring the new freestyle home. For family dining or casual entertaining, the use of interchangeable courses can simplify and consolidate culinary energy. All of the recipes in this book, except the desserts, can be used as either a first or second course; many can be paired to make one substantial course. Producing two or three compatible dishes and presenting them in whatever order suits you can be easier than planning a first course and a traditional meat dish surrounded with the customary sauce, starch, vegetable, and garnish. And it can be at least as satisfying to have two important dishes as one main dish with satellite courses and side dishes. One reason that these somewhat smaller courses are the order of the day is that fewer people want a large quantity of meat as the feature attraction anymore, and we include a whole chapter of vegetable dishes that are substantial enough to serve on their own at any point in the meal.

Many of the recipes in this book provide a virtual mini-dinner including a bit of protein, starch, and vegetable all in one dish, but with the different flavors and textures much more distinct than those in the casseroles popular a couple of decades ago. The dishes are, therefore, exceptionally useful for one-dish, weeknight suppers as well as for interchangeable parts in the new free, modular cuisine.

The recipes here can be arranged, rearranged, and interchanged in endless menu possibilities. The menus suggested in the chapters will get you started. They also address the challenge of matching wines with these new menus. The usual light-white to full-red progression doesn't always work, and so we called on our wine expert, Barbara Ensrud, to make suggestions, which we think you'll consider innovative and interesting solutions. Often one wine works throughout for more casual meals.

A Note on the Recipes

The recipe methods are divided into sections, most commonly PREPARATION, COOKING, and SERVING. The steps listed under PREPARATION can be completed at least a few hours ahead, in the afternoon for an evening party, for instance, and often earlier. The very occasional exceptions are noted. We specify when to do each step, including when to chop herbs, for instance, even though a chopped quantity is listed among the ingredients. The preparation will often include some cooking that can be done in advance, and sometimes an entire recipe method will fall under this heading, when the dish can be completed hours before serving. The COOKING section includes the final steps to be completed shortly before the meal, and SERVING outlines our suggestions for arrangement on the plate.

Quantities may be somewhat smaller than the usual main-course serving and are usually a generous appetizer portion. This size is perfect for a two- or three-course meal plus dessert in which a given dish can occupy first, second, or third position. If you're serving one of these interchangeable courses alone as lunch or a simple dinner, you may want to increase the ingredients somewhat, or the recipes can be scaled up or down to fit into more traditional menus.

Christopher Kimball   Judith Hill
Publisher   Editor-in-Chief

COOK'S Magazine

CHAPTER 1

WINE ACCOMPANI-MENTS

Ham-and-Cheese-Stuffed Mushrooms
Miniature Scallion Crêpes with Salmon Caviar and Sour Cream
Cabbage Pancakes · Shellfish in Dill Brine
Corn Bread with Ham and Maple Butter · Chicken and Herb Sausage
Cured Pork Sausage with Rice · Country Terrine · Herb Pâté
Ham and Pear Pâté · Salmon-Butter Triangles with Caviar and Dill
Fried Cheese

I n our minds, virtually all foods can and should be accompanied by
wine, but in this chapter we offer recipes that are especially
appropriate to accompany wine before a meal or at a party. Wine
complements the food with which it is served rather than
deadening the palate, as hard liquor does. It allows you to
appreciate an unusual hors d'oeuvre rather than just reach for the nearest
bowl of salted peanuts. The only hard-and-fast rule for foods made to
go with wine is to avoid vinegary preparations.

Cheese and pâté are probably the most common accompaniments to
wine, and deservedly so. See page 15 for newly available cheeses and
wine suggestions for each. Our recipe for crispy deep-fried wedges of
melting Camembert or Brie is an unusual variation on this theme. Or,
you can choose among an unusual Ham and Pear Pâté, a flavorful
Country Terrine, and a more delicate Herb Pâté. Canapés are much
maligned but are extremely practical for eating at a stand-up wine party,
and they can be fresh and delicious. We include two new ideas: Salmon-
Butter Triangles with Caviar and Dill, and Corn Bread with Ham and
Maple Butter.

All the hallmarks of the new cuisine are evident in our wine accompaniments: inventiveness and experimentation with new and unusual ingredients, rediscovery and redefinition of traditional American foods, the influence of many ethnic cuisines. The recipes range from pork sausage to crayfish, from cabbage pancakes to miniature scallion crêpes.

Though the selections in this chapter work well as hors d'oeuvre or appetizers, with the new dining habits, many of these dishes might serve as the major element in a light meal. "Grazing," or having a bit of this or that on the move rather than sitting down to a full meal, is the latest eating mode: tapas, the Spanish appetizers usually served with wine, are in vogue, and "little meals" that fall somewhere between the appetizer and main course in size and purpose are gaining popularity as the distinctions among the traditional menu categories blur and courses become interchangeable.

Easy Wine Accompaniments

In addition to the recipes in this chapter, there are many good wine accompaniments that require little or no cooking. Some of the possibilities are listed below, and our suggestions should give you ideas for even more.

Country bread spread with parsley butter and topped with smoked salmon (to make parsley butter, combine 2 tablespoons finely minced fresh parsley with ½ cup softened butter)
WINE SUGGESTION: California Fumé Blanc

Mussels steamed in wine and served hot or cold, in their shells
WINE SUGGESTION: Pinot Grigio

Picked crab heaped on thin rounds of raw zucchini

WINE SUGGESTION: White burgundy, such as Saint-Véran

Whole wild mushrooms sautéed in a light oil and dusted with chopped fresh chervil or parsley
WINE SUGGESTION: Beaujolais-Villages

Smoked meats, such as pheasant, turkey, or ham, on buttered bread
WINE SUGGESTION: Oregon Pinot Noir

Grilled ham and Gruyère sandwiches made on crustless bread and cut into quarters
WINE SUGGESTION: White Zinfandel

A variety of Mediterranean olives
WINE SUGGESTION: Chilled Fino Sherry or Spanish champagne

A mixture of raw cashews and raisins (half and half)
WINE SUGGESTION: Alsace Gewurztraminer

Toasted, lightly salted almonds or pecans
WINE SUGGESTION: Brut champagne

Tiny quiches (quiche Lorraine or any favorite recipe made in miniature tartlet shells)

WINE SUGGESTION: Vouvray or dry Chenin Blanc

Raclette cheese, melted in the oven and served with chunks of French bread
WINE SUGGESTION: Crisp white, such as Pinot Blanc or Neuchatel

Newly Available Cheeses

There are well over 1,000 varieties of cheese, and more are available in the United States than ever before. Cheeses that are new to us come from all over the world, and some are now being made here, too. For instance, California chèvres have recently gained respect and popularity. The following are proving particularly popular:

Buffalo-Milk Mozzarella—fresh Italian mozzarella, which is very different from that sold in rubbery blocks in American supermarkets. A delicate, semisoft cheese, it is available salted or unsalted, smoked or unsmoked.
WINE SUGGESTION: plain—Italian rosé, such as Chiaretto del garda; smoked—Soave or Valpolicella

Cheshire, Gloucester, and Double Gloucester—hard, cheddar-type, English cheeses. Gloucester is made with whole and

skimmed milk. Richer double Gloucester uses entirely whole milk.
WINE SUGGESTION: Light red such as Chinon or Moulin-à-Vent

Chèvre—there are at least a hundred different goats' milk cheeses produced in France alone. The range in shape, texture, and flavor is great, from mild, soft, moist, fresh cheese to very sharp, firm, and dry aged chèvre, from pyramids to rounds, cylinders, and button shapes. A tray of cheeses at various ages makes an interesting offering.
WINE SUGGESTION: white—Sancerre or Fumé Blanc; red—Rhône Reds

Dry Monterey Jack—a hard cheese, basically an American cheddar-type, produced primarily in California. It has a definite, slightly sweet taste all its own.
WINE SUGGESTION: Zinfandel, Petite Sirah, or Côte Rotie

Mascarpone—a rich, fragile, fresh Italian cheese. It has a slightly sweet, almost nutty taste and goes well with fruits; it is often used in cheese tortas, available in specialty shops, in which mascarpone and Gorgonzola are layered, sometimes with herbs or other flavorings.

WINE SUGGESTION: with fruit—Asti spumante; with Gorgonzola—Dolcetto d'Alba or Ruby port

HAM-AND-CHEESE-STUFFED MUSHROOMS

Choose medium-sized, well-formed mushrooms to hold this savory stuffing. This is a good, basic formula for stuffed mushrooms that can be varied according to the ingredients available. White bread can be used rather than rye. Instead of Westphalian ham and Jarlsberg cheese, regular baked ham and Swiss cheese are good, as are prosciutto and Fontina, or you might try other meats, such as crumbled sausage or leftover roast of any kind.

WINE SUGGESTION: Sancerre Rosé or Tavel

Preparation: Remove the stems from the 24 mushrooms and reserve them. Wipe the caps with a damp cloth. Mince the shallots and parsley. Make the bread crumbs. Dice the ham and the cheese.

In a large frying pan, melt 2 tablespoons of the butter and sauté the mushroom caps, stem sides down, for about 2 minutes. Remove and place, stem sides up, in a shallow baking pan.

Chop the ½ pound mushrooms and the reserved mushroom stems. Add the remaining 5 tablespoons of butter to the pan. Sauté the chopped mushrooms and shallots over medium heat until all the liquid has evaporated and the mixture is quite dry, 5 to 15 minutes, depending on the moistness of the mushrooms. Add the Madeira and cook until it has evaporated, 1 to 2 minutes.

Remove from the heat and combine with the parsley, bread crumbs, ham, cheese, and cream. Season with salt and pepper to taste. Fill the mushroom caps with the mixture.

½ pound mushrooms with stems plus 24 attractive, medium-sized mushrooms
3 shallots
1 teaspoon minced fresh parsley
1 cup fresh rye bread crumbs
2 ounces Westphalian ham
¼ pound Jarlsberg cheese
7 tablespoons unsalted butter
1 tablespoon Madeira
¼ cup heavy cream
Salt and black pepper

Cooking: Heat the oven to 375° F. Bake the mushroom caps for 15 minutes.

YIELD: 24 stuffed mushrooms

MINIATURE SCALLION CRÊPES WITH SALMON CAVIAR AND SOUR CREAM

Inspired by traditional blini, this innovation uses scallion-flavored crêpes as the base and jewel-like, but relatively inexpensive, red caviar as garnish.

WINE SUGGESTION: California Blanc de Blancs or Macon-Villages

Scallion Crêpes

2 eggs
1 tablespoon unsalted butter
1 scallion
½ cup flour
¼ teaspoon salt
⅛ teaspoon black pepper
¾ cup milk, plus more if necessary

⅔ cup sour cream
3 ounces salmon caviar

Preparation: *For the crêpes,* beat the eggs to combine. Melt the butter. Cut the scallion into thin slices. In a bowl, combine the flour, salt, and pepper. Add the eggs and whisk until smooth. Gradually add the milk, whisking, until the batter is free of lumps. Stir in melted butter and scallion. Cover and let the batter rest for at least 45 minutes. If you are making the batter more than 1½ hours ahead, do not add the scallion slices until the end of the resting time.

Cooking: Heat a crêpe pan or small nonstick frying pan and butter very lightly. Thin the batter with milk if necessary so that it is the consistency of heavy cream. Make the crêpes using about ½ tablespoon of the batter for each crêpe. Cook about 1 minute on the first side, turn, and cook about 30 seconds. Stack the crêpes between sheets of plastic wrap. The crêpes can be made ahead and stored in the refrigerator.

SERVING: Bring the crêpes to room temperature before using or serve while still warm. Put about ¾ teaspoon sour cream on each, spreading to within ¼ inch of the edge. Cover with about ¾ teaspoon of the caviar and fold each crêpe in half.

YIELD: about 40 crêpes

CABBAGE PANCAKES

These miniature vegetable pancakes combine cabbage, celery, onion, and bread crumbs for excellent taste and texture.

WINE SUGGESTION: Dry Chenin Blanc

Preparation: Cut the cabbage into strips. Cut the celery into ¼-inch slices.

In a large pot of boiling salted water, cook the cabbage and celery until the celery is very soft, about 10 minutes. Drain and cool under running water. Press out as much of the liquid as you can. Transfer to a food processor.

Slice the onion. In a small frying pan, heat 2 tablespoons of the oil and cook the onion over low heat, covered, for about 5 minutes. Mince the garlic and add it to the pan. Cook gently, covered, for another 5 minutes. Remove from the heat and season with salt and pepper. Add the onion and garlic to the food processor. Tear the bread into chunks, add to processor, and whir briefly just to combine.

In a small bowl, whisk the eggs. Sprinkle with the flour and whisk again until smooth. Add this mixture to the processor and whir just to chop the vegetables and distribute the eggs and flour. Do not overprocess; the pancakes should have some texture. Do not let stand or the vegetables will begin to exude moisture and thin the batter.

Cooking: In a large frying pan, heat the remaining 3 tablespoons of oil over medium-high heat. Use 1 heaping tablespoon of batter per pancake. Drop into the frying pan and smooth out to about 2 inches with the back of a spoon. Do not overcrowd the pan. When the bottoms of the pancakes are browned, turn and brown the second sides. Remove and keep warm until all the pancakes are done.

YIELD: about 8 pancakes

1 pound cabbage
1 rib celery
1 onion
5 tablespoons oil
1 clove garlic
  Salt and black pepper
3 slices white bread
2 eggs
2 tablespoons flour

SHELLFISH IN DILL BRINE

Thanks to the increasing popularity of Cajun/Creole cooking, crayfish are more widely available than ever before; however, shrimp are also wonderful made according to this Scandinavian-inspired recipe. Serve with plenty of napkins.

WINE SUGGESTION: California Riesling, such as Phelps Early Harvest

3 pounds live crayfish or *1½ pounds shrimp in the shell*
1½ bunches fresh dill
⅔ pound coarse salt

Preparation: To purge the crayfish, put them into cold water for 1 day, changing the water frequently. Transfer the crayfish to lightly salted water for 1½ hours. Discard any dead crayfish.

Fold, tie, and boil half the dill in a pot with 1½ gallons of water and ⅓ pound of the coarse salt. After 10 minutes remove the dill.

Bring the dill brine to a rapid boil and add the crayfish or shrimp, a few at a time so that the roll is not disrupted. Boil the crayfish until they float, 5 to 8 minutes; or boil the shrimp until just cooked through, about 2 minutes, depending on their size. Strain and chill.

Dissolve the remaining ⅓ pound of salt in 1½ gallons of water. Save a few sprigs for garnish and chop the remaining dill. Add it to the water. Put the crayfish or shrimp into a nonreactive container and cover with the fresh brine. Refrigerate for 24 to 48 hours.

SERVING: Remove the crayfish or shrimp from the brine and garnish with dill sprigs.

YIELD: 4 servings

CORN BREAD WITH HAM AND MAPLE BUTTER

This is an all-American hors d'oeuvre including corn bread, maple syrup, and corn kernels. For the neatest canapés, be sure to chill the prepared corn bread until the butter is firm enough to make cutting out the rounds easy.

WINE SUGGESTION: Kir or Pinot Noir Blanc

Preparation: *For the corn bread,* heat the oven to 450°F. Butter a 12- by 18-inch baking pan. Put the cornmeal, flour, baking powder, salt, and baking soda into a large bowl and stir to combine. Melt the 4 tablespoons of butter. In another bowl, mix together the buttermilk, milk, melted butter, and eggs. Add to the dry ingredients and stir just enough to combine.

Pour the mixture into the prepared baking pan and bake in the preheated oven until the corn bread begins to shrink from the sides of the pan, 10 to 15 minutes. Allow to cool in the pan.

When cool, turn the corn bread onto a baking sheet. Using a long, serrated knife, trim to an even ⅜-inch thickness.

For the maple butter, bring the butter to room temperature or soften in a microwave oven. Combine the softened butter with the maple syrup and mustard. Spread on the corn bread. Cover with the ham slices and refrigerate to firm the butter. Using a 1½-inch round cookie cutter, cut out the canapés.

SERVING: Garnish each canapé with parsley, a generous sprinkling of black pepper, and the corn kernels.

YIELD: 32 canapés

Corn Bread

2 cups yellow cornmeal, preferably stoneground
½ cup flour
2 teaspoons baking powder
1 teaspoon salt
½ teaspoon baking soda
4 tablespoons unsalted butter
1 cup buttermilk
1 cup milk
2 eggs

Maple Butter

6 ounces unsalted butter
1 tablespoon maple syrup
½ teaspoon Dijon mustard

12 thin slices smoked ham
¼ cup chopped fresh parsley
1 tablespoon coarse black pepper
Cooked corn kernels, frozen or cut from the cob, for garnish

CHICKEN AND HERB SAUSAGE

This is a light and delicate sausage flavored with fresh herbs. Chef Judy Rodgers, who developed this recipe, suggests using rabbit instead of the chicken as a variation. Another possibility is to roll the poached sausage in melted butter and then bread crumbs and finish sautéing. Though we call for packing the sausage meat into casings, you can wrap it in caul fat instead or just shape into patties and panfry.

WINE SUGGESTION: Fleurie

1 pound boneless chicken breasts
¼ pound pork butt with about 30 percent
    fat content
¼ pound fatback
1 onion
2 tablespoons chopped fresh herbs, such as
    thyme, chervil, marjoram, parsley,
    or chives
3 feet lamb casings or 1½ feet hog casings
1½ teaspoons unsalted butter
1 egg
¼ cup heavy cream
1½ teaspoons coarse salt
    White pepper to taste
2 cups Chicken Stock (page 81)

Preparation: Remove the skin from the chicken breasts and cut the meat into pieces. Cut the pork butt and fatback into chunks. Mince the onion. Chop the herbs. Put the chicken and pork butt through a meat grinder using a plate with large holes. Chill. Add fatback, grind again, and refrigerate. Rinse the lamb or hog casings well and soak in cold water for at least 1 hour.

In a frying pan, melt the butter over low heat and sauté the onion until it is translucent, about 5 minutes. Chill.

Blend together the chilled onion, egg, cream, salt, and white pepper and add to the meat mixture. Stir in the herbs just enough to distribute them well.

Fry and taste a small patty of the mixture. Adjust the seasonings. Stuff the mixture into lamb or hog casings, tie or twist into lengths, and refrigerate for at least 1 hour.

Cooking: In a saucepan, bring the stock to a simmer. Poach the sausages until just firm to the touch, about 6 minutes for lamb casings, 8 minutes for hog casings. Or grill them over a low flame or fry in a little butter over low heat.

YIELD: about 1½ pounds

CURED PORK SAUSAGE WITH RICE

For this sausage, the pork is cured in brine. This is exceedingly easy to do, but you do have to allow three to five days for curing. As in the preceding recipe, you can use casings, wrap the sausages in caul fat, or simply shape into patties and fry them.

WINE SUGGESTION: Alsace Gewurztraminer

Preparation: *For the brine,* crush the allspice, peppercorns, bay leaf, garlic, salt, and sugar in a deep nonreactive container. Add 3 quarts cold water and stir until the salt and sugar have dissolved.

Cut the pork butt in half and add to the brine. Cover and cure in the refrigerator for 3 to 5 days.

Rinse the hog casings well and soak in cold water for at least 1 hour. Cook the rice, season well with salt and pepper, and cool.

Remove the pork butt from the brine and pat it dry. Cut into chunks and grind through a plate with large holes; then refrigerate.

Chop the onions, parsley, and garlic. In a small frying pan over medium heat, sauté the onions in the butter until tender and translucent, about 5 minutes; then chill.

Combine the ground pork with the chilled onions and garlic, parsley, allspice, rice, cayenne, and black pepper. Fry a small patty of the mixture, taste, and adiust the seasoning if necessary. It will take several hours for the cayenne to flavor the mixture, so use it cautiously. Stuff the sausage mixture into the hog casings, tie or twist into lengths, and refrigerate at least 1 hour.

Cooking: In a lightly oiled frying pan, cook the sausages over low heat until they are browned and just lose their pink color, about 10 minutes.

YIELD: about 5 pounds

Brine

4 allspice berries
    Handful of whole peppercorns
1 bay leaf
3 cloves garlic
¼ cup coarse salt
¾ cup sugar

Sausage

5 pounds boneless pork butt with about 30
    percent fat content
5 feet hog casings
¾ cup white rice
    Salt and black pepper
2 onions
5 tablespoons chopped fresh parsley
4 small cloves garlic
2 tablespoons unsalted butter
1 teaspoon ground allspice
1 teaspoon cayenne
1 teaspoon cracked black pepper
    Oil for frying

COUNTRY TERRINE

Though the distinction between the two has nearly disappeared, terrines are traditionally "rougher" than pâtés, coarser in texture and stronger in seasoning. Both are weighted as they cool to make them more compact so that they will slice well. Allowing terrines or pâtés to mellow at least a day will make them taste even better.

WINE SUGGESTION: Vouvray

1½ pounds boneless beef, such as chuck
½ cup heavy cream
1½ pounds boneless pork, such as lean
    shoulder
½ pound pork fat
1 onion
2 cloves garlic
2 tablespoons chopped fresh parsley
1 tablespoon chopped fresh basil leaves
1 tablespoon unsalted butter
1 tablespoon dried thyme
2 eggs
   Salt and black pepper
1 tablespoon flour
⅓ cup brandy
10 to 12 slices bacon
3 bay leaves

Preparation and Cooking: In a meat grinder or food processor, grind the beef. Transfer to a bowl and stir in the cream. Refrigerate for 1 hour. Grind the pork and pork fat together. Chill until ready to assemble.

Chop the onion and crush the garlic. Chop the parsley and basil leaves.

In a frying pan over medium heat, sauté the onion in the butter for 5 minutes. Add the garlic, parsley, basil, and thyme. Remove from the heat and cool to room temperature.

In a large mixing bowl, combine the beef, pork, onion–herb mixture, eggs, 1 tablespoon plus 2 teaspoons salt, 1½ teaspoons pepper, flour, and brandy. Mix well. Fry a tablespoon of the mixture, taste, and adjust the seasoning.

Heat the oven to 350°F. With the bacon, line an 8-cup terrine mold or baking dish, preferably one that is attractive enough to bring to the table. Pack in the meat mixture. Put the bay leaves on top. Seal tightly with aluminum foil. Put the mold or dish in a large baking pan and add hot water to come halfway up the terrine.

Bring the water in the baking pan to a simmer on top of the stove, put the pan into the preheated oven, and bake until a skewer inserted into the center of the terrine for 30 seconds is very hot when withdrawn (160°F), 2 to 2½ hours.

Cool for 1 hour. Cover and weight down evenly with cans or other heavy objects. Refrigerate at least 24 hours.

SERVING: Serve at room temperature, either turned out and sliced or directly from the mold.

YIELD: 15 to 18 slices

HERB PÂTÉ

Fresh herbs, basil, rosemary, and thyme—flavor this elegant pâté, and a bull's-eye of egg in each slice adds drama. You can vary the pâté depending on the fresh herbs that are available.

WINE SUGGESTION: Tokay d'Alsace or Italian Tocai

Preparation and Cooking: Hard-cook 3 of the eggs and shell them. In a food processor or meat grinder, grind the pork and veal fine. Chop the onion. Mince the garlic. Chop the spinach. Mince the basil, rosemary, and thyme.

In a frying pan, sauté the onion and garlic in the butter. Add the spinach and cook for 1 minute. Transfer the spinach mixture to a large bowl and stir in the ground meat. Add the brandy, remaining egg, 1½ teaspoons salt, ¾ teaspoon pepper, basil, rosemary, thyme, and fennel seeds. Fry a small patty, taste, and adjust the seasonings.

Heat the oven to 350°F. Arrange the bacon across the bottom and sides of a 6-cup loaf pan or pâté mold, letting the slices hang over edges. Put half of the meat mixture into the pan. Place the hard-cooked eggs, lengthwise, down the center of the meat. Add the remaining meat mixture and fold the bacon slices over the top. Cover the pan with aluminum foil and set in a baking pan. Add hot water to come halfway up the pâté.

Bring the water in the baking pan to a simmer on top of the stove and then put the pan into the preheated oven and bake until a skewer inserted into the center of the pâté for 30 seconds is very hot when withdrawn (160°F), about 1¼ hours.

Remove from the oven and let stand, uncovered, for about 1 hour. Cover and weight evenly with cans or other heavy objects. Refrigerate at least 24 hours.

4 eggs
1 pound untrimmed boneless pork, such as shoulder (with fat left on)
½ pound boneless veal, such as shoulder
1 large onion
3 cloves garlic
1½ cups chopped fresh spinach
1½ tablespoons minced fresh basil leaves
1½ tablespoons minced fresh rosemary leaves
1 tablespoon minced fresh thyme leaves
1 tablespoon unsalted butter
3 tablespoons brandy
Salt and black pepper
1½ teaspoons fennel seeds
6 slices bacon

SERVING: Take the pâté from pan and remove the excess fat. Bring to room temperature.

YIELD: about 12 slices

HAM AND PEAR PÂTÉ

Diced pears, port-soaked currants, and strips of smoked ham go into this pâté from the American Restaurant in Kansas City. Apples work as well as pears; only the name need be changed.

WINE SUGGESTION: Cabernet d'Anjou Rosé

¼ pound smoked ham
¼ cup dried currants
¾ cup port
1¾ pounds boneless lean pork shoulder
¼ pound beef suet
¼ pound pork fatback
½ cup heavy cream
¼ cup brandy
2 eggs
2 firm ripe pears
2 cloves garlic
½ cup dry white wine
    Salt and black pepper
¼ teaspoon grated nutmeg
½ teaspoon ground allspice
6 slices bacon

Preparation and Cooking: Cut the ham into ⅜-inch-wide strips and soak in cold water to cover for 1 hour. Soak the currants in the port.

Grind the pork shoulder. Chop the suet and fatback. In a food processor, puree the pork, suet, and fatback in two batches until very smooth. Add half of the port from the currants and half the cream to each batch while processing.

In a small saucepan, warm the brandy and ignite it. Allow the flames to die out.

Transfer the meat mixture to a large bowl. Lightly beat the eggs and add them to the meat. Core, peel, and cut the pears into ⅜-inch dice and add to the mixture, blending well. Mince the garlic and add with the brandy, wine, 1½ teaspoons salt, 1 teaspoon pepper, nutmeg, allspice, and currants.

Heat the oven to 300°F. Line an 8-cup pàté mold or a loaf pan with bacon strips, reserving some strips for the top. Put about 2 cups of the pâté mixture on the bottom of the mold to form a 1-inch layer. Lay 3 strips drained ham lengthwise in the mold, cutting to fit if necessary. Repeat with another layer of pâté, another layer of ham strips, and finish with a final layer of pâté. Top with the remaining strips of bacon. Cover with aluminum foil (or the lid of the mold). Set in a baking pan and add hot water to come halfway up the pâté.

Bring the water in the baking pan to a simmer on top of the stove and then put into the preheated oven and bake for 2 hours. Remove the foil or lid and bake the pâté until a skewer inserted into the center of the pâté is very hot when withdrawn (160°F), about 30 minutes more.

Remove from the oven and cool for about 1 hour. Cover and weight down evenly with cans or other heavy objects. Refrigerate at least 24 hours.

SERVING: Take the pâté from the pan and remove excess fat. Bring to room temperature.

YIELD: about 12 slices

SALMON-BUTTER TRIANGLES WITH CAVIAR AND DILL

The smoked salmon butter used in these canapés is accented by dill and a splash of vodka. Golden caviar is the crowning touch.

WINE SUGGESTION: Piper-Sonoma Blanc de Noirs

Preparation: Bring the butter to room temperature or soften in a microwave oven. Chop the dill. In a food processor, puree the salmon. Gradually add the butter until well combined. Add the dill, white pepper to taste, and vodka. Whir until incorporated. Chill slightly.

Trim the edges of the bread and spread the slices evenly with the salmon butter. Cut each slice into 4 triangular wedges. Garnish with caviar and small sprigs of dill.

¼ pound unsalted butter
2 teaspoons chopped fresh dill leaves
4 ounces smoked salmon
White pepper
2 teaspoons vodka
8 thin slices white bread
1 ounce golden caviar
Several sprigs fresh dill

YIELD: 32 triangles

FRIED CHEESE

A crisp outer crust conceals a warm, runny cheese center. A variation is to use walnuts chopped very fine in place of a quarter of the bread crumbs.

WINE SUGGESTION: White burgundy, such as Saint-Véran

9 ounces Camembert or Brie, with rind
2 eggs
2 cups fresh white bread crumbs
  Oil for frying

Preparation: Cut the cheese into 12 wedges. Lightly beat the eggs. Dip the cheese wedges into the egg to coat them lightly and then dip into the crumbs.

Cooking: In a large, heavy pan or deep fryer, heat the oil to 375°F. Fry the coated wedges until golden, about 1 minute. Remove with a slotted spoon and drain on paper towels.

YIELD: 12 hors d'oeuvre

CHAPTER 2

COLD SALADS

Piquant Beef Salad
Bulgur Garden Salad · *Tortellini Salad with Red Wine–Herb Vinaigrette*
Minted Mussels · *Mussels Midia Dolma*
Seafood and Barley Salad with Lemon and Basil Vinaigrette
Avocado and Seafood with Flour Tortillas
Lobster–Grapefruit Salad Jean-Pierre Capelle · *Summer Seviche*
Cobb's Salad
Chicken and Vegetable Salad with Tomato–Cheese Mayonnaise
Smoked Chicken Salad · *Cucumber and Brie Salad*
Smoked Duck Salad
Provençale Green Bean Salad with Black Olive Vinaigrette
Sugar Snap, Red Cabbage, and Ham Salad with Walnut Vinaigrette

A cold salad used to mean simply lettuce—frequently the dreaded iceberg. But the salad has come into its own with our new lighter cooking. Following California's lead, the entire nation is now munching greens and vegetable salads, enjoying salads of shellfish or untraditional chicken salads. A great deal of creativity has been brought to bear on the whole idea of a salad. It has become a colorful arrangement of interesting comestibles, fresh and raw or carefully cooked, usually lightly dressed with a vinaigrette or sometimes more richly finished with a real homemade mayonnaise.

Our recipes, for example, include a Sugar Snap, Red Cabbage, and Ham Salad with Walnut Vinaigrette; a Seafood and Barley Salad with Lemon and Basil Vinaigrette, and a Chicken and Vegetable Salad with Tomato–Cheese Mayonnaise.

A cold salad is a natural for a summer meal and can stand alone. Any of our cold salads, such as Minted Mussels or Smoked Chicken Salad, are also eminently appropriate for a first course any time of the year, or they can be mixed and matched with recipes from other chapters, holding down first, second, or third position on a modular menu. Those that feature vegetables—the Cucumber and Brie Salad or the Provençale Green Bean Salad with Black Olive Vinaigrette—might also be served as side dishes to simple grilled chicken or meat.

The old essentials, leafy greens, are still the base of many a salad, and their treatment is important. Find, if possible, a store that handles them carefully—no bruising rubber bands, please. We find that the best way to hold greens in the refrigerator at home is swaddled in paper towels and covered loosely in a plastic bag. In any case, don't wash the leaves more than a few hours before you're ready to use them, give the greens a quick twirl in a salad spinner to dry, and pop them back into the refrigerator until just before tossing. The indispensable plastic spinner, the kind with a little knob on top for rotation, is a boon to quick drying so that dressings cling undiluted.

There are an infinity of salads to be created, and culinary innovation is nowhere more appropriate, because the goodness of a salad relies, perhaps more than that of any other type of dish, on the freshest, best ingredients that happen to be available to you. Use our recipes not only as guides to tested combinations but as inspiration to put together the finest from garden or grocer to suit your own taste.

Vinegars

Whatever else nouvelle cuisine did, it refocused the attention of American cooks on vinegar, one of the world's oldest flavoring staples. All vinegar is produced by fermenting alcohol, usually wine. Red and white wine vinegars and basic white and cider vinegars have now been joined by flavored vinegars. The varieties of these vinegars, infused with herbs or fruits, seem to be increasing almost daily.

White Vinegar

Common white vinegar made from distilled alcohol is best used for pickling.

Cider Vinegar

Another traditional favorite for pickling, cider vinegar can also be used in salads. The flavor is quite sharp, and so this vinegar should be used in small quantities, with highly flavored ingredients.

Wine Vinegar

Red and white wine vinegars are the most versatile of all. There are many excellent varieties of French wine vinegar. The best of these are produced by the "Orleans method," during which the vinegar is subjected to minimum heat in order to retain maximum flavor; these high-quality vinegars may be labeled "aged in oak."

Italian wine vinegar is less common, but there are some very good Italian red wine vinegars available. Mellow balsamic vinegars from Italy are becoming well known; these red wine vinegars undergo long aging in wooden casks.

Very good wine vinegars are now produced in America, especially in California. The best sherry vinegars, not surprisingly, come from Spain. Their distinctive flavor combines well with stronger oils such as walnut. Japanese rice wine vinegars, made from sake, are sweet tasting and mild.

Fruit and Herb Vinegars

Flavored vinegars are produced by infusion, a process whereby heated vinegar is combined with various seasonings and allowed to steep. Needless to say, the better the vinegar to start with, the better its flavor after it's infused. The range of flavored vinegars is vast, since the tastes of many herbs and fruits, especially berries, combine successfully with those of wine-based vinegars. Among the more common herb vinegars are tarragon, dill, and basil; fruit vinegars include those made with raspberries or blackberries, blueberries, and pears; and tangy chili vinegar is also popular. Herb vinegars are particularly appealing on vegetables or plain green salads. Although raspberry vinegar is featured in some of the vilest creations of nouvelle cuisine, fruit and berry vinegars can highlight the natural sweet or sour flavors of vegetables such as carrots or beets, and a tablespoon or two will enliven a salad, soup, or even a tomato sauce that seems a little flat. Like all good vinegars, these infusions combine well with oil and simple seasonings to make a classic vinaigrette.

Oils

The best oils of any type are those that are cold pressed rather than those produced by methods using heat or chemicals. Most oils sold in supermarkets are not cold-pressed oils, but health food stores and gourmet markets do offer unrefined, cold-pressed oils. All oils should be stored in a cool, dark place. The big brand-name oils usually have preservatives and will last longer, but even they can become rancid if kept for too long.

Vegetable and Seed Oils
Corn and soybean are the most common vegetable oils; the seed oils include cottonseed, safflower, and sunflower. These oils are good for cooking and frying because they can be heated to high temperatures without burning. And they're fine for salads, too. An odd member of this group is the recently popular sesame, whose flavor is too strong to use in frying or, in fact, to use in quantity at all.

Olive Oil

Also a vegetable oil, olive oil is really a category in itself. The best olive oils have traditionally come from Italy, but there are a few companies now producing excellent oil in California. There are three types of olive oil: extra virgin, virgin, and pure. *Extra virgin* oil is that which is cold pressed from the first pressing of the olives, has no additives, and is unrefined (i.e., after extraction, it is simply filtered and bottled). *Virgin* olive oil can be cold pressed from olives of lesser quality than those used for extra virgin oil, and *pure* olive oil may come from a second or third pressing. Unfortunately, while European regulations concerning the labeling of olive oils are stringent, U.S. regulations are imprecise, and the designations on American olive oils do not always match up to the European categorizations. Generally, unless the label contains the word *virgin,* the oil is probably of an inferior quality. It may consist of oil from a second or third pressing or from refined oils that have undergone a chemical process that is intended to reduce harshness in their flavor but in fact reduces flavor intensity in general.

Free fatty acid (oleic acid) content is an important factor in the stability of the finished oil. Again, the FDA has no formal label regulations for U.S. olive oils, but European labels indicate percentages of oleic acid in cold-pressed oils. Extra virgin oils contain less than 1 percent oleic acid, while the content of virgin oils may be as high as 4 percent.

The distinctive taste of olive oil makes it particularly appropriate for marinades and salad dressings, but its relatively low smoking point renders it less so for frying. Olive oil is affected by both light and air, and so it should be stored in small containers in a dark place. It is not necessary to store it in the refrigerator (where it will become cloudy and semi-solid) unless room temperature is extremely high.

Nut Oils

Peanut oil has long been available in the United States. It can be used for frying as it has a high smoking point. Peanut oil is used in many Oriental dishes and is the all-purpose oil of choice of most French chefs both for vinaigrettes and cooking. Walnut, hickory, hazelnut, and other less-common nut oils add a distinctive taste to salads. These oils cannot be used in cooking as they break down under heat. They also tend to become rancid quickly; storing them in the refrigerator is a good idea.

Greens

While the firmer-textured, more strongly flavored greens used in warm salads (see page 53) are also appropriate for use as a bed of lettuce beneath a hearty cold salad, the softer, sweeter lettuces come into their own for gently tossed green salads and other light salads.

Bibb Lettuce

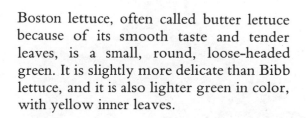

Boston or Butter Lettuce

Bibb lettuce grows in a fairly loose, egg-shaped head with dark-green exterior leaves and lighter green or white leaves toward the center. Its delicate flavor is readily enhanced by a light vinaigrette.

Boston lettuce, often called butter lettuce because of its smooth taste and tender leaves, is a small, round, loose-headed green. It is slightly more delicate than Bibb lettuce, and it is also lighter green in color, with yellow inner leaves.

leaf lettuce is a beautiful, less common loose-leaf variety, delicate, with thin, bronze-colored leaves.

Romaine

Romaine, or cos lettuce, is crisper and less fragile than the other lettuces discussed here. It grows in a long, V-shaped head, with crisp, ribbed leaves. It's an excellent basic green that keeps well.

Mache

Mache, also known as lamb's lettuce, or corn lettuce, is almost a staple of the new cuisine. The small, deep-green leaves grow in little bunches that look lovely left whole in a mixed salad. Mache has a unique, nutty flavor.

Loose-leaf Lettuce

There are many varieties of loose-leaf lettuces. Green, *curly* leaf lettuces are the most familiar, but *ruby* lettuce, with its red-edged leaves, is increasingly popular. *Oak-*

PIQUANT BEEF SALAD

Either well-done, leftover braised beef or rare roast beef can be used in this salad. Ideally the meat should be combined with the red onion vinaigrette at least an hour before serving. Even a day ahead is not too soon—the flavor just seems to get better.

Preparation: *For the vinaigrette,* mince the parsley and red onion. In a bowl, combine the mustard, parsley, onion, anchovy paste, vinegar, and salt and pepper. Slowly whisk in the oil.

Cut the beef into ½-inch cubes. Toss with about half the vinaigrette.

Preheat the broiler. Put the peppers about 3 inches from the heat source. Broil until well charred on all sides, turning as necessary. Peel, cut into quarters, and remove the seeds and ribs.

Remove the tough spines of the lettuce and the spinach stems; wash the lettuce and spinach well in cool water and drain. Tear into small pieces.

SERVING: Toss the lettuce and spinach with enough vinaigrette to coat and make a bed of greens on each plate. Top with the beef, arrange the red peppers around the outside, and garnish with the black olives. Pass any remaining dressing.

YIELD: 4 servings

Red Onion Vinaigrette

½ cup minced fresh parsley
1 red onion
1½ tablespoons Dijon mustard
½ teaspoon anchovy paste or more to taste
2 tablespoons red wine vinegar
Salt and black pepper
⅓ cup olive oil

1 pound cooked beef
4 red bell peppers
½ head romaine lettuce
¼ pound fresh spinach
½ cup black Mediterranean olives

BULGUR GARDEN SALAD

A strong Middle Eastern influence is evident in this vegetable salad from Michael McLaughlin, chef and co-owner of The Manhattan Chili Company in New York City. Crunchy bulgur adds taste and texture; a jalapeño pepper adds bite to the herb and pepper vinaigrette.

2 cups bulgur
2 large red bell peppers
2 large ripe tomatoes
3 medium-sized zucchini
4 scallions

Herb and Pepper Vinaigrette

1 cup loosely packed fresh coriander leaves
1 cup loosely packed fresh mint leaves
1 jalapeño pepper
5 tablespoons white wine vinegar
   Salt
¾ cup olive oil

   Salad greens, such as romaine, arugula,
      watercress, or Bibb to line plates
½ pound sharp, white, crumbly cheese,
      such as feta or chèvre

Preparation: In a small saucepan, bring 3 cups water to a boil. Stir in 2½ teaspoons salt and pour the boiling water over the bulgur in a bowl. Let stand, stirring once or twice, for 45 minutes. Strain the bulgur, pressing with the back of a spoon to extract any water that hasn't been absorbed; transfer to a mixing bowl.

Roast the peppers in the flame of a gas burner or under a broiler until blackened. Cool enough to handle and peel. Remove the stems, ribs, and seeds. Cut the peppers into ½-inch dice. Halve the tomatoes, squeeze out the seeds and excess juice, and cut into ½-inch dice. Cut the zucchini into ½-inch dice. Slice the scallions.

Toss the bulgur with the peppers, tomatoes, zucchini, and scallions.

For the vinaigrette, whirl the coriander, mint, jalapeño, vinegar, and ½ teaspoon salt in a food processor until smooth. With the motor running slowly add the oil. Pour the dressing over the salad and toss to combine. Taste for seasoning.

SERVING: Line 4 plates with salad greens. Mound the bulgur salad onto the greens. Crumble the cheese evenly over each salad.

YIELD: 4 servings

TORTELLINI SALAD WITH RED WINE–HERB VINAIGRETTE

Excellent cheese-filled tortellini can be purchased now both fresh and frozen. We've even seen ready-prepared tortellini in the kitchen of a Michelin-starred Parisian restaurant. Tortellini are usually served hot, but they are also delicious at room temperature, as in this salad.

Preparation and Cooking: *For the vinaigrette,* put the vinegar and herb sprig in a small bowl. Lightly crush the garlic and add it. Whisk in the mustard and salt and pepper. Slowly add the oil, whisking. Let the vinaigrette stand at room temperature for at least 1 hour. Strain, adjust the seasoning, and whisk again before using.

Bring a large pot of salted water to a boil. Stir in the tortellini and cook until tender, 7 to 12 minutes. Drain well.

Chop the onion and parsley. Dice the pepper. Cut salami *or* sausage into thin strips. In a large mixing bowl, combine warm tortellini, onion, parsley, and ½ cup of the vinaigrette. When cool, add diced pepper, olives, and salami *or* sausage. Season to taste with salt and pepper and additional vinaigrette as needed.

SERVING: Toss again and serve at room temperature.

YIELD: 4 servings

Red Wine–Herb Vinaigrette

3½ tablespoons red wine vinegar
  1 sprig fresh or a pinch dried herb, such
      as basil, oregano, or thyme
  1 clove garlic
  4 teaspoons Dijon mustard
     Salt and black pepper
⅔ cup olive oil

  1 pound fresh or frozen cheese-filled
      tortellini
½ red onion
½ cup chopped flat-leaf parsley
  1 large red bell pepper
¼ pound thinly sliced salami or other hard
      sausage
½ cup black Mediterranean olives
     Salt and black pepper

MINTED MUSSELS

This refreshing variation on classic French steamed mussels is from Marian Morash, executive chef of The Straight Wharf in Nantucket, Massachusetts.

4 pounds mussels
1 1-inch piece fresh ginger
4 cloves garlic
1 cup sweet rice wine (sake)
1 cup dry white wine
4 sprigs parsley
⅓ cup chopped fresh mint leaves
½ cup chopped fresh chives
    Salt and black pepper

Preparation: Scrub and beard the mussels. Discard any mussels that don't close when handled.

Cut the ginger into 4 slices. Crush the ginger and garlic lightly. In a bowl, combine the rice wine, garlic, and ginger.

In a large pot, bring the white wine, 1 cup of water, and parsley to a boil; cook for 3 minutes. Add the mussels, cover, and cook over high heat, shaking the pot once or twice to distribute the mussels evenly. As soon as the mussels open, about 3 minutes, transfer them, in their shells, to a large, shallow bowl. Discard any that have not opened.

Strain the mussel-cooking broth through cheesecloth and add 1 cup of the rice wine dressing mixture. Pour this mixture over the mussels. Chop the mint, add, and toss lightly. Refrigerate, tossing occasionally, for at least 4 hours—the salad can be made as much as a day ahead. Chop the chives.

SERVING: Bring to room temperature, adjust the seasoning with salt and pepper, and toss in the chives.

YIELD: 4 servings

MUSSELS MIDIA DOLMA

The inspiration for this flavorful mussel and rice salad comes from the traditional filling for Armenian stuffed grape leaves.

Preparation: Scrub and beard the mussels. Discard any mussels that don't close when handled. Mince the onion. Quarter the carrots lengthwise and slice thin.

In a large pot with 1½ cups water, cook the mussels over high heat, covered, until they open, about 3 minutes. Discard any that have not opened. Cool until easy to handle. Holding the shells over the pot to catch any liquid, open the mussels and remove the meat. Set aside the shells and meat separately. Strain the liquid through several layers of cheesecloth and reserve.

In a large, heavy saucepan, heat the olive oil. Sauté the onion and pine nuts over medium heat until the onion is soft, about 4 minutes. Add the cayenne, black pepper, cinnamon, nutmeg, allspice, thyme, dill, bay leaf, and raisins. Sauté, stirring, until the pine nuts are golden, about 5 minutes; take care that the pine nuts do not burn. Stir in the rice, chicken stock, and 2 cups of the reserved mussel liquid and bring to a boil. Cover and lower the heat to simmer. After 10 minutes, add the carrots and cook, covered, for 5 more minutes. Add the cooked mussels without stirring, quickly replace the cover, and remove from the heat.

Let the pot stand, covered, off the heat for 15 minutes. Gently stir the mussels and lemon juice into the rice mixture and cool to room temperature. Cover and chill well. Mince the parsley for garnish.

SERVING: Taste the salad and adjust the seasoning with salt and pepper. Mound the salad in the reserved shells. Garnish with parsley.

YIELD: 4 servings

5 pounds mussels
1 red onion
2 carrots
¾ cup olive oil
⅓ cup pine nuts
*   Pinch of cayenne*
½ teaspoon black pepper
¾ teaspoon ground cinnamon
¼ teaspoon grated nutmeg
1¼ teaspoons ground allspice
½ teaspoon dried thyme
1½ teaspoons minced fresh dill or ½
*   teaspoon dried dill*
1 bay leaf
¼ cup raisins
1½ cups rice
1 cup Chicken Stock (page 81)
1 teaspoon lemon juice
3 tablespoons minced fresh parsley
*   Salt and black pepper*

SEAFOOD AND BARLEY SALAD
WITH LEMON AND BASIL VINAIGRETTE

This is a perfect salad for high summer, cool and fresh tasting yet substantial enough to be the focus of a meal. To make it at other times of the year, when fresh basil is harder to come by, use parsley in the vinaigrette instead, and add 2 teaspoons dry basil.

1⅓ cups pearl barley
¾ pound shrimp
3 ribs celery
1 large red onion
¼ cup black Mediterranean olives
¾ pound bay scallops

Lemon and Basil Vinaigrette

1½ cups loosely packed fresh basil leaves
2 tablespoons lemon juice
Salt and black pepper
⅔ cup olive oil

Sprigs of basil for garnish (optional)

Preparation: Bring a large saucepan of salted water to a boil. Stir in the barley, lower the heat, and simmer, uncovered, stirring once or twice, until the barley is just tender, about 25 minutes. Drain, rinse with cold water, and drain thoroughly. Put the barley into a mixing bowl.

Shell and devein the shrimp. Slice in half lengthwise. Dice the celery and onion. Pit and chop the olives.

Bring a large pot of salted water to a boil. Add the shrimp and scallops. After 1 minute—it is not necessary that the water return to a boil—drain the seafood and cool to room temperature.

Toss the seafood together with the barley. Stir in the celery and onion.

For the vinaigrette, whir the basil, lemon juice, and ½ teaspoon salt in a food processor until smooth. With the motor still running, slowly add the oil.

Pour the dressing over the salad and toss well. Season with pepper to taste and toss again. Adjust the seasoning.

SERVING: Garnish with the chopped olives and sprigs of basil, if using. Serve cool or at room temperature.

YIELD: 4 servings

AVOCADO AND SEAFOOD WITH FLOUR TORTILLAS

Golden wedges of deep-fried tortilla contrast with the smooth, rich avocado and seafood salad.

Preparation: Scrub the clam shells. In a saucepan, simmer the scallops in salted water until they are just opaque, about 1 minute; remove with a slotted spoon. Cook the shrimp in the same cooking liquid until they turn pink, about 1½ minutes. Remove the shrimp with a slotted spoon and cook the clams in the same liquid, covered, just until the shells open, about 3 minutes. Discard any clams that do not open.

Cool the shellfish enough to handle. Peel the shrimp and remove the clams from their shells. If using bay scallops, cut them in half; if using sea scallops, cut them into eighths. Cut the shrimp and clams into the same size pieces as the scallops. Cut each tortilla into 8 wedges. Cut the avocados in half lengthwise; peel, chop, and toss them with lime juice. Add the sour cream, shellfish, cayenne, and chives and toss lightly. Season with salt and pepper to taste. If not using immediately, press plastic wrap onto the top to prevent the avocado from discoloring and refrigerate. Bring to room temperature before serving.

1½ dozen cherrystone clams or other small
  tender clams
½ pound sea or bay scallops
½ pound shrimp
6 flour tortillas
2 ripe avocados
1½ teaspoons lime juice
2 tablespoons sour cream
⅛ teaspoon cayenne
2 tablespoons minced fresh chives or
  scallion tops
Salt and black pepper
Oil for frying

Cooking: In a frying pan, heat 1 to 2 inches of oil to 375°F. Fry the tortilla wedges, being careful not to overcrowd, until golden, about 30 seconds per batch. Drain on paper towels and season with salt and pepper.

SERVING: Put some avocado salad in the center of each plate and circle with tortillas.

YIELD: 4 servings

LOBSTER–GRAPEFRUIT SALAD JEAN-PIERRE CAPELLE

Grapefruit and shellfish have a surprising affinity for one another. This elegant recipe was inspired by the langoustine and grapefruit salad Chef Jean-Pierre Capelle created at his country inn, the Domaine de Bassibe, in the Gascony region of France.

2 1½-pound lobsters
  Court Bouillon (recipe follows)
2 pink grapefruits

Grapefruit Dressing

¼ cup grapefruit juice, from above
  Salt and black pepper
¾ cup olive oil

2 ripe avocados

Preparation: Boil the lobsters, in the Court Bouillon, covered, for 10 minutes. Cool and carefully remove the meat from the shells, keeping each claw in one piece. Cut the tail into ¼-inch slices. With a knife, peel the grapefruits down to the flesh, removing all the white pith. Cut the segments away from their membranes, working over a bowl to catch the juice. Squeeze the membranes to get out all the juice.

For the dressing, whisk together the grapefruit juice and salt and pepper. Whisk in the oil.

Peel the avocados and cut the flesh into ½-inch dice. Toss lightly with just enough dressing to coat. If not using immediately, press plastic wrap over the surface.

SERVING: Put a mound of diced avocado in the center of each plate. Garnish each mound with a lobster claw. Arrange grapefruit slices around the avocado like spokes around the hub of a wheel. Put the slices of lobster between the spokes. Spoon the remaining dressing over lobster and grapefruit.

YIELD: 4 servings

COURT BOUILLON

Preparation: Chop the carrot, onion, and celery. Wash and chop the leek. With a peeler, remove 2 strips of zest from the lemon.

Cooking: In a large pan, melt the butter. Cook the carrot, onion, celery, and leek over low heat until soft, about 5 minutes. Add the wine, water, bouquet garni, peppercorns, and zest. Squeeze the juice from the lemon into the pan. Simmer for 30 minutes.

YIELD: about 3 cups

1 carrot
1 onion
1 rib celery
1 small leek, white part only
1 lemon
3 tablespoons unsalted butter
1 cup dry white wine
3 cups water
1 bouquet garni of parsley, bay leaf, and thyme
1 teaspoon whole peppercorns

SUMMER SEVICHE

Zucchini, corn, tomatoes, and lots of basil make this seviche a summer treat. It's simplicity itself to put together, but allow at least four hours to marinate the fish, or plan to begin marinating a day ahead of time.

Preparation: Cut the fish into 1-inch squares and put into a nonreactive bowl. Pour the vinegar over the fish and stir gently. Crush the garlic lightly and bury it in the fish. Refrigerate, covered, for 4 to 24 hours. Stir occasionally.

Trim zucchini and dice it. Cut ⅔ cup fresh corn kernels from the ears of corn or thaw the frozen corn. Trim the scallions and cut them into thin slices (including the green tops). One hour before serving, drain the fish, reserving ⅓ cup of the vinegar. Transfer the fish to a large mixing bowl and stir in the oil and reserved vinegar. Add the zucchini, corn, and scallions. Season with salt and pepper to taste.

Refrigerate, covered, for at least 30 minutes. Seed and chop the tomatoes.

SERVING: Add the tomatoes to the seviche and divide among 4 plates. Peel and slice the avocado and use to garnish the plates. Cut the basil leaves into fine strips and sprinkle over all.

YIELD: 4 servings

2 pounds skinned lean white fish fillets, such as sole, snapper, scrod, or halibut
½ cup white wine vinegar
1 clove garlic
1 medium-sized zucchini
2 ears corn, or ⅔ cup frozen corn kernels
4 scallions
⅓ cup olive oil
Salt and black pepper
2 ripe tomatoes
1 ripe avocado
½ cup loosely packed fresh basil leaves

COBB'S SALAD

The original Cobb's Salad was developed in 1936 by Robert Cobb, proprietor of Hollywood's famed Brown Derby restaurant. There the ingredients were carefully arranged for presentation and then tossed at tableside, a bit of showmanship that we retain in our updated version.

Chicken

2 chicken breast halves
    (about 1 pound in all)
½ small onion
⅓ cup dry white wine
1 small bay leaf
2 sprigs parsley
1 sprig fresh tarragon leaves or a pinch of
    dried thyme
    Salt and black pepper

Vinaigrette

1 small clove garlic
½ teaspoon minced fresh tarragon leaves or
    ¼ teaspoon dried tarragon
⅓ cup white wine vinegar
1 teaspoon lemon juice
1 teaspoon Dijon mustard
    Salt and black pepper
¼ cup olive oil
¾ cup vegetable oil

6 slices bacon
½ head iceberg lettuce
1 small head chicory
1 bunch watercress
1 Belgian endive
2 ripe tomatoes
3 hard-cooked eggs
3 scallions
3 ounces blue cheese
1 ripe avocado
½ lemon

Preparation: *For the chicken,* put the breasts in a saucepan. Chop the onion and add it to the pan. Add the wine, ½ cup water, bay leaf, parsley, tarragon, and salt and pepper. Bring to a simmer over medium heat. Lower the heat, cover, and poach until the chicken is just done, 20 to 25 minutes. Set aside to cool and then remove from the broth; skin the chicken, remove the meat from the bones, and cut it into ½-inch dice.

For the vinaigrette, mince the garlic and tarragon if using fresh. Whisk together the vinegar, lemon juice, mustard, salt and pepper, garlic, and tarragon. Slowly whisk in the oils.

Cook the bacon until crisp. Drain on paper towels and crumble.

Slice the iceberg lettuce and chicory into shreds and then chop crosswise. Remove the stems from the watercress. Separate the endive into leaves. Put the greens into a large, shallow bowl and toss gently to combine.

Peel and cut the tomatoes into large dice. Chop the hard-cooked eggs. Chop the scallions, including the green tops. Crumble the cheese. Peel and dice the avocado, squeeze the lemon juice over it, and toss.

Arrange the chicken, tomatoes, eggs, avocado, and cheese in rows over the greens. Sprinkle with the bacon and scallions. The salad can be assembled up to 1 hour before serving and kept chilled.

SERVING: At the table, pour the vinaigrette over the salad and toss well.

YIELD: 4 to 6 servings

CHICKEN AND VEGETABLE SALAD
WITH TOMATO–CHEESE MAYONNAISE

Homemade mayonnaise and a variety of fresh vegetables make this a special chicken salad. You can vary it as you like, perhaps by using minced herbs instead of or in addition to the tomato paste in the mayonnaise, or by substituting half the quantity of mustard for the tomato paste. And any combination of vegetables you fancy can go into the salad.

Preparation: *For the chicken,* put the breasts in a large pan in one layer. Chop the onion and add it to the pan. Add the wine, ½ cup water, parsley, bay leaf, thyme, and salt and pepper. Bring to a simmer. Lower the heat, cover, and poach until the chicken is just done, 20 to 25 minutes. Remove the chicken, reserving the poaching liquid, and cool to room temperature. Reduce the poaching liquid over high heat to 2 tablespoons, about 5 minutes, and reserve. When the chicken is cool enough to handle, skin, remove the meat from the bones, and cut it into ½-inch dice.

For the mayonnaise, whisk the egg yolks, ½ teaspoon salt, pepper, and lemon juice together. Whisk in the oils very slowly, drop by drop at first and then in a thin stream. Strain the reduced pan juices into the mayonnaise and whisk in along with the tomato paste and grated cheese.

Peel the carrots and cut into ½-inch dice. Snap the tough ends off the asparagus and discard them. Peel the stalks and cut them into 1-inch lengths. Cut the zucchini into ½-inch dice. Cook the carrots in boiling salted water for 10 minutes. After 5 minutes, add the asparagus and fresh peas, if using. Add the zucchini and frozen peas, if using, to cook during the last 2 minutes. Drain, plunge into cold water, and drain well.

Toss the chicken and vegetables with half the mayonnaise. Adjust the seasoning.

SERVING: Sprinkle the servings of salad with grated cheese and pass the remaining mayonnaise separately.

YIELD: 4 servings

Chicken

4 chicken breast halves
  (about 2 pounds in all)
½ small onion
⅓ cup dry white wine
2 sprigs parsley
1 bay leaf
  Pinch of dried thyme
  Salt and black pepper

Tomato–Cheese Mayonnaise

2 egg yolks
  Salt and black pepper
2 tablespoons lemon juice
⅔ cup vegetable oil
⅓ cup olive oil
2 teaspoons tomato paste
¼ cup grated Parmesan cheese

2 carrots
½ pound asparagus
1 medium-sized zucchini
½ cup fresh or frozen peas
  Salt and black pepper

¼ cup grated Parmesan cheese

SMOKED CHICKEN SALAD

This untraditional chicken salad, developed by famed caterer Martha Stewart, shows her love for colorful presentation and her flair for innovative combinations. It's perfect for a summer or early fall party.

Marinade

1 small onion
1 clove garlic
1 orange
¼ cup chopped fresh parsley
¼ cup olive oil
   Salt and black pepper

2 whole chicken breasts or 1¼ pounds
   smoked chicken (see Note)
¼ pound sugar snap peas
¼ pound baby pattypan squash
1 tablespoon unsalted butter
2 ounces mushrooms, such as shiitake or
   boletes
   Pinch of saffron

Vinaigrette

3 tablespoons rice wine vinegar
1 teaspoon Dijon mustard
   Salt and black pepper
6 tablespoons olive oil

½ pound red or green baby okra
½ cup golden cherry tomatoes
   Red leaf lettuce for lining the serving
   bowl
2 tablespoons fresh chervil leaves

Preparation: *For the marinade,* slice the onion and the garlic. Squeeze the orange. In a large bowl or pan, combine all the marinade ingredients. Marinate the chicken breasts in the mixture for at least 10 hours, refrigerated, before smoking.

Transfer the chicken from the marinade to a smoker rack. Smoke in a water smoker *or* covered kettle grill according to the manufacturer's directions until the juices run clear and the flesh shows no pink when the chicken is pierced, 45 to 60 minutes (see Note). Set the chicken aside to cool.

Halve the breasts, carefully remove the meat from the bones in one piece, and cut it into ⅛-inch-thick slices.

Remove the strings from the sugar snap peas. In a large pot of boiling salted water, boil the squash until tender, 3 to 4 minutes. Add the peas to cook during the last minute. Drain. Plunge into cold water and drain well.

Melt the butter in a small frying pan. Sauté the mushrooms together with the saffron over medium-high heat until lightly browned, 3 to 4 minutes. Cool.

For the vinaigrette, whisk together the vinegar, mustard, and salt and pepper in a large bowl. Whisk in the oil.

Boil the okra until tender, 4 to 5 minutes. Drain and add to the vinaigrette. (Warm okra will regain some of its color when mixed with the vinaigrette; cold okra will not.)

Halve the cherry tomatoes lengthwise. Add to the dressing with the mushrooms (reserving a few for garnish), the pattypan squash, and peas, and toss lightly. Line a serving bowl with the lettuce, fill with the vegetables, and arrange the chicken on top. Garnish with reserved mushrooms and sprinkle with chervil leaves.

YIELD: 4 servings

NOTE: The chicken can be smoked over a fire made of mesquite charcoal and mesquite wood. Use 1 bottle of white wine in the water pan instead of water for added flavor. The chicken can be smoked the day before. Or you can simply buy smoked chicken and use as is without marinating or cooking.

CUCUMBER AND BRIE SALAD

This fresh, light salad is an unusual combination of Brie, cabbage, and cucumber, accented by a balsamic vinegar dressing. It's especially good for Brie fanciers who find that the specimens usually available to them are less than perfect.

Preparation: Mince the onion. Core the cabbage and cut it into thin strips. Grate the carrot. Peel and seed the cucumbers; then quarter lengthwise and slice thin. Cut the Brie into large dice.

Put the onion, vinegar, and lemon juice in a bowl and leave for 5 minutes. Whisk in the oil. Add the cabbage, carrot, cucumber, and cheese. Season with salt and pepper to taste. Toss lightly.

½ small red onion
½ savoy cabbage
½ carrot
3 cucumbers
3 ounces Brie
1 tablespoon plus 1 teaspoon balsamic vinegar
½ teaspoon lemon juice
3 tablespoons peanut oil
Salt and black pepper
4 leaves red leaf or Boston lettuce

SERVING: Put a lettuce leaf on each of 4 chilled plates and top with the salad.

YIELD: 4 servings

SMOKED DUCK SALAD

It's easiest to smoke the duck for this salad in a smoker or kettle grill.
Directions are also given below for using a large, heavy pot as a smoker
on your stove, a method that gives excellent flavor, though it can make
a bit of a mess.

2 cups dried lentils

For Indoor Smoking

⅓ cup rice
¼ cup black-currant-flavored or other fruit-
flavored tea leaves
¼ cup packed light-brown sugar
1 cinnamon stick, broken
1 3-inch strip orange zest

4 boneless duck breasts (from 2
approximately 3½-pound ducks)
Salt and black pepper

4 cups duck or Chicken Stock (page 81)
2 red bell peppers
2 yellow bell peppers
2 cloves garlic
1 tablespoon balsamic vinegar
Salt and black pepper
2 scallions

3 tablespoons olive oil
2 teaspoons lemon juice
Arugula or mache for garnish
Black olives for garnish

Preparation: Pick over and rinse the lentils. Soak them
in water overnight and then drain, or increase cooking
time for lentils to about 1 hour.

For indoor smoking, line a large, heavy pot and its lid
with 3 to 4 thicknesses of aluminum foil, leaving a generous overhang. Combine all the indoor smoking ingredients in the prepared pot. Oil a steaming rack (or
improvise with a plate set on a measuring cup) and put
it over rice-tea mixture.

Put the duck breasts, skin side up, on the rack. Season
lightly with salt and pepper. Put the lid on the pot,
leaving the foil overhang loose. Put the pot over high
heat until a steady stream of smoke emerges, about 5
minutes. Now crimp the overhanging foil to seal
loosely and smoke for 10 minutes. Carefully open the
pot, remove the duck and rack, and immediately discard the foil and smoking mixture. Alternatively,
smoke the duck breasts in a water smoker until they test
done and are pink inside, 30 to 40 minutes, or over an
indirect fire in a kettle grill for 15 to 20 minutes. Set the
duck aside to cool.

In a saucepan, bring the lentils and stock to a boil,
covered. Lower the heat and simmer until the lentils are
just tender but not mushy and the liquid has been absorbed, about 20 minutes. Let cool.

Broil or grill the red and yellow peppers until blistered and blackened; peel and cut them into 1-inch
strips. Mince the garlic. In a bowl, toss the red and
yellow pepper strips with a light coating of balsamic
vinegar, the garlic, and salt and pepper and set aside.
Cut the scallions diagonally into thin slices.

SERVING: Season the lentils with salt and pepper and add the oil, lemon juice, and scallions. Slice the duck diagonally. Arrange the slices on a large plate, fanning them out slightly. Arrange the marinated pepper strips and lentil salad alongside. Garnish with arugula or mache and olives.

YIELD: 4 servings

PROVENÇALE GREEN BEAN SALAD WITH BLACK OLIVE VINAIGRETTE

This salad can be prepared ahead and refrigerated. Remove it from the refrigerator about 30 minutes before serving so that it will return to room temperature.

Preparation: Wash and trim the beans. Pit the olives. Slice the radishes.

In a pot of boiling water, cook the beans until just tender, 6 to 8 minutes. Drain and refresh under cold running water. Drain thoroughly.

For the vinaigrette, whisk together the olive puree, vinegar, and salt and pepper. Whisk in the oil and taste for seasoning.

1 pound thin green beans
¼ cup black Mediterranean olives
¼ cup small green Mediterranean olives
12 radishes

Black Olive Vinaigrette

1 tablespoon black olive puree (see Note)
1½ tablespoons red wine vinegar
    Salt and black pepper
¼ cup olive oil

SERVING: Toss the beans, olives, and vinaigrette together. Put on plates and garnish with the radishes. Serve at room temperature.

YIELD: 4 servings

NOTE: Black olive puree, sold in small jars, is available in specialty stores. Or puree about 4 pitted black olives to make 1 tablespoon.

SUGAR SNAP, RED CABBAGE, AND HAM SALAD WITH WALNUT VINAIGRETTE

If you don't keep walnut oil on hand, don't pass this delicious combination by. Just crush a generous handful of raw walnuts and add to a cup of any light-flavored oil, such as peanut or safflower.

½ pound sugar snap peas or *snow peas*
½ pound red cabbage
 1 tablespoon red wine vinegar

¼ cup chopped walnuts
½ pound Smithfield or *other country ham*

Walnut Vinaigrette

⅓ cup balsamic vinegar
   Salt and black pepper
¾ cup walnut oil
¼ cup vegetable oil

Preparation: Trim the peas. Shred the cabbage. Cook the peas in a large pot of boiling salted water until just tender, 3 to 5 minutes. Remove with a slotted spoon, cool under cold water, and drain well. Add the red wine vinegar and cabbage to the same water and boil until the cabbage is just tender, 1 to 2 minutes. Drain, refresh under cold water, and drain well.

Toast the walnuts in a 325°F oven until lightly browned, 5 to 10 minutes. Cut the ham into thin julienne strips.

For the dressing, whisk together the vinegar and salt and pepper. Slowly whisk in the oils.

SERVING: Toss the cabbage and peas separately in enough vinaigrette to coat them. Arrange a bed of cabbage on each salad plate. Put the peas on top and a mound of ham in the center. Sprinkle with toasted walnuts and drizzle a bit more dressing over the salads. Serve at room temperature.

YIELD: 4 servings

MENUS

Lobster–Grapefruit Salad Jean-Pierre Capelle (page 42)

Dry Chenin Blanc, such as Dry Creek Vineyard

Char-Grilled Vegetable Soup (page 80)

Dry, blended white, such as Trefethen Eshcol White

Papaya–Rum Babas (page 264)

Salmon-Butter Triangles with Caviar and Dill (page 27)

Piper-Sonoma Blanc de Noirs

Cucumber and Brie Salad (page 47)
Smoked Chicken Salad (page 46)

Côte de Brouilly (lightly chilled)

Cherry Soup with Strawberry Sherbet (page 234)

Seafood and Barley Salad with Lemon and Basil Vinaigrette (page 40)

Sancerre

Curried Lamb Chops with Banana–Almond Chutney (page 167)

Zinfandel, such as Simi or Kendall-Jackson

Espresso
Pistachio Butter Cookies (page 227)

CHAPTER 3

WARM SALADS

Grilled Sole Salad with Vegetable Dressing
Chinese Noodle Salad with Grilled Monkfish
Warm Salad with Matsutake · *Smoked Catfish–Egg Roll Salad*
Mixed Greens with Curried Clams · *Fried Chicken Salad*
Shredded Chicken · *Quail with Cracklings Salad* · *Arugula Salad*
Grilled Rabbit Salad with Country Bacon–Molasses Dressing
Warm Beef and Spinach Salad · *Oyster and Spinach Salad*
Warm Lamb and Blue Cheese Salad

Warm salads are emblematic of the new modular cuisine. They are inventive; they taste light and healthy; they can be served at various points in the meal—as a first course, a chic main course, or a cheese and salad course before dessert. Hardly a restaurant has opened in the last five years that doesn't have at least one warm salad on the menu.

Although the words *lettuce* and *salad* have long been virtually synonymous, warm salads are generally better made with less-common garden varieties. The preferred greens fall into two categories: firm and tender. Those in the first group, including radicchio (when is a green red?), endive, and dandelion, are ideal for warm salads, because their firmer textures withstand the wilting effect of warm ingredients or dressings. These greens even benefit from this bit of tenderizing. Softer but spicy-flavored greens, such as watercress and arugula, comprise the other group, whose leaves are so tender to begin with that the addition of warm ingredients makes them practically melt in your mouth. The difference between these and the more traditional soft greens is that their lively taste is a match for forceful other flavors. In fact, the firm greens are usually full flavored, too, a strong base on which to build a dish that stands on its own. In either case, firm or soft, flavorful greens in combination with warm ingredients make for a symbiotic match.

Heated goat cheese is the prototypical warm salad ingredient. The warm chèvre salad of French nouvelle cuisine launched a limitless number of possibilities that are being explored by U.S. chefs. The idea has been taken up enthusiastically by home cooks, too, largely because such dishes are quickly prepared. And a warm salad is an ideal place to showcase relatively small quantities of expensive ingredients, such as wild mushrooms or duck breast. Consider the following: a bed of many greens topped with grilled sole and a vegetable vinaigrette; curried clams on a variety of greens; warm quail set on mustard greens; lamb and blue cheese on Belgian endive. It's a long way from lettuce and tomato!

Greens

Leafy vegetables with firm texture or strong flavor—or both—are especially suited to warm salads.

Arugula

Arugula is a peppery green that has a good bite. The best arugula is small and has slender, dark-green leaves that are two to three inches long. After the plant has flowered, or if it has a slight fuzziness under the leaves, it will be tough and unpleasantly bitter. Arugula is also known as rocket and roquette.

Belgian Endive

The tightly packed, spear-shaped heads of Belgian endive are protected from light to produce their characteristic color, which shades from white at the base of the leaves to pale yellow at the tip. It should be stored in a dark place so that it doesn't turn bitter.

Curly Endive

Curly endive, also called chicory in this country, has narrow, frizzled green leaves. Because of its sharp, bitter flavor, many people prefer to use curly endive as an accent rather than the focus of a salad.

Dandelion

Like other greens, dandelions should be picked before they flower for the best texture and flavor. Jagged-edged dandelions should be bright green, and they will keep longer if the root ends and stems are not removed until cooking. The leaves have an appealing bitter flavor and are good uncooked or slightly wilted in a warm dressing.

Mustard Greens

Frilly mustard greens are among the prettiest leaves to go into a salad. They have a full, surprisingly rich, and somewhat hot flavor.

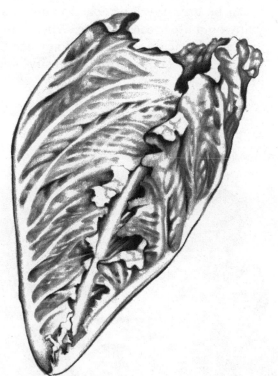

Napa Cabbage

The wide, white ribs of Napa cabbage are surrounded by crinkled yellowish-green. The head is shaped like romaine lettuce, but is more compact. This mild-flavored cabbage is best cooked very briefly or eaten raw, and small heads are generally the sweetest.

Radicchio

The darling of 1980s cooking in America, radicchio has been around for a long time in Italy. The two types you're most likely to find on the American market are the round-headed radicchio di Verona and the longer, leafier radicchio di Treviso. Radicchio has a pleasant bitterness, and it's usually better uncooked because the pretty color turns brown when heated.

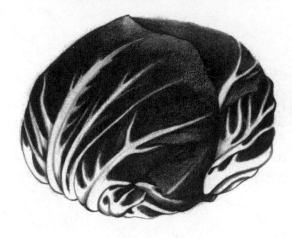

Red Cabbage

A deep, red purple, this cabbage is otherwise similar to its common green cousin. It can be used raw or cooked in any way you would use green cabbage. When cooking, add an acid, such as lemon juice or vinegar, to retain—in fact intensify—the bright color.

Savoy Cabbage

Savoy cabbage is slightly milder and more tender than red and green cabbage. Its crinkly outer leaves shade from deep green on the outside to a yellow-green inner head. It can be used interchangeably with other cabbages and is most readily available from autumn through springtime.

Spinach

As with other greens that don't like hot weather, you'll find spinach in slightly less quantity and lower quality in the summer. Spinach will stay freshest if stored with the stems intact. Thorough washing in several changes of water is always in order because spinach grows in sandy soil and the curly leaves hold a lot of grit.

Watercress

Watercress, which does in fact grow in water, has crisp, tender deep-green leaves that are at once spicy and refreshing. Choose cress with tender stems and use it quickly.

Mushrooms

There's nothing wrong with the common cultivated mushroom, but a variety of possibilities is even better. Among the types now readily available, boletes, chanterelles, matsutake, and morels are true wild mushrooms. Most shiitake, enoki, and oyster mushrooms found in stores are cultivated under carefully controlled conditions.

To prepare fresh mushrooms, gently brush off dirt and trim the stems. If the mushrooms are very dirty, wipe them with a damp paper towel or even rinse them, but do this quickly so that they don't absorb water.

Boletes

Most readily available in fall, boletes are large, meaty mushrooms also called cèpe, steinpilz, porcini, and king bolete. They have wide, convex, reddish-brown caps with "tube mouths" rather than gills and white to brownish stalks. When the boletes are young, the caps are firm and the flesh is almost crunchy. Older boletes become spongy and have fibrous stems that can be pulled into fine strands like noodles. Cut off the tube mouths of older mushrooms because they may be slimy or bitter. And don't sauté boletes past golden brown or they may become bitter.

Chanterelles

Chanterelles have a nectar fragrance somewhat like that of apricots and a sweet flavor that varies from mild to slightly spicy. You're most likely to find them in the fall or winter. Chanterelles can be recognized by their distinctive caps, which flare from bottom to top forming a sort of triangle of firm, cream-colored or yellowish flesh. Blunt, fold-like ridges run from the base of the stem to the edge of the cap. Choose chanterelles that are firm. Gently press your thumb to the cap—it should not leave an indentation. If water comes to the surface when you press, the mushrooms are too wet to pay top dollar for but can be used if they are in good condition otherwise. Spread the wet mushrooms on paper towels to dry out or cook them in a dry frying pan over medium heat, spooning out the water as it is expelled and saving the liquid for a sauce.

Enoki

Enoki have long, delicate stems with tiny caps. They are cultivated and rarely need any preparation more than trimming the brownish root ends. You can eat them raw or briefly cooked—be careful not to over-heat or they may become bitter.

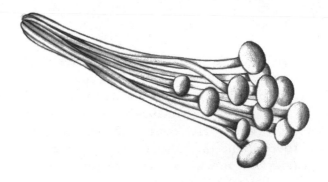

Matsutake

Matsutake are gathered from July through mid-December, although these large, thick-fleshed mushrooms may appear in stores now and then during the rest of the year, too. The Asian matsutake is a dark brown with a mild aroma. The American matsutake is stark white, with some cinnamon-color staining in age and a sweet, spicy fragrance. As long as they are still firm, the older cinnamon-streaked mushrooms are the most flavorful. Slow cooking is best to tenderize and bring out the flavor.

Morels

The convoluted morel cap looks like a thimble-shaped honeycomb. The hollow caps are a favorite hiding place for bugs and debris, and so it's a good idea to cut the mushrooms in half and brush them out before cooking. Morels vary in color from yellow to brown to black, with yellow being the type you're most likely to come across. Choose morels that are moist, spongy, and heavy for their size. Unlike other mushrooms, they should always be cooked. Morels are in season in spring and early summer.

Oyster Mushrooms

Ear-shaped oyster mushrooms derive their name from their flavor, which many people consider similar to that of the bivalve. Unlike their namesakes, though, oyster mushrooms are equally good all year round. The thick, white flesh is smooth, fragrant, and moist, and the mushrooms are flavorful but sometimes tough. The caps range from white to gray or brown, and the gills are whitish or yellow-tinged.

Shiitake

Widely used in Oriental cooking, shiitake have a light, woody scent and round, flat caps that are brown on top and whitish underneath. The caps have a pleasantly chewy texture, but the fibrous stems are tough. Save the stems to flavor a stock or sauce; strain them out before serving. Shiitake should be dry and firm with caps that curl under slightly. They are good all year.

GRILLED SOLE SALAD WITH VEGETABLE DRESSING

The unusual vinaigrette for this dish, invented by Chef Christian Lévêque at La Récolte in New York City, is excellent on hot vegetables as well as on salads—green beans, for instance, or even potatoes.

Preparation: *For the vinaigrette,* peel and chop the carrot. Chop the cauliflower and broccoli florets. Trim the beans. In a pot of boiling salted water, cook the carrot for 2 minutes. Add the cauliflower, broccoli, and beans and boil until fully cooked, about 5 minutes more. Drain. Transfer the vegetables to a blender or a food processor and whirl until pureed. Add the vinegar and 1 tablespoon of water. Slowly pour in the oil. Set the mixture aside to cool. Whisk in the cream. Add a tablespoon or so more water if the dressing seems too thick. Season with salt and pepper to taste.

Tear the arugula (if using), radicchio, Bibb lettuce, and endive into bite-sized pieces. Cut the red pepper and truffle or olives into ⅛-inch dice. Peel the zucchini and cut the skin into ⅛-inch dice. Save the flesh for another use.

Cooking: Season the sole with salt and pepper and coat it lightly with the oil. Heat a grill or broiler. Grill the fish until it just tests done, about 3 minutes.

While the fish is cooking, toss the arugula, radicchio, Bibb lettuce, and endive with just enough dressing to coat them lightly.

SERVING: Mound greens on 4 plates. Cut each fillet in half lengthwise. Place on top of the greens. Distribute the red pepper, truffle or olives, and zucchini skin over the salad and serve at once with remaining dressing on the side.

YIELD: 4 servings

Vegetable Vinaigrette

½ carrot
¼ small head cauliflower
1 stalk broccoli
6 green beans
2 tablespoons vinegar
¾ cup oil
3 tablespoons heavy cream
  Salt and black pepper

8 arugula leaves (optional)
1 small head radicchio
1 head Bibb lettuce
3 Belgian endives
1 red bell pepper
1 black truffle or 4 black olives
1 medium-sized zucchini
1 pound Dover sole fillets or other lean
  white fish
  Salt and black pepper
¼ cup olive oil, approximately

CHINESE NOODLE SALAD WITH GRILLED MONKFISH

A good example of the strong Oriental influence in contemporary American cooking, this salad was developed by Patricia Unterman at her innovative American restaurant, the Hayes St. Grill, in San Francisco.

1 pound monkfish fillets

Dressing

1 1-inch piece of fresh ginger
1 clove garlic
¼ cup rice wine vinegar
⅓ cup soy sauce
2 tablespoons lemon juice
1 cup peanut oil

4 scallions, including green tops
½ pound snow peas
1 pound shiitake mushrooms or regular
*   cultivated mushrooms*
1 pound fresh extra-thin Oriental-style
*   noodles*
1 clove garlic
5 tablespoons (approximately) peanut oil
1 thin slice fresh ginger
*   Salt and black pepper*

Preparation: Remove the skin from the monkfish. Trim the fish and cut it into 1-inch pieces. Put on 4 skewers.

For the dressing, peel and grate the ginger root. Mince the garlic. In a food processor, blend the ginger, garlic, vinegar, soy sauce, and lemon juice until smooth. Slowly add the oil. Spoon about ¼ cup of the dressing ver the fish.

Cut the scallions into 1-inch-long pieces. Remove the strings from the snow peas. Remove and discard the stems from the shiitake, if using; slice the caps or the whole cultivated mushrooms. Carefully separate the noodles. Crush the garlic.

Heat ¼ cup of the oil in a large frying pan. Add the slice of ginger and crushed garlic. When the oil begins to sizzle and the ginger and garlic become aromatic, remove them. Add mushrooms and sauté quickly over high heat until they are just cooked, 1 to 2 minutes. Add the scallions, season with salt and pepper, and stir. Remove from the pan and set aside.

In a pot of boiling salted water, blanch the snow peas until they turn bright green, about ½ minute. Drain, cool under cold water, and drain well.

In a large pot of boiling salted water, bring the noodles to a boil and cook until just done, 2 to 3 minutes. Drain and rinse with cold water. Shake and drain the noodles very well and toss with remaining tablespoon peanut oil to prevent them from sticking.

Cooking: Heat the grill or broiler. Grill or broil the skewers of monkfish until they are just firm but still juicy, 2 to 3 minutes per side.

SERVING: Toss the noodles with ½ cup of the dressing and put on individual plates. Toss the snow peas in the dressing and put alongside the noodles. Spoon the mushrooms along the opposite side. Arrange a skewer of fish diagonally over the noodles. Pass the remaining dressing separately.

YIELD: 4 servings

WARM SALAD WITH MATSUTAKE

This salad was developed by James Moore, the executive chef at the Mountain Home Inn in Mill Valley, California, and a great proponent of wild mushrooms.

Preparation: Trim the mushrooms and cut them into thin wedges. Wash and dry the greens. Mince the parsley.

Cooking: In a large frying pan, heat 2 tablespoons of the oil and the butter. Over high heat, shaking the pan constantly, cook the mushrooms for 3 minutes. Season with salt to taste. Lower the heat and simmer until the mushrooms are tender, about 15 minutes, checking to make sure the mushrooms don't get overcooked and rubbery. Remove the mushrooms with a slotted spoon. Reduce the cooking liquid over high heat to a syrupy consistency. Whisk in the remaining 6 tablespoons of oil, vinegar, coriander, allspice, parsley, and salt and pepper to taste. Toss the greens with this dressing.

1 pound matsutake or chanterelles
24 leaves firm greens, such as Belgian endive or radicchio
2 tablespoons minced fresh parsley
8 tablespoons olive oil
2 tablespoons unsalted butter
Salt and black pepper
1½ tablespoons white wine vinegar
Pinch of ground coriander
Pinch of ground allspice

SERVING: Arrange 6 leaves on each plate, overlapping to form a fan. Put the warm mushrooms in a mound, overlapping the base of each fan.

YIELD: 4 servings

SMOKED CATFISH–EGG ROLL SALAD

This rather odd-sounding combination is a delicious invention and a
good way to use the smoked catfish that has recently become available.
Other smoked fish also work well in this recipe.

Basil and Red Onion Mayonnaise

½ red onion
½ cup plus 1 tablespoon peanut oil
¼ cup shredded fresh basil, tarragon, or
   parsley leaves
   Salt and black pepper
1 teaspoon red wine vinegar
¾ teaspoon lemon juice
1 egg yolk

1½ pounds smoked catfish or other smoked
   fish, such as smoked whitefish
1 egg white
2 carrots
4 cups shredded Chinese or savoy
   cabbage
8 6-inch egg roll wrappers
   Safflower or other oil for frying
⅓ cup shredded fresh basil, tarragon, or
   parsley leaves
4 teaspoons peanut oil
4 teaspoons red wine vinegar
   Salt and black pepper
   Basil leaves for garnish (optional)

Preparation: *For the mayonnaise,* mince the onion. Heat
1 tablespoon of the peanut oil in a small frying pan over
medium heat. Sauté the onion and basil with salt and
pepper to taste until just soft, about 4 minutes. Transfer
the mixture to a bowl and add the vinegar and lemon
juice. Whisk in the yolk. Whisk in the remaining ½ cup
peanut oil very slowly, first almost drop by drop and
then in a very thin stream. Adjust the seasonings.

Remove the skin and bones from catfish and cut fish
into ½-inch chunks. Gently toss the catfish in mayonnaise.

Lightly beat the egg white. Cut the carrots with a
vegetable peeler into long, very thin strips. Cut the
cabbage into shreds.

Arrange the egg roll wrappers with one point of each
facing you. Put one-eighth of the smoked fish filling,
widthwise, slightly below the center of each wrapper,
patting it into a 2½- by 1-inch rectangle. Fold the bottom corner of the wrapper over the filling and brush
with the egg white. Fold in the left and right corners,
sealing the folds with egg white. Roll up the wrapper
away from you, sealing tightly so that all the filling is
completely enclosed. Cover egg rolls tightly with plastic wrap and refrigerate until ready to fry.

Cooking: In a deep fryer, heat the safflower oil to
375°F. Fry the egg rolls in the hot oil, being careful not
to crowd them, until evenly golden brown, about 4
minutes in all. Drain on paper towels.

Combine the cabbage, carrots, and shredded basil.
Toss with the peanut oil, vinegar, and salt and pepper
to taste.

Miniature Scallion Crêpes with Salmon Caviar and Sour Cream

Summer Seviche

Lobster–Grapefruit Salad Jean-Pierre Capelle

Smoked Duck Salad

◀Smoked Chicken
Salad

Fried Chicken Salad

Smoked Catfish–Egg Roll Salad

SERVING: Mound dressed vegetables on plates. Arrange the egg rolls on the salad mixture. Garnish with basil leaves if desired.

YIELD: 4 to 8 servings

MIXED GREENS WITH CURRIED CLAMS

Chef Arnauld Briand of El Rio Grande-Mexico City in New York City created this recipe. If you're not fond of curry, you might vary it with a Cajun seasoning mix rather than curry or another combination of spices that you like.

Preparation: *For the vinaigrette,* whisk the mustard, vinegar, and salt and pepper together in a bowl. Whisk in the oil.

Shuck the clams and drain the meat. Mix together the flour and curry powder. Coat the clams with the flour-curry powder mixture.

Cut the carrots in thin julienne strips. Tear the greens into bite-sized pieces.

Cooking: Melt the butter in a frying pan. Sauté the coated clams over high heat until just done, about 1 minute altogether. Toss the greens in the vinaigrette dressing.

SERVING: Mound greens in the center of each plate and circle with warm clams. Top with the julienned carrots.

YIELD: 4 servings

Mustard Vinaigrette

1 teaspoon Dijon mustard
2 tablespoons red wine vinegar
Salt and black pepper
6 tablespoons vegetable oil

24 small clams
3 tablespoons flour
1 tablespoon curry powder
2 carrots
2 cups red leaf lettuce
¼ pound arugula (about 2 cups)
¼ pound mache (about 2 cups)
3 to 4 tablespoons unsalted butter

FRIED CHICKEN SALAD

We've had nouvelle cuisine, *nuova cucina,* and new American cuisine; it
was only a matter of time before new Southern cuisine surfaced. This is
a good example.

2 heads Boston or *Bibb lettuce*
8 cherry tomatoes
½ cup mushrooms
1 shallot
*1 tablespoon chopped fresh tarragon leaves
    or 1 teaspoon dried tarragon, plus
    optional fresh leaves for garnish*
*1 sweet onion, such as Vidalia or 1 red
    onion*
*4 chicken breast halves
    (about 2 pounds in all)*
*½ cup flour
    Salt and black pepper*
¼ teaspoon coarse black pepper
⅓ cup milk
½ cup peanut oil
2 tablespoons white wine vinegar
2 teaspoons Dijon mustard
1 tablespoon drained capers (optional)

Preparation: Wash and dry the lettuce. Cut the cherry
tomatoes into halves. Slice the mushrooms. Mince the
shallot. Chop the tarragon if using fresh. Cut the onion
into thin slices. Arrange the lettuce leaves and tomatoes
on 4 salad plates.

Bone the chicken breasts and cut them horizontally
into ½-inch strips. In a shallow bowl, mix flour with ½
teaspoon salt and the coarse pepper. Put the milk in
another bowl.

Cooking: Heat the oil in a frying pan over medium-
high heat. Dip the chicken strips into the milk and then
into the flour mixture to coat them.

Fry the chicken on both sides until brown, about 5
minutes altogether. Drain on paper towels, reserving
the oil in the pan. Add the vinegar to the oil. Stir,
scraping the pan with a wooden spoon to deglaze it.
Whisk in the mustard, mushrooms, shallot, and tarragon and season with salt and pepper to taste.

SERVING: Put the chicken strips on the lettuce leaves and
pour on just enough vinaigrette to moisten the leaves.
Scatter the capers, if desired, and sliced onion on top of
the salads. Garnish with tarragon leaves if desired.
Serve the remaining dressing on the side.

YIELD: 4 servings

SHREDDED CHICKEN

Susan Feniger and Mary Sue Milliken developed this recipe that reflects their special combination of foreign ideas and American flair. The Orient holds sway here with the preparation and cooking of the chicken, which is then presented with avocado on a bed of watercress. Feniger and Milliken are co-chefs of The City Cafe–Border Grill and are co-owners and co-chefs of The City Restaurant, both in Los Angeles.

Preparation: *For the marinade,* grate the ginger. Mince the garlic. Blend all marinade ingredients in a bowl.

Remove the skin, fat, and any sinew from the chicken breasts. Tear the breasts into ½- by 2-inch pieces, add to the marinade, and let stand at room temperature for at least 30 minutes.

Trim, wash, and drain the watercress. Thoroughly whisk together the olive oil, lemon juice, and salt to taste.

Cooking: Heat the 6 tablespoons peanut oil in a large frying pan. When the oil is nearly smoking, add the chicken, each shred separately. Try to add as little of the marinade as possible. Cook the chicken until lightly browned on each side, no longer than 3 to 4 minutes.

SERVING: Toss the watercress with the dressing and arrange on 4 plates. Quarter the avocado, remove the skin and pit, and sprinkle the avocado with pepper. Put the avocado on top of the watercress and arrange the chicken on each salad around the avocado.

YIELD: 4 servings

Marinade

2 tablespoons grated fresh ginger
½ clove garlic
3 tablespoons sesame oil
4 teaspoons peanut oil
2 tablespoons lemon juice
2 tablespoons soy sauce
2 teaspoons cornstarch

4 boneless chicken breasts
   (about 2 pounds in all)
1 bunch watercress (about 2 cups)
4 teaspoons olive oil
2 tablespoons lemon juice
   Salt and coarse black pepper
6 tablespoons peanut oil
1 ripe avocado

QUAIL WITH CRACKLINGS SALAD

Bradley Ogden of Campton Place in San Francisco integrates American regional cooking with fresh ideas and newly available ingredients. Here the echoes are from Southern cooking—quail, cracklings, mustard greens, and corn.

Marinade

 4 small cloves garlic
½ teaspoon cracked black pepper
½ cup Madeira
½ teaspoon salt
¾ cup olive oil
10 sprigs fresh rosemary or 2 teaspoons
    dried rosemary
12 sprigs fresh thyme or 2 teaspoons dried
    thyme

 8 quail (about 4 ounces each)
¼ cup Dijon mustard
 1 pound skin and fat from pork, goose, or
    duck

Shallot Dressing

 3 cloves garlic
 4 shallots
½ teaspoon dry mustard
    Salt and coarse black pepper
½ teaspoon sugar
 4 teaspoons lemon juice
¼ cup red wine vinegar
¾ cup peanut oil

½ pound mustard greens (about 4 cups)
¼ pound arugula (about 2 cups)
12 radicchio leaves
 4 teaspoons olive oil
 1 cup corn kernels or 1 cup baby corn
 1 tablespoon unsalted butter
24 sprigs chervil or tiny sprigs parsley

Preparation: *For the marinade,* mince the garlic and mix all the marinade ingredients in a large bowl.

To bone the quail breasts, cut down both sides of the breastbone close to the bone. Slide the knife down along the ribs, removing the breast meat and wings together. Cut through the joints at the tops of the thighs and remove the thighs and legs in one piece. Rub the meat with the mustard, and put the pieces in the marinade; cover and refrigerate overnight.

For the cracklings, heat the oven to 375°F. Cut the skin from the pork, goose, *or* duck into strips about 1 inch long and ½-inch wide. Chop the fat. Put skin strips and fat into a large baking dish and cook in the preheated oven, stirring often. The fat that is rendered should remain clear yellow. If it darkens, lower the oven heat. Cook until the bits of skin turn golden brown and crisp, about 20 minutes for pork and about 10 minutes for goose and duck. Strain and cool, reserving the rendered fat. Chop the cracklings into ¼-inch dice—you should have about 2 cups.

For the dressing, mince the garlic. Slice the shallots. In a bowl, whisk together the garlic, dry mustard, salt, pepper, sugar, and lemon juice. Whisk in the vinegar, the peanut oil, and the shallots. Set aside for at least 30 minutes.

Wash and dry the mustard greens, arugula, and radicchio. Arrange the radicchio leaves on plates.

Cooking: Heat the grill or broiler. Remove the quail from the marinade and rub all over with the olive oil. Cook, skin side down, until golden and crisp, basting occasionally with a little of the reserved fat from the cracklings. Turn and continue cooking until crisp, about 8 minutes altogether.

SERVING: To assemble the salad, heat the cracklings in a large frying pan. Add the arugula and mustard greens and wilt slightly. Remove from the heat and toss with the dressing to coat. Sauté the corn in butter briefly. Arrange the dressed greens on top of the radicchio and top with the quail. Garnish with the sautéed corn kernels and chervil sprigs.

YIELD: 4 servings

ARUGULA SALAD

A savory version of crème anglaise, the sweet custard sauce, is the innovation that makes this salad unique.

Preparation: Cut the bacon into ½-inch dice. Beat the eggs lightly in a small bowl. Add vinegar, honey, paprika, and salt and pepper. Tear the arugula into bite-sized pieces.

5 ounces slab bacon
2 eggs
¼ cup cider vinegar
1½ teaspoons honey
Pinch of paprika
Salt and black pepper
¾ pound arugula (about 1½ quarts)
½ cup milk
4 tablespoons unsalted butter

Cooking: In a small frying pan over medium-high heat, cook the bacon until crisp and browned; set aside with the rendered fat.

Heat the milk and butter in a heavy saucepan until the butter has melted. Slowly add half of the milk and butter mixture to the egg mixture, whisking continuously; then add this mixture to the remaining milk and butter in the pan. Cook gently, stirring constantly, over very low heat until just thickened, about 3 minutes. Do not overheat or the eggs will curdle. Remove from the heat and quickly add the arugula, bacon, and bacon fat to the sauce and toss until well mixed.

YIELD: 4 servings

GRILLED RABBIT SALAD WITH COUNTRY BACON–MOLASSES DRESSING

Commander's Palace is famous for keeping the real New Orleans flavor in its updated dishes. Here Chef Emeril Lagasse uses Creole seasonings and a bacon-molasses dressing in a stylish new warm salad.

¼ pound boned rabbit meat
1 bell pepper
1 head red leaf lettuce
1 to 2 heads Bibb lettuce

Creole Meat Seasoning

1 teaspoon salt
¾ teaspoon granulated garlic
¾ teaspoon black pepper
¼ teaspoon paprika
Pinch of cayenne
1 tablespoon vegetable oil

Country Bacon–Molasses Dressing

¼ pound hickory smoked bacon
1 shallot
1 clove garlic
⅓ cup chopped mixed herbs, such as
    fresh basil, thyme, and chives
¼ cup red wine vinegar
2 tablespoons molasses
Salt and black pepper
Few drops of hot red pepper sauce
¼ cup olive oil

Preparation: Cut the rabbit meat into ⅛- by 1½-inch thin julienne strips. (Freezing the meat briefly—10 to 15 minutes—makes it easier to cut.) Remove the seeds from the pepper and cut into julienne strips. Wash and dry the lettuces and tear them into bite-sized pieces.

For the Creole meat seasoning, combine all the ingredients. Toss the rabbit strips and bell pepper strips in the mixture.

For the dressing, chop the bacon and sauté until golden brown. Mince the shallot, garlic, and herbs. Add to the bacon and cook until soft, about 2 minutes. Add the vinegar, molasses, salt and pepper, and hot red pepper sauce and bring to a boil. Remove from the heat, whisk in the olive oil, and keep warm.

Cooking: Heat the grill. Using a fine wire mesh basket, grill the rabbit and peppers until tender, about 2 minutes. Or sauté over high heat. Toss the rabbit, peppers, and lettuces with the warm dressing.

YIELD: 4 servings

WARM BEEF AND SPINACH SALAD

A strong Oriental influence is evident in this salad, which is essentially a
stir-fry.

Preparation: Cut the beef into 1½- by ½-inch strips.
(Freezing the meat briefly—10 to 15 minutes—makes it
easier to cut.) Mash the garlic with a pinch of coarse
salt. Pull thyme leaves from branches if using fresh.
Trim the scallions and cut them, green tops included,
diagonally into ¼-inch slices. Remove the large stems
from spinach, wash the leaves, and drain. Cut the carrot
into paper-thin diagonal slices.

1 pound trimmed boneless beef rib or
*   other tender cut*
1 clove garlic
*   Coarse salt*
1 teaspoon fresh thyme leaves or ½
*   teaspoon dried thyme*
2 small scallions
¾ pound fresh spinach
1 carrot
2 teaspoons peanut oil
*   Salt and black pepper*
4 teaspoons rice or white wine vinegar
1¼ teaspoons soy sauce
4 tablespoons unsalted butter

Cooking: In a large frying pan, heat 1 teaspoon of the
oil until very hot. Add half of the beef and season with
salt and pepper to taste. Sear over high heat, tossing,
until medium-rare, about 1½ minutes. Transfer the
meat to a large warm platter and keep it warm. Add the
remaining teaspoon of oil to the pan and cook the remaining beef. Transfer the second batch of meat to the
warm platter.

Lower the heat and add garlic and thyme to the pan.
Cook until the garlic just begins to color, about 30 seconds. Add the vinegar and soy sauce, stirring with a
wooden spoon to deglaze the pan. Add the butter and
scallions and salt and pepper to taste, stirring constantly
just until the butter melts. Remove the pan from the
heat, add the spinach and carrots, and toss. Adjust the
seasonings.

SERVING: Put the salad on warm plates and top with the
beef strips.

YIELD: 4 servings

OYSTER AND SPINACH SALAD

Jimmy Schmidt, who developed this innovative recipe, gained fame as the chef of Detroit's London Chop House and now lends his talents to the Rattlesnake Club in Denver.

6 slices bacon

Dressing

¼ cup chopped fresh chives
2 tablespoons grainy mustard
2 teaspoons dry mustard
¼ cup sherry wine vinegar
¼ cup balsamic vinegar
1 tablespoon anchovy paste
1 teaspoon hot red pepper sauce
½ cup olive oil
¼ cup bacon fat
* Salt and black pepper*

1 red onion
1 red bell pepper
6 ounces spinach (about 3 cups)
1 bunch watercress (about 2 cups)
8 radicchio leaves
24 oysters
2 cups bread crumbs
½ pound unsalted butter, clarified, or 1 cup
* vegetable oil*

Preparation: First, cook the bacon until crisp, drain on paper towels, and save ¼ cup of the fat for the dressing. *For the dressing,* chop the chives. Combine both mustards, both vinegars, and the anchovy paste. Whisk in the hot red pepper sauce, oil, bacon fat, and chives. Season with salt and pepper to taste. Transfer to a small saucepan.

Crumble the bacon. Cut the red onion and red pepper into thin julienne strips. Tear the spinach into bite-sized pieces. Cut the stems from the watercress. In a bowl, combine the bacon, onion, pepper, spinach, and half of the watercress. Arrange the radicchio leaves and the remaining watercress on 4 plates. Roll the oysters in the bread crumbs.

Cooking: In a heavy frying pan, heat butter *or* oil over medium-high heat. Sauté the coated oysters quickly on both sides until just cooked, about 1 minute altogether. Transfer to paper towels to drain. Heat the dressing just to a boil. Pour enough dressing over the bowl of greens to coat and then toss. Add the oysters and toss again.

SERVING: Distribute the oysters and greens among plates. Spoon the remaining sauce over the radicchio and watercress.

YIELD: 4 servings

WARM LAMB AND BLUE CHEESE SALAD

An invention of Michael Roberts, whose restaurant, Trumps, is a Los Angeles bastion of the new American cuisine, this salad is as quick as it is luxurious.

Preparation: Cut the lamb into ½-inch-thick slices. Crumble the blue cheese. Cut the endives lengthwise into slivers and arrange on 4 plates.

1 pound boneless rack of lamb
½ pound blue cheese, such as Roquefort or
Stilton
2 Belgian endives
½ cup oil
½ cup balsamic vinegar

Cooking: In a frying pan, heat the oil. Add the lamb and brown over high heat on both sides to rare, about 3 minutes altogether. Do this in batches if necessary; do not overcrowd the pan. Remove the lamb from the pan and add vinegar and blue cheese and cook for 30 seconds more, scraping the bottom of the pan.

SERVING: Arrange lamb over endive and spoon the cheese, vinegar, and oil over all.

YIELD: 4 servings

Raw Cashews and Raisins	Riesling *Spätlese*
Polenta Studded with Braised Mushrooms (page 104)	
Quail with Crackling Salad (page 68)	Crozes-Hermitage
Chocolate Meringue Cake (page 257)	

Red Snapper Soup (page 89)	White burgundy, such as Saint-Véran
Warm Beef and Spinach Salad (page 71)	Beaujolais-Villages (chilled)
Poached Oranges with Anise (page 228)	Quady Essencia Orange Muscat

Chilled Sorrel Soup (page 86)	California Pinot Blanc
Shredded Chicken (page 67)	Sebastiani Eye of the Swan (Pinot Noir Blanc)
Chocolate–Cherry Bavarian Pie (page 266)	

NEW SOUPS

Our new soups underline the principles of today's American cuisine. They are inventive yet solidly based on traditional American regional dishes, and they clearly reflect the many cultures that have melded to form America. Oriental seasonings are combined with Italian pasta; Creole and Cajun traditions are evident.

Many—in fact almost half—of the recipes in this chapter are based on shellfish or finfish. This is not surprising; more types of fish and shellfish have become available throughout the country, and in all courses of a meal, Americans have been turning away from a heavy emphasis on meat and toward lighter fish and poultry.

Several of these soups are updated versions of old standbys: a new barley soup, a lentil soup suitable for a dinner party, an unusual sorrel soup. On the other hand, many cooks love making soup because they can indulge their creative urges—you can put almost anything in a soup. While the new American cuisine has suffered somewhat at the hands of those who have put together unusual combinations with little apparent thought other than to shock, other chefs have made real discoveries. It is often the unusual ingredient that really completes the dish: the sage in the fish soup, the coconut in the shellfish soup. Soup is often thought of as a "comforting" food, and so it is, but that doesn't mean it must be dull.

Of Herbs and Spices and Seasoning the New Soups

In addition to the seasonings traditionally associated with soup, there are some recently available herbs and spices that now appear frequently in soups, as well as in other sorts of recipes.

Basil

There are more than a dozen varieties of basil, which fall basically into two groups. The first, with the more familiar taste, includes sweet, bush, and fine-leaf French basil. The members of the second group have the sweet basil taste with an added flavor from which they take their names, such as cinnamon basil and licorice basil. The flavored basils seem to hold up better in cooking than do the basils of the first group, which are best added raw at the last minute.

Cayenne and Other Peppers

Americans have finally lost their timidity concerning hot and spicy foods, a blessing that is obvious in the recipes in this chapter: Half a dozen of them use some form of hot pepper, from the jalapeños in the Fish and Shellfish Soup with Coriander and Coconut to the hot red pepper sauce used in Son of a Gun Seafood Stew and the cayenne in the Lentil Soup with Quail or Pork. When using fresh peppers, remember that the membranes as well as the seeds are especially hot and should be removed if a milder flavor is desired. Paprika has been rescued from the dubious culinary function of adding color only. Always buy Hungarian paprika, which ranges from sweet to very hot, and keep it in the refrigerator to protect its flavor.

Coriander

Coriander's recent rediscovery is a deserved one, for it can add a fresh taste to many recipes. Coriander, Chinese parsley, and cilantro are all one and the same. Coriander is important in Chinese, Indian, and Thai cooking, as well as Tex-Mex and Mexican dishes. The leaves look somewhat like Italian parsley, although they are a bit more feathered; when there's any doubt, coriander can always be identified by its pungent smell.

Parsley

Parsley has always been a standard in soup making, but only recently has it really been appreciated as more than part of a bouquet garni. The flat-leafed Italian variety has gained popularity for its stronger taste, but curly parsley (of which there are 37 varieties) is still ubiquitous—deservedly so, since its flavor complements so many others. Generally, the two types can be used interchangeably, although you may sometimes wish to use slightly more of the curly variety since it is milder.

Saffron

The best way to buy saffron, the most costly seasoning in the world, is in threads because they retain flavor longer than does powdered saffron and they are likelier to be genuine than the easier-to-fake powder; if possible, choose dark-orange threads that show no white streaks. Toasting the threads in a 350°F oven for about 3 minutes releases the pungent oils; you can then powder the toasted saffron and either add it directly to a dish or steep it in liquid first. Or you can steep untoasted strands in liquid for about 10 minutes before using or add the strands to hot oil to release their color and flavor.

SPRING VEGETABLE SOUP

The classic preparation of spring peas in France is to steam them with
butter, lettuce, and tiny onions. The same flavors are united here in a
soup.

Preparation: Shell the peas if using fresh. Chop the
lettuce and slice the scallions, including the green tops.
Mince the thyme if using fresh.

In a large pot of boiling water, cook the peas for
about 5 minutes. Add the lettuce and continue to cook
until it is tender, about 5 minutes. Drain the lettuce and
peas, refresh under cold water, and drain again, pressing gently with the back of a spoon to remove any
excess moisture.

In a saucepan, sauté all but a couple of tablespoons of
the scallions in the butter over medium-low heat until
soft, about 3 minutes. Add the lettuce and peas and toss
to coat. Add the flour, thyme, and salt and pepper to
taste. Toss again. Cook, stirring, about 3 minutes. Stir
in about ½ cup of the chicken stock.

Transfer the mixture to a food processor and puree.
Return the puree to a saucepan, stir in remaining 2½
cups of chicken stock and the wine, and slowly bring to
a boil, stirring. Lower the heat and simmer, stirring
often, about 5 minutes. Adjust the seasoning.

SERVING: Reheat the soup if it has been made ahead. Top
each serving with a spoonful of crème fraîche and some
of the reserved scallions.

YIELD: about 1½ quarts

¾ cup green peas, fresh or frozen
2 heads romaine lettuce (about 1½ pounds)
6 scallions
3 teaspoons minced fresh thyme leaves or
    ¾ teaspoon dried thyme
4 tablespoons unsalted butter
4 teaspoons flour
    Salt and black pepper
3 cups Chicken Stock (page 81)
⅓ cup white wine
4 tablespoons crème fraîche

CHAR-GRILLED VEGETABLE SOUP

Norman Van Aken, of Louie's Backyard in Key West, Florida,
combines charcoal-grilled eggplant, zucchini, yellow and red peppers,
and leeks with cream to create an exquisitely flavored vegetable soup.

2 medium-sized leeks
1 medium-sized eggplant
1 small zucchini
1 small yellow summer squash
1 small yellow bell pepper
1 small red bell pepper
  Salt and black pepper
  Olive oil for coating
3 ribs celery
1 small onion
6 tablespoons unsalted butter
¼ cup chopped fresh basil leaves
1 bay leaf
½ cup Chicken Stock (page 81)
3 cups heavy cream, plus more if necessary

Preparation and Cooking: Cut off and discard the green leaves from the leeks, cut the bulbs in half, and wash. In a saucepan, blanch the leeks in boiling salted water to cover until just tender, about 5 minutes. Drain.

Heat the grill. Halve the eggplant lengthwise. Cut one half into ¼-inch-thick lengthwise slices. Cut the zucchini and yellow squash into ¼-inch-thick lengthwise slices. Season the leeks, eggplant slices, zucchini, yellow squash, and yellow and red peppers with salt and pepper and coat lightly with olive oil.

Grill the eggplant half until quite soft, about 10 minutes. Remove from the grill to cool. Grill the seasoned vegetables, in batches if necessary, until charred evenly, 3 to 5 minutes for the eggplant slices, squashes, and leeks, and 10 minutes for the peppers. Put the eggplant slices, squashes, and leeks into a bowl. Peel and seed the peppers and add them to the bowl with the other vegetables.

Chop the celery and onion. Scrape flesh out of cooled, grilled eggplant half and discard the skin. Chop the flesh. In a large pot, heat the butter until it is foamy. Add the celery and onion and cook until they are soft, about 4 minutes. Chop the basil. Add the chopped eggplant and basil. Season with salt and pepper and add the bay leaf. Cook for 5 minutes over medium heat. Add the stock and cook gently for 10 to 12 minutes. Add the cream and bring to a boil; then remove from the heat.

Puree the soup in a blender and strain. Return to a clean pot and simmer for 15 minutes.

Final Cooking: Reheat the soup if it has been made ahead. Cut the grilled leeks, eggplant slices, zucchini, and yellow squash crosswise into thin strips. Cut the peppers lengthwise into thin strips. Return the leeks, eggplant, zucchini, yellow squash, and peppers to the bowl and mix to distribute the vegetables evenly. Stir two thirds of the vegetable mixture into the strained soup. Season with salt and pepper. Add more cream if you prefer a mellower flavor.

SERVING: Ladle the soup into warm bowls and garnish with the remaining vegetable mixture.

YIELD: about 1½ quarts

CHICKEN STOCK

Chicken stock is the most versatile of all stocks. It can be used almost any time stock is called for—certainly it can substitute for veal stock, and often even for fish stock. We salt stocks very lightly if at all so that, if reduced when used in a recipe, they don't become overpoweringly salty.

Preparation: Heat the oven to 450° F. Put the chicken in a large roasting pan. Quarter the carrot, celery, and onion and add them to the pan. Sprinkle the oil over all.

Roast in the preheated oven, stirring occasionally, until the vegetables and bones are lightly browned, about 30 minutes. Transfer to a stockpot. Add the parsley, bay leaf, thyme, peppercorns, a little salt, and water to cover well. Bring to a boil, skimming off any foam that rises to the top. Lower the heat and simmer until the stock is reduced to about 2 quarts, about 3 hours.

Strain. The stock can be refrigerated for about a week, or it can be frozen.

3 pounds chicken carcasses, necks, and/or wings
1 carrot
1 rib celery
1 onion
¼ cup oil
6 parsley sprigs
1 bay leaf
½ teaspoon dried thyme
10 whole peppercorns
Salt

YIELD: about 2 quarts

COLD CREAM OF BROWN RICE SOUP WITH SORREL

The sharp taste of sorrel enhances this unusual and satisfying cold soup. For the suavest consistency, serve just as it begins to set. You'll need a good, strong homemade stock, for both its flavor and its natural gelatin.

2 quarts Chicken Stock (page 81)
½ cup brown rice
2 teaspoons salt
2 eggs
½ cup heavy cream
1½ cups loosely packed sorrel leaves

Preparation: Bring the stock to a boil. Lower the heat slightly and cook, uncovered, until reduced to about 1 quart, about 45 minutes.

In a saucepan, bring 3 quarts of water to a boil. Stir in the brown rice and salt. Lower the heat and cook, stirring once or twice, until the rice is just tender, about 30 minutes. Drain, rinse briefly under cold water, and drain well.

Final Cooking: Bring the stock to a simmer and remove from the heat to cool slightly. In a medium-sized bowl, whisk together the eggs and cream. Slowly whisk the hot stock into the egg mixture; pour it in a very thin stream to avoid overheating the eggs and curdling them. Return the stock to a saucepan and cook over low heat, stirring constantly, until the soup is steaming and slightly thickened, 3 to 5 minutes.

Transfer the soup to a bowl. Set the bowl in a larger bowl of ice water. Stir the soup until it is thick and silky and just beginning to set, 10 to 15 minutes. Adjust the seasoning.

SERVING: With a sharp knife, shred the sorrel. Divide the rice among 4 soup bowls. Ladle the chilled soup over the rice and sprinkle with the sorrel.

YIELD: about 1½ quarts

THE TRELLIS CHEESE SOUP

Chef Marcel Desaulniers of The Trellis in Williamsburg, Virginia,
prefers to use Oregon Tillamook cheddar for this smooth cheese soup.
However, you can substitute any good medium-sharp yellow cheddar to
make this delicious recipe.

Preparation and Cooking: Cut the onion, carrot, and celery into thin slices. Shred the cheese.

In a heavy saucepan, melt the butter. Add the flour to make a roux. Over low heat, cook thoroughly but don't brown, stirring often, about 10 minutes and remove the roux from the heat. Meanwhile, heat the chicken stock.

Gradually add the hot chicken stock to the cooked roux, stirring constantly over medium heat until the mixture is smooth and bubbly, 3 to 4 minutes; simmer over low heat for 5 minutes, stirring often. In a frying pan, heat the oil and sauté the onion, carrot, and celery over medium-low heat for 5 minutes. Add the sautéed vegetables to the soup and allow to simmer, stirring often, until the vegetables are cooked, about 8 to 10 minutes.

Final Cooking: Remove the soup from the heat (or reheat if made ahead to this point) and gradually stir in the shredded cheese. Continue to stir until all of the cheese has been added and the soup is smooth. Season with salt and pepper to taste.

YIELD: about 1½ quarts

1 large onion
1 carrot
2 ribs celery
9 ounces Oregon Tillamook cheddar cheese or *other medium-sharp yellow cheddar*
6 tablespoons unsalted butter
4½ tablespoons flour
4½ cups Chicken Stock (page 81)
1½ tablespoons vegetable oil
Salt and black pepper

OYSTER AND ARTICHOKE SOUP

Paul Prudhomme's stamp on his ravishing combination of oysters and artichokes is evident. The soup relies on the Cajun seasonings that have made K-Paul's Louisiana Kitchen a New Orleans landmark.

2 dozen oysters
1 lemon
3 tablespoons olive oil
2 tablespoons salt
2 teaspoons garlic powder
5 artichokes (each 6 to 7 ounces)

Seasoning Mix

2 teaspoons salt
1 teaspoon sweet paprika
¾ teaspoon white pepper
¾ teaspoon onion powder
¾ teaspoon garlic powder
¼ teaspoon cayenne
¼ teaspoon dried thyme
   Pinch of black pepper
   Pinch of dried oregano

1 small onion
10 tablespoons unsalted butter
1⅓ cups heavy cream
2 tablespoons plus 2 teaspoons flour
6 scallions
3 tablespoons minced fresh parsley

Preparation and Cooking: Shuck the oysters into a large bowl. Add a quart of cold water to the oysters. Stir and then refrigerate for at least 1 hour. Strain through a fine sieve, reserving the liquid. Refrigerate the oysters and oyster water separately until ready to use.

Cut the lemon in half. In a large saucepan, combine 3 quarts of water with the olive oil, salt, garlic powder, and lemon halves. Cover and bring to a boil over high heat. Add the artichokes and boil, covered, just until leaves can be pulled off easily, about 20 minutes. Stir occasionally and rotate the artichokes once or twice during cooking.

Drain the artichokes and cool slightly. Remove the outer leaves and scrape off the edible fleshy part from the bottom of each. Remove the tender innermost leaves and chop. Use a small spoon to scoop away the fuzzy chokes and discard, leaving the artichoke bottoms intact. Cut away the stems, trim their ends, and peel away the stringy skin if necessary. Chop the stems' tender centers. Put all the pulp into one container. Cut the artichoke bottoms into thin slices and put them in a separate container. Set aside.

For the Seasoning Mix, combine all the ingredients in a small bowl. Mix thoroughly and set aside.

Mince the onion. In a large saucepan, melt 6 table-spoons of the butter over high heat. Add the minced onion and sauté until it is soft, about 3 minutes, stirring occasionally. Add the reserved chopped artichoke pulp and 5 teaspoons of the Seasoning Mix. Stir well. Cook until the mixture starts to stick to the pan, about 5 minutes, stirring fairly often and scraping the bottom of the pan well. Add ⅔ cup of the oyster liquid, scraping the bottom of the pan with a wooden spoon to deglaze it. Cook, stirring frequently, until most of the liquid has evaporated, about 3 minutes more. Add 1⅓ cups more oyster liquid and the remaining Seasoning Mix. Bring to a boil, stirring once or twice. Cover the pan, lower the heat to medium, and cook for 10 minutes, stirring once. Stir in ⅔ cup more oyster liquid (reserve any remaining to use in a seafood stock) and the cream. Turn the heat to high and bring to a boil, stirring occasionally.

In a frying pan, melt the remaining 4 tablespoons of butter over medium-low heat. Gradually add the flour, whisking until well blended and smooth. Remove from the heat. When the cream mixture reaches a strong boil, slowly add butter-flour mixture, stirring constantly.

Chop the scallions and mince the parsley.

Final Cooking: Return the soup to a boil, stirring constantly. Stir in the scallions, parsley, and reserved sliced artichokes. Cook for about 1 minute, stirring. Stir in the oysters and bring the soup to a boil, stirring occasionally. Remove from the heat, cover the pan, and let sit until oysters are thoroughly heated, about 15 minutes.

YIELD: about 2 quarts

CHILLED SORREL SOUP

Sour sorrel has become increasingly popular in American cooking. It has a special affinity for fish and is combined here with a luxurious variety of fish and shellfish in an unusual new soup. The soup can be varied according to the fish and shellfish available.

1 shallot
1 teaspoon chopped fresh thyme leaves or
    ¼ teaspoon dried thyme
1 clove garlic
    Pinch of coarse salt
¼ pound sorrel, plus a few small leaves
    for garnish
2 carrots
3 ribs celery
1 leek
½ cup shredded savoy cabbage
⅓ pound swordfish steak or ¼ pound
    fillet
⅓ pound salmon steak or ¼ pound fillet
⅓ pound large shrimp
2 small boiling potatoes
1½ teaspoons olive oil
½ cup dry white wine
5 cups cold water
    Salt and black pepper
⅓ pound bay scallops
2 ripe avocados
1 teaspoon lemon juice
¼ cup sour cream

Preparation and Cooking: Mince the shallot. Chop the thyme if using fresh thyme leaves. Mash the garlic with a pinch of coarse salt. Reserve a few small leaves of the sorrel for garnish and clean and remove stems from about three quarters of the rest; cut the leaves crosswise into strips. Cut the carrots into thin slices. Pull the strings off the celery and dice the ribs. Cut the leek in half lengthwise, wash and then cut into thin slices. Slice the cabbage into thin shreds. Remove the skin and bones from the swordfish and salmon and cut them into ½-inch dice. Peel and devein the shrimp and cut them into halves lengthwise. Peel the potatoes and cut them into small dice.

In a large saucepan, heat the olive oil and add the shallot. Cook over medium-high heat until soft, about 1 minute. Add thyme and garlic and sauté until the garlic is soft, about 3 minutes. Stir in the cut sorrel and all the carrots, celery, leek, cabbage, and potatoes. Add the wine, water, and salt and pepper. Cover and bring just to a boil. Lower the heat and simmer until all the ingredients are tender, about 8 minutes.

Remove from the heat and stir in the swordfish, salmon, shrimp, and scallops. Cool to room temperature and then cover and chill in the refrigerator.

Final Assembly: Remove the stems from the remaining quarter of the sorrel and cut the leaves crosswise into thin strips. Peel the avocados, coat them with the lemon juice, and push them through a sieve. In a bowl, whisk together the mashed avocado and sour cream. Gently stir the avocado mixture into the chilled soup with the remaining cut sorrel. Adjust the seasonings with salt and pepper.

SERVING: Garnish with sorrel leaves.

YIELD: about 2 quarts

SON OF A GUN SEAFOOD STEW

This hearty soup is from Chef Jim Heywood of American Bounty, the student-operated showcase restaurant of The Culinary Institute of America in Poughkeepsie, New York.

Preparation and Cooking: Chop the garlic. Cut the leek into thick slices. Dice the green pepper. Cut the mushrooms into thick slices. Peel, seed, and dice the tomatoes. Mince the parsley. Slice the olives. Cut the monkfish into bite-sized pieces. Peel the shrimp. If using sea scallops, cut them into bite-sized pieces. Cut the crabmeat into bite-sized pieces.

In a large frying pan, heat the olive oil. Sauté the garlic, leek, and green pepper over medium heat until soft, 4 to 5 minutes. Add the mushrooms and cook 2 minutes more, being careful not to brown them. Add the tomatoes, Pernod, thyme, basil, parsley, tomato puree, olives, fish stock, salt, and red pepper sauce to taste. Bring to a boil and then simmer, covered, for 5 minutes.

Final Cooking: Add the seafood to the simmering soup or return the soup to a simmer if it was made ahead and then add the seafood. Cover and continue to simmer until all the seafood is just cooked, about 10 minutes. Season with salt to taste.

SERVING: Serve with garlic croûtes. Put a dollop of sour cream on top of the croûtes before adding to soup if desired.

YIELD: about 2 quarts

NOTE: For the garlic croûtes, cut ½-inch-thick slices of French bread from a loaf about 3 inches in diameter. You should have one croûte for each person being served. Rub the slices with a cut garlic clove, brush both sides of each slice lightly with olive oil, and toast on both sides under a broiler. Watch carefully because they burn easily. These can be made ahead and kept in an airtight container.

1 clove garlic
1 small leek
1 small green bell pepper
2 mushrooms
2 plum tomatoes
1 teaspoon minced fresh parsley
½ cup sliced ripe olives
½ pound monkfish fillets
½ pound small shrimp
½ pound bay scallops or *sea scallops*
½ pound crabmeat
2 tablespoons olive oil
¼ cup Pernod
1 teaspoon dried thyme
1 teaspoon dried basil
¼ cup tomato puree
½ cup Fish Stock (page 97)
Salt
Hot red pepper sauce
Garlic croûtes (see Note)
Sour cream for garnish (optional)

FISH AND SHELLFISH SOUP WITH CORIANDER AND COCONUT

Joyce Goldstein of Square One in San Francisco offers a fish stew flavored with coriander, saffron, and coconut. Steeping the saffron threads in white wine helps release their color and flavor.

16 clams
16 mussels
2 onions
2 green bell peppers
4 cloves garlic
2 jalapeño peppers
¼ teaspoon saffron threads
1 tablespoon dry white wine
8 ripe plum tomatoes
1 pound firm white fish fillets, such as
  angler, rockfish, or red snapper
16 shrimp
2 tablespoons shredded coconut (optional)
2 tablespoons chopped fresh coriander
  leaves
4 tablespoons unsalted butter
1 tablespoon ground coriander
½ cup canned sweetened coconut cream
5 cups Fish Stock (page 97)
1 lime
  Salt and black pepper
¼ pound lobster meat (optional)
¼ pound crabmeat (optional)

Preparation and Cooking: Wash the clams and mussels. Chop the onions and green peppers. Mince the garlic and jalapeño peppers. Steep the saffron in the white wine for 5 minutes. Peel and seed the tomatoes; then cut them into ½-inch pieces. Cut the fish into 2-inch pieces. Peel and devein the shrimp. Toast the coconut if using it. Chop the coriander leaves.

In a saucepan, sauté the onions in the butter over medium heat until soft, about 5 minutes. Add the green peppers, garlic, jalapeños, and ground coriander and sauté for 5 minutes. Add the saffron, coconut cream, fish stock, and tomatoes and simmer for 2 minutes. Squeeze 2 to 3 tablespoons lime juice into the soup and season with salt and pepper.

Final Cooking: Add the clams to the soup and cook, covered, for 2 minutes. Add the fish, shrimp, optional shellfish, and mussels and cook, covered, until the clams and mussels open and the fish is done but still firm, 5 to 6 minutes. Discard any clams or mussels that have not opened.

SERVING: Serve the hot soup sprinkled with chopped coriander and, if desired, toasted coconut.

YIELD: about 2 quarts

RED SNAPPER SOUP

Jonathan Waxman, co-owner and chef of the popular restaurants Jams, Bud's, and Hulot's in New York City, devised this Mediterranean-accented soup. The skin is left on the red snapper because it looks so pretty.

Preparation and Cooking: Cut the shallots in half. Slice the carrot and onion. Cut the fennel into small pieces. Remove the zest from the orange in strips. Squeeze the juices from the orange and lemon into a large saucepan. Cut the fish into 1-inch pieces. Dice the potatoes.

In a large frying pan, heat 2 tablespoons of the olive oil. Add the shallots, carrot, onion, fennel, and potatoes and sauté over medium heat until tender, about 6 minutes. Season lightly with salt and pepper and set aside.

Add the 2 cups of water to the orange and lemon juices along with orange zest, sage, parsley, and bay leaves. Bring to a simmer and then cook over low heat, skimming occasionally, for 30 minutes. Strain the liquid and return to the pan. Season with salt and pepper to taste. Add the fish stock and the remaining 4 tablespoons of olive oil.

Final Cooking: Bring the soup to a boil. Add the snapper pieces and cook for 3 minutes. Add the sautéed vegetables and cook until the fish just tests done, about 2 minutes more.

YIELD: about 1½ quarts

8 shallots
1 carrot
1 red onion
1 bulb fennel
1 orange
1 lemon
1 pound red snapper fillets with skin
3 whole, tiny new potatoes or 2 red potatoes
6 tablespoons olive oil
  Salt and black pepper
2 cups water
1 sprig fresh sage or ¼ teaspoon dried sage
1 sprig parsley
2 bay leaves
1 cup Fish Stock (page 97)

TURKEY AND BARLEY SOUP

Homemade turkey stock adds depth of flavor to this hearty winter soup, but chicken stock could certainly be substituted.

5 cups Turkey Stock (page 91)
⅔ cup pearl barley
1 pound boneless turkey breast
1 cup snow peas
2 tablespoons unsalted butter
  Salt and black pepper

Preparation: Make the stock. Cook the barley in salted water to cover until tender, about 1 hour. Drain.

Cut the turkey into bite-sized pieces. Remove strings from the snow peas and cut the snow peas on the diagonal into ⅛-inch-wide strips.

Cooking: Heat the stock. In a large frying pan, melt the butter and add the turkey. Season with salt and pepper to taste. Sauté over high heat until just cooked through, about 3 minutes. Add the snow peas and stir to combine. Add the barley, turkey, and snow peas to the stock and adjust the seasonings. Return just to a simmer.

YIELD: 4 servings

BARLEY SOUP

From Seppi Renggli, chef of The Four Seasons in New York City, this is a personal version of a traditional favorite. His barley soup is enriched with heavy cream and served with grated Parmesan cheese. It can be made entirely ahead of time.

3 slices bacon
1 small onion
2 cloves garlic
1 small carrot
1 small kohlrabi
1 small celery root
1 small leek
¼ head savoy cabbage
2 tablespoons butter or lard

Preparation and Cooking: Chop the bacon and onion. Mince the garlic. Dice the carrot, kohlrabi, and celery root. Wash and chop the leek. Shred the cabbage.

In a large pot, melt the butter and add the bacon. Sauté over medium heat until the bacon is golden and the fat is rendered, about 5 minutes. Add the onion and garlic and cook over low heat, stirring often, for 5 minutes. Add the remaining vegetables and cook over low heat, covered, for 5 minutes. Add the thyme, stock, and barley with any water that hasn't been absorbed. Bring to a boil and then simmer, partially covered, until the barley is tender, about 1 hour. Add the cream, season with salt and pepper and nutmeg, and heat through.

SERVING: Top with grated Parmesan cheese if desired.

YIELD: about 2 quarts

¼ teaspoon dried thyme
1 quart Chicken Stock (page 81) or beef
    stock
½ cup pearl barley
1 pint heavy cream
    Salt and black pepper
    Pinch of grated nutmeg
    Grated Parmesan cheese (optional)

TURKEY STOCK

Preparation: Heat the oven to 400°F. Using a cleaver or the heel of a French knife, chop the turkey into smaller pieces. Put the turkey into a roasting pan, sprinkle lightly with salt and pepper, and roast until golden, about 40 minutes, stirring occasionally.

Chop the celery, carrots, onions, and garlic. Add the chopped vegetables, parsley, thyme, peppercorns, and bay leaf to the turkey and cook for about 5 minutes more; put the mixture into a large stockpot. Add wine to the roasting pan and scrape with a wooden spoon over high heat to deglaze; pour into the pot along with enough cold water to cover well, about 2½ quarts. Bring just to a boil, skim, and lower the heat to a gentle simmer. Simmer for about 3 hours, skimming as necessary. Strain and season with salt and pepper to taste.

YIELD: about 1½ quarts

4 pounds turkey wings and/or
    drumsticks
    Salt and black pepper
3 ribs celery
2 carrots
2 onions
2 cloves garlic
10 to 15 parsley stems
    ½ teaspoon dried thyme
    6 whole peppercorns
    1 bay leaf
    ½ cup dry white wine

LENTIL SOUP WITH QUAIL OR PORK

Wolfgang Puck of Spago, in Los Angeles, updates an old standard by adding grilled quail to a satisfying lentil soup laced with red wine and Madeira. The quail can be sautéed rather than grilled, and pork can substitute for the quail with excellent results.

⅔ cup dried lentils
4 quail (see Note)
4 tablespoons balsamic vinegar
2 carrots
1 rib celery
5 mushrooms
1 onion
½ teaspoon dried thyme
¼ teaspoon dried rosemary
4 juniper berries
¼ cup dry red wine
¼ cup Madeira
8 tablespoons unsalted butter
¼ pound slab bacon
1 quart Chicken Stock (page 81) or water
1 small bouquet garni of parsley, bay leaf, thyme, and leek
Salt and black pepper
Cayenne
1 parsnip
1 small orange
1 tablespoon chopped fresh parsley

Preparation: Pick over lentils. Soak them overnight in cold water to cover and then drain, or increase the cooking time for the lentils to about 1 hour.

Heat the oven to 400°F. Cut the meat away from the quail bones in pieces as large as possible. Reserve the bones. Set the meat aside in a bowl with 1 tablespoon of the vinegar. Chop 1 of the carrots, the celery, mushrooms, and onion.

In a small roasting pan, roast the quail bones in the preheated oven with the chopped carrot, celery, mushrooms, and half of the onion, turning occasionally, until brown, about 30 minutes. Transfer the pan to the stove top and add the thyme, rosemary, and juniper berries. Add the wine and Madeira and simmer, scraping the bottom of the pan with a wooden spoon to deglaze. Add enough water to cover, and boil to reduce the liquid to about 1 cup, about 25 minutes. Strain and discard the bones and vegetables.

In a pot, melt 6 tablespoons of the butter. Sauté the remaining onion until soft, about 6 minutes. Add the bacon and sauté for 5 minutes. Add the remaining 3 tablespoons vinegar, lentils, and chicken stock. Add the bouquet garni and salt, pepper, and cayenne to taste. Cook, skimming occasionally, until the lentils are soft, about 20 minutes. Remove and discard the bouquet garni. Remove the bacon and cut it into thin strips. Set aside ¼ cup of the lentils and puree the remaining lentils in blender or food processor and then push through a sieve.

Cut the remaining carrot and the peeled parsnip into small dice. Grate the zest from the orange. In a frying pan, sauté the carrot and parsnip with the orange zest in the remaining 2 tablespoons of butter until tender. Chop parsley.

Cooking: Heat the grill if using. Grill quail meat or sauté it in butter in a frying pan over medium-high heat, keeping breasts slightly pink, about 4 minutes. Combine the quail stock, bacon, whole lentils, lentil puree, and carrot-parsnip mixture. Add more stock or water if the soup is too thick, which may well be the case if the lentils were not presoaked and have therefore absorbed a good deal of the liquid; bring to a boil. Season with salt and pepper to taste.

SERVING: Divide the soup among 4 soup plates. Put the quail meat on top and sprinkle with the chopped parsley.

YIELD: about 2 quarts

NOTE: Three-quarter pound of pork chops, the bones used for the stock and the meat cut into ¼-inch-thick slices, can be substituted for the quail.

VENISON SOUP WITH DILL DUMPLINGS

Game has recently become popular again with American diners. In this new soup, the venison is first marinated in white wine and then simmered for an hour and a half, so the less expensive shoulder cut can be used. Miniature dill dumplings complement the flavorful melange.

Cooked Game Marinade

1 onion
1 carrot
1 rib celery
4 cloves garlic
1 bottle dry white wine (about 3½ cups)
¾ cup white or red wine vinegar
3 sprigs parsley
2 bay leaves
6 whole peppercorns

2 pounds venison shoulder or other lean
    stewing meat such as beef
4 sprigs dill
2 sprigs marjoram, or ½ teaspoon dried
    marjoram
6 thick slices bacon
6 cups venison, beef, or Chicken Stock
    (page 81)
2 cups cold water
1 tablespoon chopped fresh marjoram
    leaves or 1 teaspoon dried marjoram
1 small bay leaf
3 onions
3 carrots
1 red bell pepper
1 rib celery
3 cloves garlic
½ pound green beans
⅓ pound mushrooms
2 tablespoons vegetable oil, if necessary
⅓ cup medium-hot Hungarian paprika
1 1-pound can whole tomatoes in puree
    Salt and black pepper
    Miniature Dill Dumplings
     (recipe follows)
1½ cups sour cream
    Small sprigs dill for garnish

Preparation and Cooking: *For the marinade,* slice the onion, carrot, and celery. Crush the garlic. In a saucepan, bring the wine, vinegar, onion, carrot, celery, garlic, parsley sprigs, and bay leaves to a boil. Cover and simmer for 30 minutes. Add the peppercorns for the last 5 minutes. Cool completely.

Trim the meat. Strain the cooled marinade over the meat. Add the dill sprigs and marjoram and turn the meat pieces over to combine the ingredients. Cover and refrigerate for 1 to 2 days, turning the meat occasionally.

Cut the bacon into 1-inch squares and cook over medium heat in a heavy frying pan until golden brown and the fat has been rendered, 8 to 10 minutes. Drain the bacon and reserve the bacon fat.

Drain the venison or other meat and discard the marinade. Cut the meat into ½- to ¾-inch cubes and pat dry. Put 2 tablespoons of the reserved bacon fat in a frying pan. Then put an additional 2 tablespoons of the reserved bacon fat into a large, heavy pot.

Heat the fat in both the frying pan and pot over medium-high heat. Add one fourth of the meat to each pan and cook, stirring occasionally, until the meat is lightly browned, about 5 minutes. With a slotted spoon, transfer the meat from both frying pan and pot to a plate. Repeat with the remaining meat, adding bacon fat as necessary. Pour any excess fat from the pot into the frying pan and return all meat to the pot. Add the stock, water, marjoram, and bay leaf. Bring to a boil and skim. Lower the heat and simmer, covered.

Cut onions, carrots, red pepper, and celery into large dice. Mince the garlic. Cut the green beans into 1-inch lengths. Cut mushrooms into thick slices. Set aside.

Add the vegetable oil to frying pan if there isn't enough bacon fat. Add the onions, carrots, red pepper, celery, and garlic. Cook over medium heat, tossing occasionally, until the vegetables begin to soften, about 10 minutes. Add the paprika, lower heat, and cook for about 2 minutes. Add the tomatoes and cook, breaking up tomatoes, until slightly thickened, about 3 minutes.

Add the vegetable mixture to soup pot, stirring to combine; then skim. Simmer, partially covered, skimming when necessary, until the meat is tender, about 1½ hours total cooking time for the meat. Remove the bay leaf.

With a slotted spoon, transfer about 1 cup of the vegetables with a little of the liquid from the soup to a food processor or food mill. Puree until smooth and return the puree to the soup. If you prefer a thicker soup, repeat with another ½ cup of the vegetables. Add the green beans, mushrooms, reserved bacon, and salt and pepper. Simmer, uncovered, until the beans are tender, about 10 minutes. Remove the soup from the heat and prepare the Miniature Dill Dumplings.

SERVING: Reheat the soup if necessary. Either add half of the sour cream to the soup or serve all the cream on the side. To add it to the hot soup, whisk ¾ cup of the sour cream in a small bowl. Whisk in a few tablespoons of the hot soup. Add another few tablespoons of soup and whisk again. Stir the sour cream mixture into the soup. Do not allow the soup to boil once the sour cream has been added. Add the dumplings. Top each serving with an additional dollop of sour cream and a small sprig of dill.

YIELD: about 2 quarts

MINIATURE DILL DUMPLINGS

1¼ cups flour
½ teaspoon salt
2 tablespoons chopped fresh dill leaves
1 egg
1 egg yolk
⅓ cup water

Preparation: Sift the flour and salt into a mixing bowl. Add the dill. In another bowl, beat together the egg, egg yolk, and water until blended. Make a well in the flour, add the egg mixture, and gradually stir in the flour until incorporated. Stir briefly, just until the dough is soft and smooth. Do not overbeat.

Let the mixture rest while you bring a large pot of salted water to a boil. Dip 2 teaspoons into boiling water; then scoop up an irregular ½ teaspoonful of the dough, and use the other spoon to push it into water. Repeat, working quickly, until you have used up the dough. Simmer the dumplings, uncovered, for 3 to 4 minutes after they have risen to the surface, turning periodically. (Cut into one to be sure the center is done.) Drain the dumplings well before adding them to the soup.

YIELD: about 24 dumplings

PERSIAN MEATBALL AND YOGURT SOUP

Joyce Goldstein opened her San Francisco restaurant in 1984. The chef/owner of Square One makes good use of ideas from various areas of the world as is evident in her Fish and Shellfish Soup with Coriander and Coconut (page 88) and in this hearty soup with a Mideastern accent.

½ cup dried lentils
1 small onion
½ pound ground lamb
2 eggs
   Salt and black pepper
1 teaspoon ground cinnamon
3 cups plain yogurt
¼ cup basmati rice
1 tablespoon flour
½ teaspoon ground turmeric
5 cups Chicken Stock (page 81) or lamb stock

Preparation and Cooking: Pick over lentils and soak for 5 hours or overnight in cold water to cover. Drain.

Grate the onion into a bowl. Add the lamb, 1 of the eggs, salt and pepper, and ½ teaspoon of the cinnamon. Combine well and form into tiny meatballs.

Put the yogurt into a large saucepan. Combine the rice, remaining egg, flour, turmeric, and remaining ½ teaspoon cinnamon and stir into the yogurt in the saucepan. Add 4 cups of the stock and the lentils. Cook gently over low heat until slightly thickened, about 15 minutes.

Chop the parsley and scallions. Add the remaining cup of stock, meatballs, parsley, and scallions. If using dried mint, add it now. Simmer 10 to 15 minutes.

Final Cooking: In a small frying pan, melt the butter. Mince the garlic and sauté in the butter until soft but not colored, about 3 minutes. Add to the hot soup and adjust the seasoning with salt and pepper.

SERVING: If using fresh mint leaves, chop and sprinkle them over the soup.

YIELD: about 2 quarts

¼ cup chopped fresh parsley
2 scallions
2 tablespoons chopped fresh mint leaves,
*   or 1 tablespoon dried mint*
2 tablespoons unsalted butter
2 cloves garlic

FISH STOCK

Fish stock should be made from the bones of lean fish. Avoid strong-flavored fat fish, such as mackerel and bluefish. The whole head will contribute flavor, but always remove and discard the gills. To avoid bitterness, fish bones should not be cooked longer than about 20 minutes, making this the quickest of all stocks.

Preparation: Chop the onion and celery. Rinse the fish bones and cut them into pieces.

In a stockpot, melt the butter. Add the onion and celery and cook over low heat until soft, 5 to 10 minutes. Add the bones and cook, stirring well, for 2 minutes. Add water to cover, the parsley, bay leaf, thyme, salt, and peppercorns and bring to simmer. Simmer for 20 minutes, skimming off any foam that rises to the top.

Strain. The stock can be refrigerated for a week or so, or it can be frozen.

YIELD: about 1 quart

1 onion
2 ribs celery
2 pounds bones from lean fish, such as cod,
*   flounder, or whiting*
1 tablespoon unsalted butter
4 parsley sprigs
1 bay leaf
*   Pinch of dried thyme*
*   Pinch of salt*
5 whole peppercorns

Oyster and Artichoke Soup (page 84)	Alsace Sylvaner
Chicken and Vegetable Salad (page 45)	Côte de Beaune-Villages
Biscoitos de Porto (page 231)	Port, such as Cockburn's Reserve Porto

Miniature Scallion Crêpes with Salmon Caviar and Sour Cream (page 18)	California Blanc de Blancs
Warm Salad with Matsutake (page 63)	Medium-bodied red Rhône, such as Gigondas
Venison Soup with Dill Dumplings (page 94)	
Pastry Cornucopia (page 254)	Sweet Madeira, such as Bual

Turkey and Barley Soup (page 90) *Café Fanny Basil Sandwiches (page 192)*	Vin Gris, such as Sanford
Raspberries and Sliced Peaches	

CHAPTER 5

VEGETABLE COURSES

Risotto with Artichokes · *Onion and Fennel Frittata*
Polenta Studded with Braised Mushrooms · *Braised Mushrooms with Kasha*
Zucchini "Pasta" with Tomato–Clam Sauce
Grits, Greens, and Garlic Soufflé
Green Bean and Roasted Red Pepper Frittata · *Pumpkin and Bean Stew*
Asparagus Shortcake with Ham · *Sweet Potato Tamales*
Eggplant Rollatini Stuffed with Prosciutto and Sun-Dried Tomatoes
Feta–Vegetable Pie with Herbed Crust · *Cabbage Pie*
Eggplant and Smoked Cheese Pie · *Braised Mushroom Soufflé*

We can't claim to understand vegetarians. It's easy, though, to see the attraction of vegetable courses. Most of us lead much less physically active lives than our grandparents did, and so, alas, we simply don't need to take in as many calories. Since vegetables are generally less fattening than meat, they're a natural new focus. We can prepare them just as scrumptiously as we do meat and still be ahead in the calorie battle.

The vegetable recipes in this chapter do not eschew meat. Stock is frequently used, and sometimes a touch of meat or fish for added flavor and texture. Grains are important in such dishes as Braised Mushrooms with Kasha, Risotto with Artichokes, and the fantastic Sweet Potato Tamales that use fresh corn in the tamale dough. There are four egg dishes, including a Grits, Greens, and Garlic Soufflé from the new Southern cuisine, and cheese comes into play frequently, as in the Eggplant and Smoked Cheese Pie. In a couple of cases, vegetables are used as a conscious substitute for the meat or pasta of a traditional dish —Zucchini "Pasta" with Tomato–Clam Sauce and Eggplant Rollatini—

but mainly ours are innovative recipes featuring vegetables for their own sake. They have not been conceived as side dishes but to stand solo as complete courses.

A star of the new freestyle cuisine, vegetable dishes are liable to show up anywhere—first, second, or third course at dinner, as a brunch feature, or on their own as a simple lunch or supper. Or you might turn the expected meat-vegetable balance around and serve vegetables as the main attraction and a small portion of meat on the side—perhaps a hearty piece of Cabbage Pie flanked by a single sausage or Green Bean and Roasted Red Pepper Frittata with a slice of ham. It's a new emphasis that works.

Asparagus

While asparagus is not native to America, it has been grown here at least since the eighteenth century. European asparagus is generally white, and there is some white asparagus now grown in California, but most American asparagus is the familiar green. Despite the cachet white asparagus seems to have, our green asparagus usually is more tender, less bitter, and less stringy (and less expensive). If you care, it also has more vitamins, high in A, B, and C.

The main asparagus season runs from March 1 to about May 15, peaking in mid-April. However, harvesting can begin as early as mid-January in parts of California, and imported asparagus now is available, at least in larger cities, during other months as well. Look for asparagus spears that have an excellent green color and tightly furled heads that have not begun to sprout. Avoid spears that look raggedy or have woody bottoms. As long as the spear is fresh and young, its thickness does not affect flavor: Fatter spears are just as good as the slender ones. Try to choose spears that are all of the same thickness so that they will cook evenly.

A slight, built-in difficulty is that there is more cellulose—the cause of toughness—in the stem than in the tip. Much of the cellulose is in the skin, and so peeling helps equalize the cooking time. A taste test will prove to you that the flavor is better, too,

Special pots have been devised that boil the stalks while steaming the tips. For green asparagus, especially when peeled, such equipment is entirely unnecessary. Boil flat in a saucepan or, if the spears are long, a large frying pan until the stalks bend slightly when picked up by the butt end. At this point the tips will be cooked through, and the stems retain a suggestion of crunch.

Eggplant

The first eggplants introduced to England, in the sixteenth century, were a small, white species that does indeed resemble a large egg. Most eggplants contain bitter juices and taste best when these juices are removed. Disgorging, as it is called, involves simply salting the flesh and giving the bitter juices time to leach out. Pro-

longed heat also diminishes the bitter taste, and, therefore, eggplant should be thoroughly cooked.

When buying eggplant, look for those that feel heavy for their size and have smooth, glossy skins and good color. Avoid any with puckered skin or any that yield to your touch.

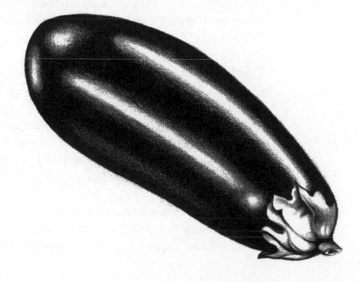

RISOTTO WITH ARTICHOKES

Risotto, the most common rice dish in Italy, is becoming increasingly popular in the United States. The term *risotto* refers to the method of cooking, which is always the same. Rice, butter, onion, stock, wine, and cheese are pretty much constants, but various regions in Italy have their own local versions, including different additional ingredients. As rice may absorb more or less liquid or cook at varying rates, play the cooking time by ear and add stock or water as needed. The end result should be a creamy mass, with soft grains of rice suspended in thickened, saucelike liquid.

1 clove garlic
¼ cup chopped fresh flat-leaf parsley
¼ cup grated Parmesan cheese
1 large artichoke or 2 smaller artichokes
*   Juice of ½ lemon*
6 tablespoons (approximately) olive oil
3 cups (approximately) Chicken Stock
*   (page 81)*
*   Salt and black pepper*
½ small onion
¾ cup Italian Arborio or other rice
⅔ cup dry white wine
2 tablespoons unsalted butter

Preparation: Slice the garlic as thin as possible. Chop the parsley. Grate the cheese. Snap off the artichoke stem and remove the tough outer leaves until only pale yellow inner leaves remain. Cut the artichoke in half lengthwise, and, with a paring knife, cut out the fuzzy choke. Use a grapefruit spoon or teaspoon to dig out the fuzzy fibers and then wipe the heart clean. Rub the artichoke at once with lemon juice to prevent discoloration. Slice each artichoke half crosswise as thin as possible and toss with lemon juice.

In a saucepan, heat 3 tablespoons of the oil. Sauté the artichoke slices and garlic over medium heat until the garlic is soft, about 3 minutes. Add ⅓ cup of the chicken stock, 3 tablespoons of the parsley, and pepper to taste. Simmer until the artichoke is just tender, about 30 minutes. Chop the onion.

Cooking: Heat the remaining 3 tablespoons of oil in a saucepan. Cook the onion until soft, about 3 minutes. Add the rice and stir for 1 minute to coat. Stir in the wine. Cook, stirring, over medium-high heat until most of the wine has evaporated, about 4 minutes.

Heat the remaining stock and add about ⅔ cup to the rice. Cook, stirring continuously, until all the liquid has been absorbed.

Stir the artichoke mixture into the risotto. Add more stock, ⅓ cup at a time, stirring continuously. Wait until most of the liquid has been absorbed before adding more stock. When all the liquid has been absorbed, the grains should be soft but still whole and the remaining liquid thickened to a creamy consistency. This should take about 20 minutes altogether. Stir in the butter and 3 tablespoons of the cheese. Season with salt and pepper to taste.

SERVING: Serve the risotto at once, sprinkled with the remaining cheese and the parsley.

YIELD: 4 servings

ONION AND FENNEL FRITTATA

Frittatas are quickly prepared, versatile creations that are equally good warm or at room temperature. Martha Stewart, who in her work as a caterer must be both practical and inventive, developed this recipe using the complementary combination of onions and fennel to lend distinction to the simple dish.

Preparation: Cut the onions into thin slices. Cut the fennel lengthwise into thin slices. Heat the oil in a round, 2-quart baking pan or a large, ovenproof frying pan over medium heat. Sauté the onions in the oil until translucent, about 5 minutes. Remove the onions from pan and sauté the fennel over high heat until the edges darken. Return the onions to the pan and arrange the vegetables attractively in the pan.

3 large onions
2 medium-sized fennel bulbs
½ cup olive oil
14 eggs
Salt and black pepper

Cooking: Heat the oven to 425°F. In a large bowl, beat the eggs until well mixed but not fluffy. Pour the eggs over fennel and onions. Sprinkle liberally with salt and pepper. Bake on the middle rack of the preheated oven until puffed and golden brown and the center is cooked through, 25 to 30 minutes.

SERVING: Serve hot, warm, or at room temperature, cut into wedges.

YIELD: 8 servings

POLENTA STUDDED WITH BRAISED MUSHROOMS

Chef James Moore of the Mountain Home Inn in Mill Valley,
California, updates a traditional ethnic dish by adding wild mushrooms
to cheesy Italian polenta. He favors hedgehogs, but virtually any
mushroom could be used, including the standard cultivated variety.

Braised Mushrooms (recipe follows)
¼ cup chopped fresh parsley
*½ pound Parmesan or other sharp, hard
 cheese*
4½ cups Chicken Stock (page 81) or water
1 cup yellow cornmeal
Salt

Preparation: Make the Braised Mushrooms. Chop the
parsley. Grate the cheese.

Cooking: In a heavy saucepan, bring the stock to a
boil. Gradually add the cornmeal, stirring constantly.
When the mixture thickens, add the parsley. Simmer,
stirring, until the mixture is thick enough to come away
from the side of the pan when the pan is tilted, 30 to 40
minutes altogether. Add the cheese and salt to taste.
Heat the mushrooms.

SERVING: Mound the polenta on a warm platter. Using
a spoon, make shallow indentations in its surface. Put
warm Braised Mushrooms in these indentations and
pour the remaining braising liquid over the polenta.
Serve immediately.

YIELD: 4 servings

BRAISED MUSHROOMS

12 shallots
¼ cup chopped fresh parsley
1 pound hedgehog or other mushrooms
4 cups Chicken Stock (page 81)

Preparation: Mince the shallots. Chop the parsley.
Chop the stems of the mushrooms and leave the caps
whole.

Cooking: In a saucepan, cook the stock, two thirds of
the shallots, parsley, and mushroom stems over medium heat, uncovered, for 10 minutes. Strain, pressing
out the liquid from the solids before discarding them.
    Add the mushroom caps and remaining shallots,
parsley, and mushroom stems to the stock and bring to

a simmer. Simmer, covered, until the mushrooms are tender, 7 to 10 minutes. Remove mushrooms with a slotted spoon.

Reduce the braising liquid over high heat to 1 cup, 20 to 25 minutes, and return the mushrooms to the liquid.

BRAISED MUSHROOMS WITH KASHA

This simple recipe from James Moore of the Mountain Home Inn in Mill Valley, California, uses, for choice, boletes, the wild mushroom some swear is the best of all. Other mushrooms work well in this recipe, too.

Preparation: Mince the onion and thyme if using fresh. Cut the mushrooms into thick slices.

In a saucepan, sauté onion and kasha in 2 tablespoons of the butter until the onion is soft and the kasha is browned, about 5 minutes. If using dried thyme, add it now. Add 1 cup of the stock and simmer, covered, until the kasha is tender, about 30 minutes, adding up to 2 cups more stock as the liquid is absorbed.

Meanwhile, in a frying pan, heat the remaining 4 tablespoons of butter and the olive oil. Sauté the mushrooms until firm, about 5 minutes. Season with salt and pepper to taste. Add the sherry and scrape bottom of the pan with a wooden spoon to deglaze. Add the remaining cup of stock and simmer, covered, until the mushrooms are tender, about 5 minutes. Remove the mushrooms with a slotted spoon and reduce the liquid over high heat until it is the consistency of a light sauce.

Stir in minced fresh thyme, if using. Season with salt and pepper to taste.

SERVING: Mound the kasha on plates and put the mushrooms and sauce over the kasha. Sprinkle with the thyme leaves if desired.

YIELD: 4 servings

½ onion
1 tablespoon minced fresh thyme leaves or 1 teaspoon dried thyme
1 pound boletes, matsutake, or other mushrooms
1 cup kasha (buckwheat groats)
6 tablespoons unsalted butter
3 to 4 cups Chicken Stock (page 81)
2 tablespoons olive oil
Salt and black pepper
1 tablespoon dry sherry
Fresh thyme leaves for garnish (optional)

ZUCCHINI "PASTA" WITH TOMATO–CLAM SAUCE

Julienned squash is treated as pasta in this inventive dish that gives a new elegance to two favorite summer vegetables—zucchini and tomatoes.

Tomato–Clam Sauce

4 tomatoes
4½ tablespoons olive oil
¼ cup slivered black olives
2 dozen hard-shell clams, such as
   cherrystones
2 teaspoons vinegar
Salt

Zucchini "Pasta"

4 large zucchini
2 cloves garlic
2 tablespoons olive oil
1 teaspoon dried marjoram
¼ teaspoon crushed dried hot red pepper
Salt

Chopped fresh parsley for garnish

Preparation: *For the sauce,* peel and chop the tomatoes. Cook them in a frying pan with 2 tablespoons of the oil over medium heat until the excess moisture has evaporated, about 5 minutes. Stir in olives and set the mixture aside to cool.

Scrub the clams. In a large saucepan, heat the remaining 2½ tablespoons of oil over high heat. Add the clams to the pan, cover, and shake the pan continuously over the heat so that clams cook evenly, 3 to 4 minutes. Discard any unopened clams. Reserve some unshucked clams for garnish. Shuck the remaining clams over a bowl to catch the juices. Add the clams to the tomato sauce. Pour the juice through a cheesecloth-lined strainer into the sauce.

Cooking: *For the "pasta,"* cut the zucchini into ⅛- by 5-inch julienne strips. Mince the garlic. Heat the oil in a large frying pan over high heat. Add about half of the zucchini, or enough to cover the bottom of the pan, and sauté, stirring, for about 2 minutes. Stir in half of the garlic, marjoram, and hot pepper flakes, and salt to taste, and cook until zucchini softens and browns lightly, 3 to 4 minutes more. Drain in a sieve, catching the oil in a bowl, and keep the zucchini warm. Use the drained oil to sauté the remaining zucchini, garlic, marjoram, and hot pepper flakes, and salt to taste.

Meanwhile, reheat the sauce. Add the vinegar and season with salt to taste.

SERVING: Pour the sauce over the zucchini "pasta," sprinkle with parsley, and garnish with the reserved whole clams.

YIELD: 4 servings

GRITS, GREENS, AND GARLIC SOUFFLÉ

This recipe is an example of the new Southern cuisine, which uses traditional ingredients and foods in lighter, fresher, more colorful ways. Two familiar side dishes, grits and turnip greens, are reincarnated in a garlicky soufflé.

Preparation: Grate the cheese. Mince the garlic. Chop the turnip greens. Butter a 1-quart soufflé dish or casserole and sprinkle with the bread crumbs.

Cooking: Heat the oven to 350°F. In a saucepan, bring 1 cup of water, the milk, and salt to a gentle boil. Stir in the grits. Return the mixture to a boil, stirring constantly. Lower the heat and simmer, stirring often, until thick, about 5 minutes. Remove from the heat and add ½ cup of the cheese, along with the butter, half and half, pepper, and garlic.

Separate the eggs. In a bowl, lightly beat the egg yolks. Add to the hot grits mixture and stir until the cheese and butter have melted. Cook for about 10 minutes.

In ½ cup boiling salted water, blanch the turnip greens; then drain and squeeze them dry. Mix the greens with the bacon grease and spread them on the bottom of the prepared dish. Sprinkle the remaining cheese over the greens.

In another bowl, beat the egg whites until stiff. Gently fold the egg whites into the grits mixture. Pour the mixture over the cheese and smooth the top with a spatula. Bake in the preheated oven until puffed and browned, 40 to 45 minutes.

YIELD: 4 servings

2½ ounces sharp cheddar cheese
2 cloves garlic
⅓ cup chopped fresh or frozen turnip greens
1 tablespoon dry bread crumbs
1 cup milk
½ teaspoon salt
½ cup quick-cooking grits
4 tablespoons unsalted butter
¼ cup half and half
¼ teaspoon coarse black pepper
2 eggs
1 tablespoon bacon grease

GREEN BEAN AND ROASTED RED PEPPER FRITTATA

The combination of roasted red bell peppers and fresh green beans makes this a colorful as well as delicious and easy dish that can be made ahead of time.

1 large red bell pepper
1 pound green beans
1 small onion
¾ cup grated Parmesan cheese
2 tablespoons olive oil
8 eggs
*   Salt and black pepper*

Preparation: Put red pepper under the broiler or directly on a gas flame until charred and blackened all over, about 10 minutes altogether. Peel, cut the pepper in half, seed, and cut lengthwise into 1-inch-wide strips.

Wash and trim the beans. Cut the onion into thin slices. Grate the cheese.

In a large pot of boiling water, cook the beans until tender, 5 to 10 minutes. Drain and refresh under cold, running water; then drain again.

Heat the oil in a 12-inch round baking pan or oven-proof frying pan over medium heat. Add the onion and sauté until softened, about 4 minutes. Remove from the heat. Arrange the beans over the onion slices. Put the red pepper strips on top of the beans, arranging them in a star design.

Cooking: Heat the oven to 425°F. Lightly whisk the eggs with salt and pepper to taste. Pour the eggs over the vegetables and sprinkle with the cheese.

Bake in the preheated oven until the sides puff up, the eggs are a light golden color, and a knife inserted into the center comes out clean, about 20 minutes.

SERVING: Serve hot, warm, or at room temperature, cut into wedges.

YIELD: 4 servings

PUMPKIN AND BEAN STEW

Town & Country Food and Wine Editor, James Villas, has mounted a crusade for a comeback of old-fashioned country food. He advocates a return to "true, basic, rustic cooking," and if his delectable vegetable stew is representative of the type, we're all for it.

Preparation and Cooking: Sort beans and soak overnight in enough cold water to cover by at least 2 inches. Drain and rinse the beans.

Chop the onion. Mince the garlic and chile pepper. Chop the green pepper and tomato. Dice the ham. Peel and remove the seeds from the pumpkin; then cut the flesh into 1-inch chunks.

In a large, heavy casserole, heat the butter and oil. Add the onion, garlic, chile pepper, and green pepper. Sauté over medium heat, stirring occasionally, until soft, about 5 minutes. Add the beans, tomato, ham, stock, thyme, summer savory, and pepper to taste and stir well.

Bring to a boil, lower the heat, cover, and simmer until the beans are just tender, 1 to 2 hours.

Stir the pumpkin into the beans and add more stock or water if the stew is too thick. Cover and continue to simmer until pumpkin is tender, about 30 minutes.

SERVING: Reheat the stew over low heat if made ahead. Season with salt and pepper to taste and serve.

YIELD: about 1½ quarts

1 cup dried Great Northern beans
1 large onion
1 clove garlic
½ small chile pepper
½ green bell pepper
1 large tomato
¼ pound cured country ham
1½ pounds pumpkin or butternut squash
1½ tablespoons unsalted butter
¼ cup olive oil
1 cup Chicken Stock, plus more if necessary (page 81)
¼ teaspoon dried thyme
¼ teaspoon dried summer savory
    Salt and black pepper

ASPARAGUS SHORTCAKE WITH HAM

A few years ago, shortcake came back into vogue, and every spring and summer menu included the familiar strawberry version. Shortcake is an American dish that deserves uninterrupted popularity. This savory version, a treat for asparagus lovers, is made with herb biscuits and served with a rich, lemony sauce.

Herb Biscuits

2 teaspoons minced fresh parsley
2 teaspoons minced fresh chives or
    scallion tops
1 cup flour
2 teaspoons baking powder
½ teaspoon salt
4½ tablespoons cold unsalted butter
⅓ cup milk

2 pounds asparagus
4 ⅛-inch-thick slices ham
9 tablespoons unsalted butter
1 egg yolk
1 tablespoon lemon juice
    Salt and black pepper
1 teaspoon minced fresh parsley
1 teaspoon minced fresh chives or scallion
    tops

Preparation: *For the biscuits,* mince all the parsley and chives, 1 tablespoon each. Mix the flour, baking powder, and salt in a bowl. Cut or rub in 3½ tablespoons of the butter until it is the consistency of meal with a few pea-sized lumps remaining. Stir in 2 teaspoons each of the parsley and chives. Add the milk all at once and stir in with a fork.

Press or roll the dough to a ½-inch thickness and stamp out 4 biscuits with a 2½-inch cutter. Put them on an unbuttered baking pan. Melt the remaining tablespoon of butter. Brush the tops with the melted butter and refrigerate biscuits.

Snap the ends off the asparagus spears and peel the stalks. Cut off bottoms of asparagus stalks, leaving tip ends 4 inches long. In a saucepan, cook the bottoms of the stalks, uncovered, in boiling salted water to cover for 10 minutes. Transfer with a slotted spoon to a food processor, reserving the cooking liquid in the pan. Puree the stalk bottoms and set the puree aside. With a 3-inch cutter, stamp out 4 rounds from the ham slices.

Cooking: Heat the oven to 425°F. Bring the asparagus cooking liquid back to a boil. Boil the asparagus tips, uncovered, for 4 minutes. Transfer with a slotted spoon to paper towels to drain. Continue boiling the cooking liquid to reduce it to ⅓ cup, about 5 minutes.

Bake the biscuits in the preheated oven until golden brown on top, about 15 minutes.

In a large frying pan, sauté the ham rounds in 1 tablespoon of the butter over medium heat until lightly browned, about 1 minute per side. Remove from the heat.

Split the baked biscuits and lay them open on the baking pan. On each bottom half, put a round of sautéed ham and top with asparagus tips, alternating tip ends so that they face opposite directions. Return the pan to the turned-off oven to keep warm while making the sauce.

Combine asparagus puree, reduced cooking liquid, egg yolk, and lemon juice in a small heavy pan. Whisk over low heat until the sauce thickens slightly, being careful not to boil, 3 to 4 minutes. Remove the pan from the heat and whisk in the remaining 8 tablespoons of butter by tablespoons, adding another tablespoon as soon as the preceding one is nearly incorporated. The butter should not melt completely but should soften to form a creamy sauce. Season with salt and pepper to taste.

SERVING: Put the ham-and-asparagus-topped biscuit halves on individual warm plates. Pour the sauce over and around the biscuits and top with the biscuit tops. Sprinkle the remaining parsley and chives over all and serve immediately.

YIELD: 4 servings

SWEET POTATO TAMALES

Stephan Pyles is chef and co-owner of the Routh Street Cafe in Dallas,
Texas. His sweet potato tamales are a worthwhile innovation on a
Mexican tradition. The taste is incredible, and they can be made nearly
entirely ahead of time.

Tamales

    18 large corn husks
     2 large sweet potatoes
  1½ cups fresh (from about 5 cobs) or
         frozen corn kernels
  2½ cups Chicken Stock (page 81)
     1 tablespoon maple syrup
       Salt
    10 tablespoons lard or shortening
     ½ teaspoon cayenne
     ¼ teaspoon ground cumin
  1¼ cups yellow cornmeal, preferably
         stoneground

Tamale Sauce

     ½ red bell pepper
     ½ yellow bell pepper
     1 small onion
     1 clove garlic
     1 tablespoon chopped fresh coriander
         leaves
     2 cups cooking liquid from sweet potatoes
     1 cup heavy cream
       Salt

     8 whole fresh coriander leaves for garnish
         (optional)

Preparation: *For the tamales,* soak the corn husks in
cold water for 20 minutes. Peel the sweet potatoes and
cut them into ½-inch dice. Put the sweet potatoes in a
saucepan with 2 cups of the stock. Add the maple syrup
and salt to taste and bring to a boil. Lower the heat and
simmer for 3 minutes. Drain the sweet potatoes and
reserve the stock for the sauce. Plunge the sweet potatoes into ice water to cool and then drain.

In a food processor, grind the corn kernels until very
smooth, about 3 minutes. Remove from the processor
and set aside. Put the lard or shortening into the processor and whir until light and fluffy, scraping down the
sides as necessary. Add 1 teaspoon salt, cayenne, and
cumin. Gradually add the cornmeal to the processor and
whir until incorporated. Add the ground corn kernels
and whir for 1 minute. Add the remaining ½ cup of
stock gradually in 2 additions, waiting 2 minutes between additions. Set the tamale dough aside.

Drain the corn husks and pat dry with paper towels,
Tear 16 ¼-inch strips from 2 of the husks and set aside
for tying the tamales.

For each tamale, use 2 husks. Put the wide ends together with a 2-inch overlap. Spread one eighth of the
tamale dough in the center of each pair of husks, leaving
a margin of 1 inch at each end. Put about one eighth of
the sweet potatoes on top of the dough. Roll up the
corn husks so that filling is completely enclosed. Twist
and tie each end with the reserved strips.

Cooking: In a steamer or in a strainer set in a pot and
covered, steam the tamales until the dough comes away
easily from the husks, 30 to 35 minutes. The water
should always be bubbling but never violently boiling.

The tamales can be kept warm for 30 to 45 minutes in the steamer with the heat turned off.

For the sauce, while the tamales are steaming, or earlier if you like, seed the red and yellow bell peppers and cut them into dice. Dice the onion. Mince the garlic. Chop the coriander leaves.

Heat the reserved cooking liquid from the sweet potatoes in a saucepan. Add the peppers, onion, garlic, and cream. Bring to a boil and reduce by half, 10 to 15 minutes. Season with salt to taste. The sauce can be made ahead and reheated. Just before serving, stir in the chopped coriander.

SERVING: Slice down the center of the tamales end to end. Push the ends gently toward the center and coat each tamale with some sauce. Garnish with the coriander leaves.

YIELD: 4 servings

EGGPLANT ROLLATINI STUFFED WITH PROSCIUTTO AND SUN-DRIED TOMATOES

In this hearty, full-flavored dish, eggplant slices are stuffed with leeks, cheese, prosciutto, and sun-dried tomatoes and topped with either of two sauces.

1 large eggplant (about 1 pound)
 Coarse salt
 Oil for frying
 Black pepper
 Flour for dredging

Tomato–Prosciutto Filling

2 small leeks
2 ounces prosciutto
2 ounces sun-dried tomatoes
¼ pound mozzarella cheese
1 ounce Parmesan cheese
    (about ¼ cup grated)
3 tablespoons unsalted butter
¾ pound ricotta cheese
1 egg
 Pinch of grated nutmeg
 Salt and black pepper

 Cream Sauce or Tomato Sauce
    (recipes follow)

Preparation: Cut the unpeeled eggplant into ¼-inch-thick slices, cutting diagonally to get the largest possible slices. Lightly sprinkle slices on both sides with coarse salt. Drain in a colander for 20 minutes. Rinse under cold water and drain again. Heat ¼ inch of oil in a large frying pan. Sprinkle the eggplant with pepper. Dredge each eggplant slice in flour, shaking off any excess. Fry the slices, being careful not to overcrowd the pan, until golden brown, 1 to 2 minutes per side. Replenish the oil as necessary. Drain on paper twoels.

For the filling, chop the white part of the leeks only. Mince the prosciutto. If the sun-dried tomatoes are not packed in oil, reconstitute them in warm water to cover. Chop the tomatoes. Grate the mozzarella and Parmesan. Melt the butter in a small frying pan and sauté the leeks over medium heat for 1 minute. Add the prosciutto and sun-dried tomatoes and continue sautéing until the leeks are soft, 2 to 3 minutes.

Butter a baking dish. Put the cheeses in a bowl and combine with leek mixture and egg. Season with nutmeg and salt and pepper to taste. Spread a few tablespoons of the filling on each eggplant slice and roll the slice into a cylinder. Spread one third of the Cream or Tomato Sauce in the prepared baking dish. Arrange the stuffed eggplant slices on top, seam side down; spoon the remaining sauce over them.

Cooking: Heat the oven to 350°F. Bake in the preheated oven until filling is thoroughly heated, about 30 minutes.

YIELD: 4 servings

CREAM SAUCE

Preparation: Quarter the onion. Flatten the garlic. Put the milk, cream, onion, garlic, herbs, cloves, allspice, and peppercorns into a small saucepan. Simmer gently for 20 minutes.

In another saucepan, melt the butter. Whisk in the flour to make a roux and cook over medium heat for 2 minutes. Remove both mixtures from the heat.

Strain the cream mixture into the roux, whisking vigorously. Return the pan to the heat and bring to a boil, whisking, and cook for 3 minutes, stirring frequently. The sauce should be thick. Season with salt, cayenne, and nutmeg to taste.

YIELD: 1½ cups

1 small onion
1 clove garlic
1 cup milk
1 cup cream
1 bay leaf
  Pinch of dried thyme
2 sprigs parsley
2 whole cloves
2 allspice berries
5 whole peppercorns
3 tablespoons unsalted butter
3 tablespoons flour
  Salt
  Cayenne
  Nutmeg for grating

TOMATO SAUCE

Preparation: Chop the onion. Peel, seed, and chop the tomatoes. Mince the fresh basil if using.

In a frying pan, melt the butter. Add the onion and sauté over medium heat until softened, about 4 minutes. If using dried basil, add it now. Add wine and cook for about 1 minute. Add the chopped tomatoes and salt and pepper to taste. Simmer over medium-low heat for about 2 minutes. Add minced fresh basil and simmer until slightly thickened, about 3 minutes.

YIELD: 1½ cups

1 small onion
1 pound plum tomatoes
4 teaspoons minced fresh basil leaves or
    1 teaspoon dried basil
2 tablespoons unsalted butter
2 tablespoons dry red or *white wine*
  Salt and black pepper

FETA–VEGETABLE PIE WITH HERBED CRUST

The flavor of whole wheat is excellent in pie crusts, but when overdone, the texture of the pastry suffers. Here white flour is used in a proportion of four to one of whole wheat.

Herbed Crust

> 2 tablespoons minced fresh herbs, such as chives, parsley, rosemary, or basil or a mixture
> 1½ ounces cream cheese (3 tablespoons)
> 6 tablespoons unsalted butter
> 1 cup all-purpose flour
> ¼ cup whole-wheat flour
> ¼ teaspoon salt
> 1 egg yolk
> 2 to 3 tablespoons cold water
> 1 tablespoon Dijon mustard

Vegetable–Cheese Filling

> 3 medium-sized yellow summer squash
> 8 thin asparagus stalks
> 3 medium-sized carrots
> 2 tablespoons minced fresh chives or scallion tops
> ¼ cup minced fresh herbs, such as parsley, basil, or rosemary or a mixture
> ½ pound fresh spinach
> Salt and black pepper
> Nutmeg for grating
> ¼ cup pine nuts
> 2 eggs
> ½ pound feta cheese (about 1 cup)
> ¾ pound ricotta cheese (about 1½ cups)
> ½ teaspoon dry mustard

Preparation: *For the crust,* mince the herbs. Cut the cream cheese and butter separately into pieces and chill. Whir the flours and salt in a food processor to mix. Add the herbs, egg yolk, and chilled cream cheese and whir to blend. Add the cold butter and whir until it is the size of small peas. With the motor running, add the cold water a little at a time, until the mixture can be lightly pressed together. Shape into a flat disc and wrap in plastic wrap. Refrigerate until workable, about 30 minutes.

Heat the oven to 450°F. On a lightly floured surface, roll the dough to a 12-inch round. Brush off any excess flour. Press the dough into an 8-inch cake pan with removable bottom or a deep tart pan. Prick the bottom of the crust with a fork. Refrigerate at least 20 minutes or freeze for 5 minutes.

Line crust with buttered aluminum foil, shiny side down, and fill with dried beans or pie weights.

Bake the pie shell on the bottom rack in the preheated oven for 10 minutes. Lower the oven temperature to 350°F, bake for an additional 10 minutes, and then remove the foil and beans. Return to the oven and continue baking until the crust is firm and dry, about 10 minutes. Brush the pie shell with Dijon mustard and return it to the oven until the mustard is dry, about 5 minutes. Remove from the oven and cool.

For the filling, cut the unpeeled squash in half lengthwise. Remove the seeds and cut the flesh into ½-inch dice. Cut the asparagus stalks on the diagonal into ½-inch pieces, leaving the tips whole. Cut the carrots on the diagonal into ¼-inch-thick slices. Mince all the herbs. Wash the spinach.

Blanch the squash in boiling salted water for 30 seconds. Drain. Season with salt and pepper. Blanch the asparagus for 1 minute, and season with salt and pepper. Separate the tips from the stalks. Blanch the carrots for 3 minutes, and toss them with the chives. Grate the nutmeg over the asparagus stalks and toss with the herbs. Cook the spinach in boiling salted water until limp, about 30 seconds. Rinse with cold water, squeeze out all the excess water, and chop. Season with salt and pepper to taste.

Toast the pine nuts in a 325°F oven until golden, 5 to 10 minutes. In a large bowl, beat the eggs to combine. Crumble in the feta cheese. Add the spinach, ricotta, dry mustard, and asparagus stalks and season with salt and pepper to taste.

Put one third of the spinach mixture into the pie shell. Layer with the carrot slices, reserving 12 slices. Add another layer of spinach and then a layer of squash. Top with the remaining spinach mixture. Garnish with the asparagus tips and reserved carrot slices. Sprinkle with the pine nuts.

Cooking: Heat the oven to 350°F. Bake in the preheated oven until the filling is set, about 1½ hours. Cover the top with aluminum foil if it is browning too fast. Remove from the oven and cool for 20 minutes before serving.

YIELD: 4 servings

CABBAGE PIE

This hearty vegetable pie is flavored with Madeira and baked in a whole-wheat poppy seed pie shell.

Poppy Seed Whole-Wheat Pastry

⅓ cup whole-wheat flour
1¼ cups all-purpose flour
½ teaspoon salt
⅛ teaspoon black pepper
4 teaspoons dark poppy seeds
2 ounces cream cheese (4 tablespoons)
7 tablespoons unsalted butter
1 egg yolk
3 tablespoons (approximately) cold water

Cabbage Filling

1 red bell pepper
1 large onion
1 rib celery
¼ pound mushrooms
3 cloves garlic
1½ pounds Napa cabbage or green cabbage
¼ cup vegetable oil
1½ cups beef stock
1 bay leaf
 Salt and black pepper
3 tablespoons flour
¼ cup Madeira or port
¼ pound Swiss cheese
½ cup bread crumbs
½ teaspoon paprika

Preparation: *For the pie crust,* combine the flours, salt, pepper, and poppy seeds. Work in the cold cream cheese and butter with a pastry blender or your fingertips until the mixture is the texture of coarse meal with a few pea-size pieces left. Whisk the egg yolk with 1 tablespoon water. Add the yolk mixture and enough cold water so that the dough just holds together when lightly pressed. Wrap in plastic wrap and refrigerate for 30 minutes.

On a lightly floured work surface, roll the dough to about a ⅛-inch thickness. Press the dough into a deep 10-inch pie pan. Flute the edge. Prick the bottom of the crust. Refrigerate for at least 20 minutes or freeze for 5 minutes.

Line the crust with aluminum foil and fill with dried beans or pie weights.

Heat the oven to 450°F. Bake for 10 minutes in the preheated oven. Lower the oven temperature to 350°F and bake until set, about 7 minutes. Remove the foil and bake until golden brown, about 10 minutes.

For the filling, roast the red pepper under the broiler or over a gas flame until the skin is blackened. Cool enough to handle and then peel, remove the stem and seeds, and cut the flesh into ½-inch dice. Cut the onion, celery, and mushrooms into thin slices. Mince the garlic. Cut the cabbage into thin shreds.

In a large frying pan, heat the oil. Add the onion and celery and cook, covered, over low heat for about 7 minutes. Add the mushrooms and garlic and sauté, uncovered, for 1 minute. Add the cabbage, ½ cup of the stock, the bay leaf, and salt and pepper to taste. Stir, cover, and simmer for 15 minutes. Remove the cover, raise the heat to medium-high, and cook until the excess liquid has evaporated. Discard the bay leaf. Stir in the red pepper.

In a small bowl, whisk the flour with the Madeira and the remaining cup of stock. If lumps form, strain. Pour over the vegetables. Cook over high heat, stirring occasionally, until the mixture is thick, about 10 minutes. Cook for about 15 minutes. Spoon the cooled filling into the baked shell and smooth the top of the pie.

Grate the cheese and combine with the bread crumbs and paprika. Sprinkle the mixture over the pie and lightly pat into an even layer.

Cooking: Heat the oven to 375°F. Bake the pie in the preheated oven until the filling is hot and bubbly and top lightly browned, about 20 minutes.

SERVING: Let the pie set for 10 minutes; then cut into wedges.

YIELD: 6 to 8 servings

EGGPLANT AND SMOKED CHEESE PIE

Two distinctive flavors, those of eggplant and a smoked cheese, such as mozzarella, complement one another in this satisfying pie.

Pastry

1⅓ cups all-purpose flour
⅔ cup cake flour
1 scant teaspoon salt
¼ pound unsalted butter
1 egg
4 to 5 tablespoons cold water

Eggplant–Smoked Cheese Filling

1 large eggplant (about 1 pound)
Coarse salt
1 medium-sized onion
2 medium-sized leeks
1 clove garlic
1 tablespoon chopped fresh parsley
2 teaspoons chopped fresh basil leaves
or ¾ teaspoon dried basil
6 ounces smoked mozzarella or other
smoked cheese
3 tablespoons unsalted butter
⅓ cup heavy cream
Salt and black pepper
Cayenne

Parsley or basil sprigs for garnish

Preparation: *For the pastry,* whir both flours, the salt, and butter in a food processor until the mixture is the consistency of cornmeal. Add the egg and cold water and whir just until dough comes together into a ball. Wrap tightly in plastic wrap and chill for 30 minutes. Heat the oven to 400°F.

Roll out the dough and line a 12-inch tart pan. Prick the dough with a fork and refrigerate at least 20 minutes or freeze for 5 minutes. Bake the crust in the preheated oven for 15 minutes.

For the filling, halve and score the eggplant by cutting deep crisscross gashes through the flesh, almost to the skin. Sprinkle the eggplant with coarse salt and let drain for 20 minutes. Mince the onion, the white part of the leeks, and the garlic. Chop the parsley and basil if using fresh. Cut the cheese into ⅛-inch-thick slices.

Heat the oven to 400°F. Rinse the eggplant under cold water and blot dry with paper towels.

Oil a baking sheet. Put the eggplant on the baking sheet and bake in the preheated oven until soft, about 20 minutes. Set aside to cool.

Melt the butter in a large frying pan. Sauté onion, leeks, and garlic over medium heat until soft, about 5 minutes.

Scrape the eggplant flesh out of the skin and chop it. Add the eggplant, parsley, and basil to the onion mixture and sauté for 3 minutes. Add the cream and simmer until cream has been absorbed, about 2 minutes. Add salt and pepper and cayenne to taste.

Spoon the filling into the prepared crust. Arrange the cheese slices in a ring around edge of pie on top of the filling.

Cooking: Bake the pie in the preheated oven until the cheese is melted and the filling is hot, about 25 minutes.

SERVING: Garnish with parsley or basil sprigs.

YIELD: 6 to 8 servings

BRAISED MUSHROOM SOUFFLÉ

Here is another recipe from our wild-mushroom champion, James Moore of the Mountain Home Inn in Mill Valley, California. We find that the soufflé is also delicious made with plain cultivated white mushrooms from the supermarket.

Preparation: Make the Braised Mushrooms. Reserve 8 whole mushrooms for garnish. Squeeze the rest by the handful to remove any excess liquid; then dice the mushrooms. Dice the onion. Chop the thyme if using fresh. Grate the cheeses. Butter a 1½-quart soufflé dish or casserole and sprinkle with 1 tablespoon of the Parmesan cheese.

Braised Mushrooms (page 104)
1 small white onion
1½ teaspoons chopped fresh thyme leaves
or ½ teaspoon dried thyme
6 tablespoons grated Parmesan cheese
5 tablespoons grated Gruyère cheese
3 tablespoons unsalted butter
3 tablespoons flour
⅓ cup heavy cream
Salt and black pepper
1 egg yolk
5 egg whites
¼ teaspoon cream of tartar

Cooking: Heat the oven to 375°F. In a saucepan, melt the 3 tablespoons of butter. Whisk in the flour and simmer 5 minutes, stirring constantly. Do not allow the mixture to color. Whisk in the cream and reduced mushroom liquid. Add the onion, thyme, salt and pepper, and diced braised mushrooms. Bring to a boil, stirring, and then simmer 30 minutes. Remove from the heat and whisk in the egg yolk. Set aside to cool somewhat.

In a mixing bowl, beat the egg whites with the cream of tartar until stiff peaks form.

Stir the remaining 5 tablespoons of Parmesan cheese and the Gruyère cheese into the cream mixture. Stir in one third of the egg whites to lighten and then fold in the remaining whites. Pour the mixture into the prepared soufflé dish and smooth the top.

Bake on the lower rack of the preheated oven until just set, about 25 minutes. The center should still be quite soft.

SERVING: Serve immediately garnished with the reserved whole braised mushroom caps.

YIELD: 4 servings

Zucchini "Pasta" with Tomato–Clam Sauce
   (page 106)

──────
                                  Pinot Grigio

Green Bean and Roasted Red Pepper Frittata
   (page 108)

Ancho Chocolate Soufflé (page 244)   Asti Spumante

Corn Bread with Ham and Maple Butter   Kir (white wine with cassis)
   (page 21)

Fried Chicken Salad (page 66)

──────
                                  Beaujolais Nouveau (chilled)

Grits, Greens, and Garlic Soufflé (page 107)

Winter Compote with Raspberry Sauce
   (page 232)

Grilled Lamb Sausage with Watercress and
   Warm Potato Salad (page 162)

──────
                                  Côtes-du-Rhône

Eggplant and Smoked Cheese Pie (page 120)

Banana–Caramel Soup (page 238)

CHAPTER 6

PASTA

Egg Pasta · Noodles with Celery Cabbage · Olive Pasta
Cornmeal Pasta with Ham and Pepper Sauce
Pasta with Winter Vegetables
Fettuccine with Shellfish and Mushrooms
Pasta with Beef Jerky, Asparagus, and Pimiento
Jalapeño Pasta with Lobster and Cucumber
Pasta with Smoked Salmon and Sweet Onion Sauce
Pasta with Grilled Chicken and Dill Pesto Sauce
Green and White Ravioli in Broth · Pasta with Squid and Basil

There seems to be no end to the appeal of pasta. It is always satisfying and is also infinitely flexible. It can become a luxury dish with the addition of special ingredients, as in our Jalapeño Pasta with Lobster and Cucumber or Pasta with Smoked Salmon and Sweet Onion Sauce. Other new combinations use traditional American foods in unexpected ways, for example in Pasta with Beef Jerky, Asparagus, and Pimiento. Any popular cooking method can be incorporated into a pasta dish, even grilling, as in our Pasta with Grilled Chicken and Dill Pesto Sauce. Another trend, the renewed appeal of such "unglamorous" vegetables as cabbage, is also reflected in contemporary pasta innovations. The hearty Noodles with Celery Cabbage, for instance, is a delectable combination.

All of these examples are virtually instant when made with commercial pasta, which means they're perfect either for easy entertaining or for a quick family dinner, another reason for their appeal. In the traditional Italian menu, the pasta course precedes the entree, while Americans have long considered traditional spaghetti, lasagne, or macaroni the main course. In the new freestyle cuisine, we now integrate it anywhere we please.

Not only what's put on it, but the pasta itself can be varied both in flavor—we include green, jalapeño, and corn variations on our basic egg pasta recipe—and in shape. There are literally hundreds of different sorts of pasta. The major categories, however, reduce the welter to four basic types: two egg-enriched varieties, the flat egg noodle pastas and the stuffed pastas, and two flour and water varieties, the hollow pasta tubes, such as macaroni, and the spaghetti-type pastas.

Fresh pastas are made with eggs and flour and perhaps a touch of salt. Though purists consider adding oil amateurish, most American cooks use at least a touch to make rolling easier. And, more and more, good-quality fresh pasta is available commercially. Frankly, we consider quality dry pasta at least as good as, often better than most of the fresh pasta sold. Homemade is always a treat. Try taste tests with the different dry brands and commercial fresh pastas available in your area and see what's best. If you make your own, throw it into the competition, too, or simply reserve it for when you have time to stir it together and roll it out. With the exception of one ravioli dish, all the recipes in this chapter can be made with either dry or fresh pasta.

A Directory to the Pasta Shapes Used in This Chapter

Bavettine: very narrow flat noodles

Capelli d'Angelo: "angel's hair," long, very fine pasta

Capellini: very fine spaghetti

Cavatelli: ribbed shells

Conchiglie: smooth or ridged "conch shells"

Farfalle: bow-shaped, "butterfly" pasta

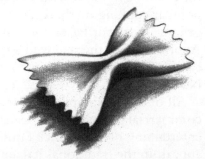

Fedelini: another very fine spaghetti similar to capellini

Fettucce: the widest fettuccine "ribbons"

Fettuccine: narrow noodles

Fusilli: spiral-shaped pasta, corkscrews

Linguine: narrow, flat noodles, some-times with slightly beveled edges
Lumache: shell-shaped "snails" of pasta

Perciatelli: long, thin macaroni
Ravioli: stuffed pasta squares

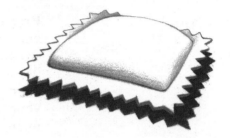

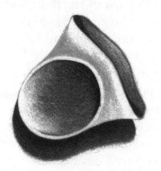

Ricciolini: small twisted pasta

Mafalde: broad, rippled noodles

Rotelle: wagon-wheel shaped pasta (also called rotini) or corkscrew pasta

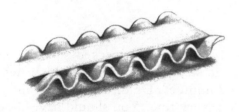

Pappardelle: broad, flat noodles

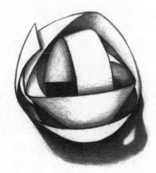

Tagliatelle: flat noodles of various widths, a Bolognese specialty similar to the Roman fettuccine
Trenette: narrow but relatively thick noodles
Ziti: large, slightly curved macaroni

EGG PASTA

1¼ to 1½ cups flour
1 teaspoon salt
2 eggs
2 teaspoons oil

Preparation: Put 1¼ cups of the flour and the salt on a work surface or into a large bowl. Make a well in the center, break the eggs into it, and add the oil. Combine the eggs and oil and then gradually incorporate the flour. The dough will be soft but should not stick to your fingers when poked. Knead the dough for 8 to 10 minutes, adding more flour as necessary to keep the dough from sticking. Let rest under a bowl or plastic wrap until ready to use, or refrigerate, covered tightly in plastic wrap, for up to 3 days.

YIELD: about ¾ pound fresh pasta

VARIATIONS

Green Pasta
Cook about 1 cup loosely packed spinach leaves, stripped of their stems, in boiling salted water until softened, 1 to 2 minutes. Drain, squeeze out the excess water, and chop very fine. You should have about 1½ tablespoons. Add the spinach to the well in the flour. Incorporate with the eggs and oil.

Cornmeal Pasta
Substitute ½ cup yellow cornmeal for ½ cup of the flour.

Jalapeño Pasta
Mince 2 jalapeño peppers or other fresh chiles. Sauté them in ½ teaspoon of oil in a small frying pan over low heat, stirring occasionally. Being careful not to scorch, cook until all the moisture has evaporated, about 5 minutes. Cool and then add the peppers to the well in the flour and incorporate with the eggs and oil.

NOODLES WITH CELERY CABBAGE

Celery, or Chinese, cabbage is a member of the mustard family and has a piquant, slightly spicy flavor. If it is unavailable, mild, sweet Napa cabbage makes a delicious substitute.

Preparation: If using fresh pasta, roll the dough as thin as possible by hand or machine. Cut into ½-inch-wide strips.

Cut the onion into thin slices. Mince the garlic. Separate the cabbage leaves, rinse well, and cut across the rib into thin slices. Peel and shred the carrot. Mince the sage and lemon zest.

In a large frying pan, melt the butter over medium heat, add the onion, and cook, covered, for 5 minutes. Add the garlic and cook, stirring, for 1 minute. Add the cabbage and carrot, stir well, and pour in ½ cup water. Add the sage, lemon zest, and salt and pepper to taste. Simmer, covered, until the cabbage is tender, about 25 minutes.

Thin the sour cream with the milk.

Cooking: In a large pot of boiling salted water, cook the noodles until just tender, about 2 minutes for fresh or 8 minutes for dry. Drain well, toss with the oil, and season with salt and pepper.

While the pasta is cooking, reheat the cabbage sauce if necessary. Stir in the cottage cheese and cook just to warm the cheese and melt it slightly. Season with salt and pepper to taste.

SERVING: Heap the noodles on warm plates, ladle the sauce over each portion, and top with the sour cream.

YIELD: 4 servings

*¾ pound Egg Pasta (page 126) or ½
    pound dry pasta, such as wide egg
    noodles, mafalde, or trenette*
1 small onion
1 clove garlic
¾ pound celery cabbage or Napa cabbage
1 carrot
*½ teaspoon minced fresh sage leaves or ¼
    teaspoon dried sage*
¾ teaspoon minced lemon zest
*1½ tablespoons unsalted butter
    Salt and black pepper*
1½ tablespoons sour cream
*1½ tablespoons milk
    Olive oil for tossing*
¾ cup large-curd cottage cheese

OLIVE PASTA

Use olive oil in the pasta, if you're making your own. The sauce calls
for both green olives, which are picked unripe and then cured, and black
olives, which are ripened on the tree.

¾ pound fresh Egg or Green Pasta (page
126) or ½ pound dry pasta, such as
linguine, bavettine, or perciatelli
1 small red bell pepper
1 clove garlic
Coarse salt
⅔ cup sliced black Mediterranean olives
¼ cup sliced green olives
6 scallion tops
1½ tablespoons olive oil
Salt and coarse black pepper

Preparation: If using fresh pasta, roll dough as thin as possible by hand or machine. Cut the dough into ⅛-inch-wide strips, or as thin as the machine will allow.

Roast the red pepper under the broiler or over a gas flame until blistered and blackened. Remove the skin and seeds and cut the flesh into ¼-inch dice. Crush the garlic with a pinch of coarse salt. Slice the black and green olives. Chop the green scallion tops.

Cooking: Cook the pasta in a large pot of boiling salted water until just tender, about 2 minutes for fresh or 8 minutes for dry. Drain.

Heat the oil in a large frying pan over medium heat. Add the garlic, stir, and then add the olives. Add the pasta and heat. Toss the pasta with the scallions and red pepper and add salt and pepper to taste.

YIELD: 4 servings

CORNMEAL PASTA WITH HAM AND PEPPER SAUCE

Here cornmeal or other pasta is tossed with smoked ham, olive oil,
Parmesan cheese, hot pepper flakes, and basil to make a spicy dish in no
time flat.

¾ pound Cornmeal Pasta (page 126) or ½
pound dry pasta, such as tagliatelle,
fettuccine, or fettucce
⅓ pound smoked ham
2 tablespoons grated Parmesan cheese

Preparation: If using fresh pasta, roll the dough as thin as possible by hand or machine. Cut into ⅙-inch-wide strips.

Dice the ham. Grate the cheese.

Chilled Sorrel Soup

Venison Soup
with Dill Dumplings

Cabbage Pie

Feta–Vegetable Pie with Herbed Crust

Olive Pasta

Cooking: Drop the pasta into boiling salted water and cook until just done, about 2 minutes for fresh or 8 minutes for dry. Drain. Mince the basil. Toss warm pasta with the ham, olive oil, Parmesan, salt, black pepper, hot pepper flakes, and basil.

YIELD: 4 servings

1 tablespoon minced fresh basil leaves
¼ cup olive oil
½ teaspoon salt
¼ teaspoon coarse black pepper
¼ teaspoon crushed dried hot red pepper

PASTA WITH WINTER VEGETABLES

This unusual, yet quick and easy pasta comes from Barry Wine, chef and co-owner of the Quilted Giraffe in New York City.

Preparation: If using fresh pasta, roll the dough as thin as possible by hand or machine. Cut into ⅙-inch-wide strips.

Cut the fennel in half and remove the hearts. Separate the layers and cut them into thin strips. Cut off the dark green tops of the leeks; then cut the leek bulbs in half, rinse thoroughly, and slice. Peel the celery root and cut it into thin slices. Seed the red pepper and cut the flesh into thin strips. Slice the truffles if using.

In a saucepan, bring the cream to a boil. Lower the heat to a simmer and cook for about 5 minutes. Turn off the heat and add truffles if using, fennel, leeks, and celery root. Season with salt and pepper to taste and let sit, covered, for at least 30 minutes.

¾ pound Egg Pasta (page 126) or ½ pound dry fettuccine
1 medium-sized bulb fennel
3 medium-sized leeks
1 small celery root
1 red bell pepper
2 ounces black truffles (optional)
2¼ cups heavy cream
Salt and black pepper
Fresh chervil leaves (optional)

Cooking: Cook the fettuccine in a pot of boiling salted water until just tender, about 2 minutes for fresh or 10 minutes for dry. Drain.

Reheat the vegetable mixture over low heat and add the red pepper strips.

SERVING: Put the fettuccine on warm plates. Ladle the sauce over it and garnish with chervil if desired.

YIELD: 4 servings

FETTUCCINE WITH SHELLFISH AND MUSHROOMS

Chanterelles have a sweet flavor and a fragrance sometimes compared to that of apricots. Chef James Moore of the Mountain Home Inn in Mill Valley, California, pairs these aromatic wild mushrooms with fresh crayfish in an unusual dish that combines ingredients from Oriental, Italian, and new American cooking. This recipe works as well with cultivated mushrooms and shrimp, too.

1½ pounds live crayfish or 1 pound raw shrimp
¾ pound Egg Pasta (page 126) or ½ pound dry fettuccine
¾ pound chanterelles or other mushrooms
3 tablespoons grated Parmesan cheese, plus more for serving
3 tablespoons chopped fresh herbs, such as chervil, chives, and/or parsley
3 tablespoons dry white wine
3 slices unpeeled fresh ginger
¼ sheet pressed seaweed, optional
3 Szechuan peppercorns or other hot peppercorns
1½ cups Fish Stock (page 97)
3 tablespoons heavy cream
2 tablespoons lime juice
Salt and black pepper
4 tablespoons unsalted butter

Preparation: To purge the crayfish, put them into cold water for 1 day, changing water frequently. Transfer crayfish to lightly salted water for 1½ hours and discard any dead crayfish.

If using fresh pasta, roll the dough as thin as possible by hand or machine. Cut into ⅙-inch-wide strips.

Put the crayfish or shrimp in a large pot of boiling salted water and bring the water back to a boil. Immediately lower to a simmer and cook 2 minutes for crayfish or a bit longer for shrimp, until they turn bright pink. Separate the crayfish bodies from tails. Shell the crayfish tails or the shrimp. Cut the mushrooms into wedges. Grate the Parmesan cheese. Chop the herbs.

Cooking: In a saucepan, combine the wine, ginger, seaweed, peppercorns, and stock. Simmer for 10 minutes over medium heat. Strain and return the liquid to pot. Add the cream and simmer to reduce to a light sauce, about 5 minutes. Season with lime juice and salt and pepper to taste.

In a frying pan, melt the butter. Sauté the mushrooms for 3 minutes and then simmer until tender, 15 to 20 minutes. Remove the mushrooms with a slotted spoon and reduce the liquid by half. Add the shellfish just to warm.

Cook the pasta in a large pot of boiling salted water until tender, about 2 minutes for fresh or 10 minutes for dry. Drain. Toss the pasta with the mushrooms and reduced liquid. Add the sauce, sprinkle with the 3 tablespoons of Parmesan cheese, and toss again. Season with salt and pepper to taste.

SERVING: Garnish with chopped herbs. Pass extra Parmesan cheese.

YIELD: 4 servings

PASTA WITH BEEF JERKY, ASPARAGUS, AND PIMIENTO

Traditional American beef jerky is combined with fresh asparagus and pimiento for an interesting melange of colors and flavors.

Preparation: If using fresh pasta, roll the dough as thin as possible by hand or machine. Cut into ⅙-inch-wide strips.

Trim the asparagus and cut on the diagonal into 1-inch pieces. Mince the garlic. Cut the beef jerky into ¼-inch dice or 1-inch shreds. Dice the pimiento. Grate the cheese.

Cooking: Cook the asparagus in boiling salted water to cover until just tender, about 5 minutes. Drain.

In a saucepan, heat the butter and oil. Add the garlic and sauté for about 1 minute. Add the jerky and cook until slightly softened, about 1 minute. Add the pimiento and asparagus.

In a pot of boiling salted water, cook the pasta until just tender, about 2 minutes for fresh or 10 minutes for dry. Drain.

Toss the pasta with the jerky mixture. Add the cheese, toss again, and adjust the seasoning with salt and pepper.

YIELD: 4 servings

¾ pound Cornmeal Pasta (page 126) or ½ pound dry pasta, such as rotelle, farfalle, or fettuccine
½ pound asparagus
1 clove garlic
3 ounces beef jerky or other cured meat
3 ounces pimiento
2 tablespoons grated Parmesan cheese
5 tablespoons unsalted butter
2½ tablespoons olive oil
Salt and black pepper

JALAPEÑO PASTA WITH LOBSTER AND CUCUMBER

Hot jalapeños and cool green cucumbers add new flavors to this
luxurious combination of lobster and cream. It's a great way to stretch
one expensive crustacean to serve four.

*¾ pound Jalapeño Pasta (page 126) or ½
    pound dry pasta, such as wide egg
    noodles or pappardelle*
1 2-pound lobster
1 clove garlic
1 medium-sized cucumber
2 jalapeño peppers, if using dry pasta
1½ cups heavy cream
*3 tablespoons unsalted butter
    Salt and black pepper*

Preparation: If using fresh pasta, roll the dough as thin
as possible by hand or machine. Cut into ½-inch-wide
strips.

Bring a large pot of salted water to a boil and cook
the lobster until it turns bright red, about 10 minutes.
Remove the lobster from pot, reserving the water.
When the lobster is cool enough to handle, remove the
meat from the shell and cut it into bite-sized pieces.

Halve the garlic. Score cucumber with a citrus zester
or the tines of a fork and cut in half lengthwise. Remove
the seeds and cut cucumber into thin half-moons.
Mince the jalapeños.

Cooking: In a small saucepan, simmer the cream with
the garlic until it is reduced to 1 cup, about 15 minutes.
Remove and discard the garlic.

Meanwhile, return the lobster water to a boil. Add
the pasta and cook until just tender, about 2 minutes for
fresh or 8 minutes for dry. Drain.

Melt 1 tablespoon of the butter in a frying pan and
sauté the cucumber over medium heat for about 2 minutes. Reheat the lobster in the remaining 2 tablespoons
of butter.

Toss the pasta with the cucumbers and reduced garlic
cream. Season with salt and pepper to taste.

SERVING: Put the pasta on warm plates and top each
portion with lobster pieces.

YIELD: 4 servings

PASTA WITH SMOKED SALMON AND SWEET ONION SAUCE

The traditional combination of smoked salmon and onions works perfectly in this quick pasta dish.

Preparation: If using fresh pasta, roll the dough as thin as possible by hand or machine. Cut into ⅛-inch-wide strips.

Cut the onions into thin slices. Slice the scallions, including about 2 inches of the green tops. Mince the garlic. Cut smoked salmon into thin strips.

Cooking: In a large frying pan, cook the onions in 4 tablespoons of the butter over low heat until soft but not colored, about 6 minutes. Add the scallions and garlic and sauté about 1½ minutes. Add wine and stock and cook over medium-high heat for 1 to 2 minutes. Lower the heat, stir in crème fraîche or cream, and season with salt and pepper to taste.

Meanwhile, in a large pot of boiling salted water, cook the pasta until just tender, about 2 minutes for fresh or 8 minutes for dry. Drain.

Toss the sauce, remaining 2 tablespoons of butter, and hot pasta together. Toss in the smoked salmon.

SERVING: Serve on warm plates, garnished with salmon roe if desired.

YIELD: 4 servings

¾ pound Egg Pasta or Cornmeal Pasta (page 126) or ½ pound dry pasta, such as linguine, ziti, or bavettine
2 sweet onions, such as Vidalia or Maui or red onions
8 scallions
1 clove garlic
2 ounces smoked salmon
6 tablespoons unsalted butter
½ cup dry white wine
½ cup Chicken Stock (page 81)
¼ cup crème fraîche or heavy cream
Salt and black pepper
2 tablespoons salmon roe for garnish (optional)

PASTA WITH GRILLED CHICKEN AND DILL PESTO SAUCE

Grilled yellow squash and cherry tomatoes, grilled chunks of chicken, and pasta dressed with a garlicky walnut–dill pesto make a perfect summer combination.

¾ pound Egg Pasta (page 126) or ½ pound dry pasta, such as fusilli or ricciolini

Dill Pesto

1 tablespoon unsalted butter
⅓ cup grated Parmesan cheese
⅓ cup walnuts
⅓ cup fresh dill sprigs
⅓ cup parsley sprigs
1 clove garlic
⅓ cup olive oil, plus more for brushing
Salt and black pepper

1 pound boneless chicken breasts (about 3 breasts)
3 small yellow summer squash
12 cherry tomatoes

Preparation: If using fresh pasta, roll the dough as thin as possible by hand or machine. Cut into ⅙-inch-wide strips.

For the Dill Pesto, bring the butter to room temperature or soften in a microwave oven. Grate the cheese. In a food processor, whir the walnuts, dill, parsley, and garlic until chopped fine. With the motor running, pour in ⅓ cup of the oil in a thin stream. Add cheese and butter and whir until well blended. Add salt and pepper to taste.

Cut the chicken breasts into 1-inch cubes and put on skewers. Cut the squash into ½-inch slices and string loosely on skewers. Put the tomatoes on a skewer.

Cooking: Heat the grill. Brush the chicken and vegetables with oil. Grill the squash until tender and slightly charred, about 8 minutes per side. Grill the meat until slightly charred, about 3 minutes per side. Grill the tomatoes about 1 minute per side.

In a pot of boiling salted water, cook the pasta until just tender, about 2 minutes for fresh or 10 minutes for dry. Thin the pesto sauce with about 2 tablespoons of the pasta cooking liquid. Drain the pasta. Remove the meat and vegetables from skewers, toss with pasta, and heat through. Toss in the pesto to coat. Season with salt and pepper to taste.

YIELD: 4 servings

GREEN AND WHITE RAVIOLI IN BROTH

Here, colorful green and white squares filled with an herb-flavored chicken, pork, and prosciutto mixture are served in homemade chicken broth.

Preparation: *For the filling,* bring the stock to a simmer. Add the chicken breasts and simmer for 30 minutes. Remove from the stock. When cool, bone and finely grind the meat in a food processor or meat grinder. Blanch the escarole for 2 minutes in a large amount of boiling salted water. Drain, rinse in cold water, and squeeze dry. Cut 1½ cups of the escarole into fine strips. Mince the remaining escarole. Mince the garlic. Chop the prosciutto.

Melt the butter in a large frying pan. Add the pork and garlic and cook until the pork is no longer pink, 5 to 6 minutes. Add the ground chicken, prosciutto, tarragon, savory, salt, and pepper, and minced escarole. Remove from the heat and cool slightly. Lightly beat the egg and stir it in.

Roll both doughs as thin as possible by hand or machine. Put one sheet of dough on a lightly floured work surface. Beginning 1 inch from the edge, drop teaspoons of the filling 1½ inches apart. Use half of the filling to cover half of the sheet of dough. With your fingers or a pastry brush dipped in water, draw lines between the rows of filling. Fold the uncovered half of sheet over the filling and seal between the rows. Using a knife or scalloped cutting wheel, cut into 1½-inch ravioli. Repeat with the second sheet of pasta.

Cooking: Add the oil to boiling salted water. Drop the ravioli into the water and cook until just tender, about 3 minutes. Reheat the broth. Drain the ravioli and add them to the hot broth along with the escarole strips.

YIELD: 4 servings

Filling

1 quart Chicken Stock (page 81)
2 chicken breasts, about 1 pound
1 large head escarole
1 clove garlic
2 ounces prosciutto
2 tablespoons unsalted butter
¼ pound ground pork
2 tablespoons fresh tarragon leaves or 2
*   teaspoons dried tarragon*
2 tablespoons fresh savory leaves or 2
*   teaspoons dried savory*
1 teaspoon salt
⅛ teaspoon black pepper
1 egg

½ recipe Egg Pasta (page 126)
½ recipe Green Pasta (page 126)
2 tablespoons oil

PASTA WITH SQUID AND BASIL

This is a good use for squid, which has recently become widely popular and generally available. Cutting it in thin strips and cooking it very quickly insures its tenderness.

¾ pound Egg Pasta or Jalapeño Pasta
(page 126) or ½ pound dry pasta,
such as capelli d'angelo, capellini, or
fedelini
⅔ pound squid
4 plum tomatoes or 3 regular tomatoes
1½ tablespoons shredded flat-leaf parsley
1 scallion
3 cloves garlic
1½ tablespoons olive oil
Salt and black pepper
⅔ cup heavy cream
4 tablespoons shredded fresh basil leaves,
plus whole leaves for garnish

Preparation: If using fresh pasta, roll the dough as thin as possible by hand or machine. Cut into ⅛-inch-wide strips.

If you get whole squid, cut the tentacles and body from the squid head and discard the head and ink sac. Remove and discard the purple skin. Cut the fins from the body. Turn the body inside out and wash under cool running water. Discard the cartilage found in body. Keep tentacles whole. Cut the fins and body into ⅛-inch-wide slices.

Core, peel, seed, and chop the tomatoes. Cut the parsley in shreds. Chop the scallion, green top included.

Cooking: Cook the pasta with the unpeeled garlic in boiling salted water until just done, about 2 minutes for fresh or 6 minutes for dry. Drain. Pick out the whole garlic, peel, and mince.

In a large frying pan, heat the olive oil over medium-high heat until very hot. Add the squid pieces. Season with salt and pepper to taste. Cook, tossing frequently, until the squid turns opaque, about 30 seconds. Add the cream, cooked pasta, and reserved garlic. Adjust the seasonings and heat through. Cut the basil in shreds. Toss the pasta with the tomatoes, parsley, scallion, and shredded basil. Season with salt and pepper to taste.

SERVING: Garnish with plenty of basil leaves.

YIELD: 4 servings

MENUS

Olive Pasta *(page 128)*

Dry Italian white, such as Frescobaldi Pomino

Chicken Stuffed with Grape Leaves
  (page 155)
Grilled Tomatoes

Chianti Classico

Pinwheel Cake *(page 250)*

Fried Cheese *(page 28)*

Sparkling wine, such as Bouvet Brut

Pasta with Squid and Basil *(page 136)*

Veal Sausage with Greens *(page 161)*

Pouilly-Fumé

Champagne–Cassis Ice *(page 229)*

Ham and Pear Pâté *(page 26)*

Chilled Bardolino

Green and White Ravioli in Broth *(page 135)*
Focaccia *(page 180)*

Oyster and Spinach Salad *(page 72)*

Italian Chardonnay

Chocolate–Mint Pastries *(page 262)*

CHAPTER 7

SAUTÉS AND STIR-FRIES

Pork and Broccoli Stir-Fry with Potatoes and Sesame Seeds
Salmon Sauté with Corn and Sugar Snap Peas
Sauté of Chicken Thighs with Leeks and Mushrooms
Chicken Leg Sauté with Mushrooms and Lovage
Sauté of Chicken Breasts, Summer Squash, and Yellow Pepper
Pork Tenderloin Sauté with Summer Apples and Plums
Stir-Fried Chinese String Beans with Sausage and Oyster Sauce
Tarragon Chicken and Kale Stir-Fry
Stir-Fried Napa Cabbage and Smoked Pork

Both sautés and stir-fries are ideal for experimenting with new combinations and newly available ingredients. Once you've mastered the basic techniques (see sidebars in this chapter), your own combinations, based on what's best in the market, will come easily. Salmon Sauté with Corn and Sugar Snap Peas and Chicken Leg Sauté with Mushrooms and Lovage are two examples among our innovative sautés. Stir-fries have traditionally been limited to Oriental ingredients, but unusual recipes like Tarragon Chicken and Kale Stir-Fry or Pork and Broccoli Stir-Fry with Potatoes and Sesame Seeds demonstrate how readily the influences of other cuisines can be adapted to this method.

In addition to having extreme flexibility, sautés and stir-fries are quickly made. The short cooking times mean that most dishes can be prepared almost entirely at the last minute. The vegetable garnish for a sauté is prepared in the same pan used to cook the main ingredient, and a stir-fry is by nature a one-pan recipe. Streamlined new sautés omit the time-consuming sauces that were part of the classic French preparation; stir-frying quickly produces bright melanges of perfectly cooked, just-tender ingredients. Though short on preparation time, unusual and flavorful dishes like our Pork Tenderloin Sauté with Summer Apples and Plums, or Stir-Fried Chinese String Beans with Sausage and Oyster Sauce, would stand out on any menu.

Sautés

The word *sauté* refers not only to a widely used technique of cooking rapidly in a small amount of fat, but also to a specific type of dish in traditional French cuisine. Classically, a sauté was made from small, usually tender, pieces of meat or poultry. After the meat was seared in butter or oil, the pan was deglazed with an already prepared sauce, often a garnishing vegetable was added, and the whole mixture was simmered briefly until the sauce was reduced to a few tablespoons of flavorful essence.

This type of preparation was based on the assumption that sauces such as the classic *espagnole* were on hand. The realities of modern cookery led to the substitution of simple flour-thickened wine and/or stock for these time-consuming sauces. Contemporary cooks have shortened the process even further. Now, after browning, the meat or poultry in a sauté often simmers in a liquid, or combination of liquids, frequently stock and wine, that has not been previously thickened. This liquid is often boiled down later to strengthen the flavor of the sauce.

Special sauté pans called *sautoirs* have long been used in France and are still the best vessels for a sauté, though a regular frying pan can certainly be used. *Sautoirs* are fashioned of copper, heavy stainless steel, or aluminum and are made with straight rather than sloping sides. The metal in a well-made *sautoir* is heavy so that it can take intense heat and conduct heat evenly. Because a *sautoir* is deeper than an ordinary frying pan, it can hold more ingredients, and the straight sides mean that the bottom is the same size as the top opening, providing a large cooking surface. Furthermore, the high, straight sides hold in moisture, which helps cook the meat to juicy tenderness.

Because butter alone browns too quickly over high heat, sautés require using butter mixed with a small amount of oil (to raise the smoking point). Clarified butter can also be used—melted butter with the milk solids, which burn most easily, separated out from the butterfat—which also results in a higher smoking point.

The quick cooking that characterizes a sauté demands tender meat cut into pieces small enough to cook in a relatively short time. Chicken parts, veal chops or scallops, and lamb rib chops are obvious candidates. Equally appropriate are *médaillons* cut from the center of the pork loin or a pork or veal tenderloin, cutlets sliced from a boneless turkey breast, or fish steaks. A sauté garnish is a good place to show off colorful fresh produce, with variations depending on what's good in the market.

Stir-Fries

The technique of stir-frying, developed centuries ago by the Chinese, has been adopted with enthusiasm by American cooks. It is an exceptionally quick way to make a meal and lends itself to all sorts of ingredients and even to combinations with other cooking techniques so that our new stir-fries might seem unfamiliar to an Oriental chef.

A well-seasoned wok is the pan of choice for stir-frying, but a large frying pan can also be used. The wok is desirable because it provides a large surface area, with enough space to allow the ingredients to cook quickly and evenly. The wok is also large enough so that more quickly cooked ingredients can be pushed to one side to keep warm while longer-cooking ingredients are finished.

Because the actual stir-frying takes so little time, good advance preparation is essential. For the best results, all cleaning, chopping, measuring, and so forth of ingredients should be done before the wok or frying pan is heated. In Oriental cooking, preparing the raw ingredients for a stir-fry is really an art; the meat or poultry, vegetables, and other ingredients should be cut into uniform slivers or strips so that they will cook evenly. Once the cooking starts, slowing down may result in overcooked meats or limp vegetables, so it makes sense to set up the prepared ingredients as close as possible to the cooking area for easy access.

To start cooking, heat oil in a well-seasoned wok or large frying pan over high heat almost to the smoking point; a very light haze of white smoke should appear. Almost any kind of good cooking oil is acceptable—except olive oil, which has a low smoking point. Peanut oil is often used in Oriental cooking. Swirl the heated oil around to coat the entire inside surface of the pan.

Add the stir-fry ingredients, one at a time, their order determined by their required cooking times. Slower-cooking ingredients are added first so that all ingredients finish cooking at the same time. To maintain a constant high temperature, avoid overcrowding the pan. Stir to keep the ingredients moving the whole time. Keep the heat as high as possible without scorching the ingredients and keep enough oil in the pan to prevent sticking.

To finish, add any final seasonings and thicken the cooking liquid if desired. To do so, push the cooked ingredients aside to make a well in the center of the pan and add cornstarch dissolved in cold water (traditionally) or another thickener. Stir until smooth, and serve the stir-fry immediately.

PORK AND BROCCOLI STIR-FRY WITH POTATOES AND SESAME SEEDS

This all-American reinterpretation of an Oriental dish adds new potatoes and a tart apple for unexpected flavor.

Preparation: Toast the sesame seeds in a 325°F oven until golden, 5 to 10 minutes. Peel the broccoli stems. Cut the stems on the diagonal into ⅛-inch-thick slices. Cut the tops into florets. Blanch the broccoli in boiling salted water until just tender, about 4 minutes. Drain, plunge immediately into cold water, and drain again. Cut the carrot on the diagonal into ⅛-inch-thick slices. Mince the garlic and the ginger. Trim the pork of all sinew and cut it into ¼-inch-thick by 1½-inch-long strips. (Freezing the meat just before slicing makes cutting easier.) Trim the leeks, leaving about 3 inches of green part, halve, and wash. Cut crosswise into ⅛-inch-thick slices.

Dissolve the cornstarch in the stock and 2 tablespoons soy sauce. Just before stir-frying, cut the unpeeled potatoes into ⅛-inch by 1½-inch julienne strips and rinse them with cold water. Cut the unpeeled apple into eighths, core, and then cut crosswise into ⅛-inch-thick slices.

Cooking: Heat 2 tablespoons of the oil in a wok or very large frying pan over high heat. When very hot, add the carrot. Cook for 1 minute and then add the potatoes. Season with salt and pepper. Fry, stirring, until the potatoes start to turn golden, about 2 minutes. Leaving the wok over high heat, stir in the garlic and ginger, add the pork strips, add more oil if necessary, and stir-fry to sear, about 2 minutes. Add the leeks and stir-fry until they are bright green, 30 seconds. Stir in the broccoli and make a well in the center of the wok. Stir the soy sauce, stock, and cornstarch into the well. Add the sliced apple and cook until the liquid thickens. Add the cashews, sesame seeds, and sesame oil. Season with salt and pepper and soy sauce to taste.

YIELD: 4 servings

2 tablespoons sesame seeds
1 pound broccoli
1 large carrot
1 clove garlic
2 teaspoons minced fresh ginger
1 pound boneless pork loin
2 medium-sized leeks
2 teaspoons cornstarch
2 tablespoons cold Chicken Stock (page 81)
2 tablespoons soy sauce, plus more for seasoning
2 small red potatoes (about ½ pound in all)
1 tart apple (such as Cortland, Empire, or Granny Smith)
2 to 3 tablespoons peanut oil
Salt and black pepper
½ cup whole cashews
Few drops sesame oil (optional)

SALMON SAUTÉ WITH CORN AND SUGAR SNAP PEAS

The unusual combination of salmon, fresh corn, and sugar snap peas makes a delicious and colorful sauté.

2 shallots
1 small hot red pepper
6 ears corn or 2 cups frozen corn kernels
14 sugar snap peas
1 scallion
1 tablespoon minced fresh chives
  Minced fresh parsley for garnish
4 salmon steaks (about 2 pounds in all)
  Salt and black pepper
¼ pound unsalted butter, clarified, or 4
    tablespoons unsalted butter plus 2
    tablespoons vegetable oil

Preparation: Mince the shallots. Core, seed, and mince the hot red pepper. Cut the corn from the cobs or thaw the frozen corn. Trim the sugar snap peas and scallion. Cut them on the diagonal into thin slices. Mince the chives and parsley. Season the salmon with salt and pepper.

Cooking: In a heavy frying pan, heat the clarified butter or butter and oil over medium-high heat. Add the salmon and sear on the first side for about 1 minute. Turn the salmon over, add the shallots and hot red pepper, and cook for 2 minutes more. Add ⅓ cup of water, cover, and cook for 3 minutes. Add the corn, cover, and cook for about 3 minutes more. Test the salmon by gently pulling the flesh away from the center bone. It should just stick to the bone slightly. Gently stir in the peas, scallion, and chives. Season with salt and pepper to taste and heat through.

SERVING: Put the salmon steaks on warm plates and spoon the vegetables around each. Sprinkle with the parsley.

YIELD: 4 servings

SAUTÉ OF CHICKEN THIGHS WITH LEEKS AND MUSHROOMS

Wild mushrooms, such as morels, and leeks add elegance to a simple dish based on chicken thighs. This is also an excellent everyday recipe when made with plain mushrooms and onions.

Preparation: Thoroughly rinse the leeks and morels. Cut the leeks into julienne. Trim the tough stems from the morels and halve any very large ones. Sprinkle the chicken with salt and pepper.

2 small leeks
¼ pound fresh morels or other mushrooms
4 chicken thighs (about 1⅓ pounds in all)
Salt and black pepper
2 tablespoons unsalted butter
½ cup dry white wine
¼ cup Chicken Stock (page 81)
½ cup heavy cream
⅛ teaspoon grated nutmeg

Cooking: In a large frying pan, melt the butter. Sauté the chicken, skin side down, over medium heat until golden, about 4 minutes. Turn and sauté about 2 minutes more. Add the leeks and cook about 3 minutes. Add the wine and stock and bring to a simmer. Cover the pan and simmer gently, turning the chicken once, until done, 10 to 12 minutes. Remove the chicken to serving plates and keep it warm.

Reduce the pan juices over high heat until slightly thickened, about 1 minute. Add the morels, lower the heat, and stir in the cream. Simmer gently until the sauce coats the back of a spoon, 2 to 3 minutes. Season lightly with nutmeg and salt and pepper. Pour over the chicken.

YIELD: 4 servings

CHICKEN LEG SAUTÉ WITH MUSHROOMS AND LOVAGE

Chicken, mushrooms, and cream are a time-tested combination. Here lovage adds a new note. You can substitute celery leaves and a touch of lemon juice for the herb.

2 shallots
12 fresh or dried boletes or fresh shiitake
*   mushrooms (see Note)*
4 chicken thighs
4 chicken drumsticks
*   Salt and black pepper*
4 tablespoons unsalted butter, clarified, or
*   2 tablespoons butter plus 1 tablespoon*
*   vegetable oil*
1 cup Chicken Stock (page 81)
1 cup heavy cream
2 teaspoons arrowroot
1 tablespoon fresh lovage leaves

Preparation: Mince the shallots. Remove the stems from mushrooms and save for another dish. Cut the mushroom caps into thin slices. Season the chicken with salt and pepper.

Cooking: In a heavy frying pan, heat the clarified butter or butter and oil and add the chicken. Sear chicken parts lightly on all sides over medium-high heat but don't brown. Add the shallots and then the stock. Bring to a boil, lower the heat, and simmer gently for 10 minutes. Turn the chicken and add the cream. Continue to cook until the chicken just tests done, about 10 minutes. Stir in the mushrooms and reduced soaking liquid if using dried boletes. Dissolve the arrowroot in 2 teaspoons of cold water and stir in. Season with salt and pepper to taste and simmer for about 30 seconds more.

SERVING: To make the dish more attractive, cut off the knob ends of the cooked thighs and drumsticks. Coat 4 warm plates with the sauce and arrange a drumstick and a thigh on each plate. Sprinkle the sauce with lovage. Serve immediately.

YIELD: 4 servings

NOTE: If using dried bolete mushrooms, put them in a bowl, cover with warm water, and soak until they are quite soft, about 30 minutes. Transfer the mushrooms to a strainer. Pour the soaking liquid through a coffee filter paper into a saucepan and reduce to a syrup over high heat. Fill a bowl with cold water and dip the strainer of mushrooms up and down in the water to remove any remaining dirt.

SAUTÉ OF CHICKEN BREASTS, SUMMER SQUASH, AND YELLOW PEPPER

This beautiful and elegant new sauté takes only minutes to cook. Yellow squash and yellow bell pepper are accented by bright green mint.

Preparation: Remove the tendon from each chicken breast and pound the breasts to flatten them. Season with salt and pepper. Remove the zest from the orange in a long strip. Cut the skin from the squash in strips and then cut the strips crosswise into thin shreds. Reserve the squash flesh for another use. Cut yellow pepper into ¼- by 1½-inch strips. Mince the mint leaves.

Cooking: In a heavy frying pan, heat the clarified butter or butter and oil over medium-high heat. Sear the chicken on both sides, about 2 minutes altogether. Add the Lillet and orange zest and cook until the sauce is reduced to about 2 tablespoons. Discard the zest and add the cream. Turn the breasts over and stir in squash and yellow pepper. Cook, turning the breasts often, until chicken just tests done and the vegetables are tender, about 3 minutes.

SERVING: Coat 4 warm plates with the sauce, including the vegetables. Cut the chicken breasts on the diagonal into thick slices, arrange on the plates, and sprinkle with the chopped mint.

YIELD: 4 servings

4 skinned and boned chicken breasts
(about 1½ pounds in all)
Salt and black pepper
1 orange
2 medium-sized yellow summer squash
1 yellow bell pepper
1½ tablespoons minced fresh mint leaves
4 tablespoons unsalted butter, clarified, or
2 tablespoons butter plus 1
tablespoon vegetable oil
¾ cup white Lillet apéritif
1 cup heavy cream

PORK TENDERLOIN SAUTÉ WITH SUMMER APPLES AND PLUMS

The marriage of pork and fruit is a natural. Plums are not much used in cooking, but they work beautifully here in combination with apples, ruby port, and apple brandy.

1⅓ *pounds pork tenderloin*
   Salt and black pepper
2 *shallots*
3 *ripe plums*
   Minced fresh parsley for garnish
3 *tart apples*
½ *lemon*
6 *tablespoons unsalted butter, clarified, or*
   2 tablespoons butter plus 2
   tablespoons vegetable oil
¾ *cup ruby port*
¼ *cup Calvados or other apple brandy*
½ *cup Chicken Stock (page 81)*
¼ *cup crème fraîche*

Preparation: Cut the pork into ¼-inch-thick slices. Season with salt and pepper. Mince the shallots. Quarter and pit the plums. Mince the parsley. Peel and core the apples and cut them into ¼-inch-thick wedges. Squeeze the lemon juice over apples and toss.

Cooking: In a heavy frying pan, heat the clarified butter or butter and oil over medium-high heat. Lightly brown the pork on 1 side, turn, strew the shallots around the meat, and cook until soft, about 3 minutes. Add the port, Calvados, stock, plums, and apples. Lower the heat to medium, cover, and simmer just until the pork loses its pink color, about 5 minutes. Remove the meat and a few apple slices for garnish and keep warm.

Puree the remaining fruit and cooking liquid in a food processor or by pushing through a sieve. Return the puree to the pan and bring to a boil. Whisk in the crème fraîche. Season with salt and pepper to taste.

SERVING: Coat 4 warm plates with the sauce. Arrange the pork on the sauce and garnish with the reserved apple slices. Sprinkle with the parsley.

YIELD: 4 servings

STIR-FRIED CHINESE STRING BEANS WITH SAUSAGE AND OYSTER SAUCE

If Chinese sausages are unavailable, hot Italian sausages will do equally well in this strongly flavored Oriental vegetable dish.

Preparation: Mince the garlic and ginger. Wash and trim the string beans. Cut the sausage into 1-inch pieces. In a small bowl, mix the soy sauce with 2 tablespoons of water.

Cooking: Heat the oil in a wok or large frying pan over high heat almost to the smoking point. Add half the garlic and half the ginger. Cook, stirring, until light golden brown, about 2 seconds. Add the sausages and cook for 5 minutes, stirring constantly. Remove the sausages with a slotted spoon and keep them warm. Add the beans to the wok and cook, stirring constantly, until just tender, about 4 to 5 minutes. Add the remaining garlic and ginger and return the sausages to the pan. Pour in the soy sauce mixture and cook for 1 minute.

SERVING: Arrange the beans on a serving platter and pour the sauce from the wok over them. Drizzle with the oyster sauce. Serve with a small bowl of oyster sauce on the side.

YIELD: 4 servings

1 tablespoon minced garlic
1 tablespoon minced fresh ginger
1 pound Chinese string beans
2 Chinese sausages or ¾ pound hot Italian sausage
2 tablespoons dark soy sauce
1½ teaspoons oil
Oyster sauce for serving

TARRAGON CHICKEN AND KALE STIR-FRY

Only the cooking technique is Oriental in this unusual stir-fry. The chicken and kale are served over buttered toast; tarragon and lime spark the sauce, which includes an egg yolk and cream liaison.

¾ pound tender, small-leaf kale
1 shallot
1 pound boneless chicken thigh meat
*   (about 4 thighs)*
*   Salt and black pepper*
2 egg yolks
¼ cup heavy cream
2 limes
2 tablespoons fresh tarragon leaves, plus
*   optional sprigs for garnish or 2*
*   teaspoons dried tarragon*
4 slices French bread
*   Unsalted butter for spreading*
1½ tablespoons vegetable oil
¼ cup Chicken Stock (page 81)

Preparation: Remove ribs from the kale and blanch the leaves in plenty of boiling salted water until tender, about 10 minutes. Plunge into cold water to stop the cooking. Drain and squeeze out the excess water.

Mince the shallot. Cut the chicken into ¼-inch-wide strips and season with salt and pepper. (Freezing the meat just before slicing makes it easier to cut.) Whisk together the egg yolks and cream. Squeeze 1 lime to make 2 tablespoons juice. Cut the other lime into wedges for garnish. If using fresh tarragon, remove the stems and chop the leaves.

Cooking: Toast the bread. Spread each side generously with butter and keep warm. If you wish to garnish with fried tarragon, heat an inch of oil in a frying pan to 350°F. Carefully add a few tarragon sprigs with long tongs (the oil will splatter). Do not overcrowd. Fry until crisp, about 15 seconds. Drain on paper towels and season with salt.

Heat the oil in a wok or a large frying pan over high heat. Add the shallots and cook, stirring, until soft but not colored, about 30 seconds. Add the chicken and sauté until all the meat is seared, about 3 minutes. Add the kale, chopped tarragon, stock, and salt and pepper to taste, stirring, until the kale is heated through, about 2 minutes. Remove from the heat and add yolk-cream mixture, stirring constantly. Return to the stove and cook over very low heat until the mixture starts to thicken, being careful not to boil, about 2 minutes. Add the lime juice and season with salt and pepper to taste.

SERVING: Put the toast on warm plates and top with the chicken and kale. Garnish with sprigs of deep-fried or fresh tarragon, if desired, and lime wedges.

YIELD: 4 servings

STIR-FRIED NAPA CABBAGE AND SMOKED PORK

The mild, slightly sweet cabbage sets off the smoky taste of the meat in this stir-fry, and chopped peanuts add a satisfying crunch.

Preparation: Mince the garlic. Cut the cabbage into 1-inch square pieces or thin shreds. Cut scallions on the diagonal into ½-inch slices. Crush peanuts with the side of a cleaver or whir in a food processor into small pieces. Cut the carrots into thin slices on the diagonal. Remove the pork from the bones and cut the meat into 1- by 1½-inch strips. Blanch the peas in boiling water until tender, about 1 minute.

1 clove garlic
1 pound Napa cabbage
4 scallions
½ cup roasted peanuts
2 carrots
1½ pounds smoked pork chops or 14 ounces smoked ham
½ cup shelled peas, fresh or frozen
2 tablespoons peanut oil
Salt and black pepper

Cooking: In a wok or large, heavy frying pan, heat the oil over high heat until very hot. Add the garlic and cook until golden, about 30 seconds. Add the cabbage and cook, stirring, for 2 minutes. Add the scallions, peanuts, carrots, and salt and pepper to taste. Cook, stirring, until the cabbage softens a little but is still crisp, about 1½ minutes. Add the peas and cook for about 1½ minutes. Add the pork and cook for 1 minute.

YIELD: 4 servings

MENUS

Arugula Salad (page 69)
———

*Salmon Sauté with Corn and Sugar Snap Peas
(page 142)*

Raspberry–Pistachio Bombe (page 246)

Sauvignon Blanc, such as Concannon or
Silverado

———————————————

*Stir-Fried Chinese String Beans with Sausage
and Oyster Sauce (page 147)*

Tomato and Mozzarella Tart (page 179)

Pear and Cinnamon Basil Sorbet (page 228)

Gewurztraminer, such as Monticello or
Clos du Bois

———————————————

Italian Merlot, such as Lazzarini

———————————————

*Avocado and Seafood with Flour Tortillas
(page 41)*
———

*Chicken Leg Sauté with Mushrooms and
Lovage (page 144)*

Watermelon and String Cheese

Washington State Riesling, such as Arbor
Crest or Hogue

———————————————

CHAPTER 8

GRILLED FOODS

Grill-Poached Snapper Stuffed with Fennel
Warm Oriental Grilled Tuna or Swordfish and Bean Salad
Chicken Stuffed with Grape Leaves
Grilled Salmon with Mustard and Leeks
Peppery Lemon–Rosemary Chicken Winglets
Grilled Ginger Duck Breasts with Peaches
Grilled Pigeon with Garlic Sauce · Mushroom-Filled Sausages
Veal Sausage with Greens
Grilled Lamb Sausage with Watercress and Warm Potato Salad
Skewered Portuguese Scallops
Grilled Sweetbreads with Potato Pancakes and Bolete Butter
Grilled Lamb on Cabbage Leaves
Curried Lamb Chops with Banana–Almond Chutney

Grilled foods are an important part of the new cuisine. While the innovative young chefs responsible for the new California cuisine were among the first to rediscover grilling, cooks in restaurants and backyards throughout the country quickly picked up the trend. And fare other than the traditional steaks and hamburgers have been found to be equally delicious when grilled. Fish, vegetables, and all sorts of meats and poultry can be quickly cooked over an open fire, and the resultant flavor is memorable. Yet it is not only the intense taste and short cooking time that have made grilling so popular—food cooked this way is so flavorful in itself it can be deliciously lighter, served without heavy, complicated sauces and often accompanied only by a few select grilled vegetables.

Many foods to be grilled are marinated first, to impart flavor and to tenderize the meat or poultry that will be quickly cooked. An acid, such as wine, vinegar, or lemon juice, in the marinade tenderizes by breaking down tough connective tissues. Sherry and other fortified wines are excellent choices for marinades because their high sugar content gives the finished food a shiny, lightly caramelized finish. The oil added to a marinade cuts the acidity and helps to keep food from becoming too dry, while herbs, spices, and other ingredients imbue the food with additional flavor. Once food is removed from its marinade and set on the grill, the marinade, primarily if wine-based, can often be quickly reduced and transformed into an accompanying light sauce.

Many of the recipes in this chapter call for marination. Tuna steaks are treated for several hours with an Oriental wine-and-soy-sauce combination; pigeon is marinated in a mixture including several *heads* of garlic; and lamb steaks are allowed to steep in an orange, coriander, and sherry marinade for anywhere from five hours to three days. We generally recommend about five hours marinating for assured permeation, but don't let this dissuade you, even if you're in a hurry. Simply marinate for as much time as you have. Even a brief bath will have an effect on flavor. Only the leg of lamb slices in Grilled Lamb on Cabbage Leaves actually require hours of marination to tenderize. Our salmon steaks, on the other hand, are not marinated at all, but brushed with a simple mustard sauce as they grill; chicken wings receive a lemon-rosemary basting sauce; and, of course, flavorful sausages, of which there are three varieties here, mushroom-filled, veal and greens, and lamb, require no marination before grilling.

With the new popularity of grilled foods has come a number of other changes. The grill fire is no longer a mere charcoal fire, but one that may be of various fruit woods, such as cherry and fig, or of maple and corncobs, or other combinations. Mesquite has by now become ubiquitous—and, some believe, highly overrated. Grapevine cuttings, although not yet widely available, are prized for the flavor they add to grilled foods. We hold that plain old charcoal still produces a marvelous effect, too.

Though grilling always seems to add an extra relish, any dish in this chapter can be broiled or sautéed during the winter in cold climes. Also, home grilling has moved from the outdoor barbecue to the indoor char-broiler, making grilled dishes like ours a year-round possibility instead of just a summer treat.

Indoor Grilling

If the barbecue is rained out, you can always cook the meat under the oven broiler or sauté it. But for those inclement days, or for apartment dwellers, one of the newest indulgences is an indoor grill. There are currently three types on the market: units that are part of the stove, separate units that are installed in a kitchen counter, and professional models.

Several manufacturers now offer optional grilling units as part of the package available with their stoves. These units range in price from $350 to $1,000. Generally, the grill is set into the cooktop alongside or between the burners. These units require special venting, of course, which is supplied by the individual manufacturer. They often use down-venting. Both electric and gas units are available, but the electric grills do not get as hot as the gas ones.

Separate drop-in units are another possibility. They run about $500 to $600 not including the fan and venting hood, which are essential. The fan and hood must be carefully placed, and cross drafts in the kitchen can interfere with proper venting. All the drop-in models currently sold can be covered to provide additional counter space when not in use. Theoretically, if properly vented, an outdoor grill could be set into a properly insulated kitchen counter.

The professional char-broiling units used in restaurants are a problematic choice for the home cook. Like professional ranges, they are expensive, get very hot, and require elaborate ventilation. All the professional grilling units need separate venting hoods and powerful fans, and they also use a great deal of energy. Still, with the ever-increasing popularity of grilled foods, it is no doubt only a matter of time before a variety of practical, less-expensive indoor grilling units become available to the home cook.

GRILL-POACHED SNAPPER STUFFED WITH FENNEL

Fresh fennel, here with its taste accented by anise-flavored Pernod, is a perfect complement to red snapper. Other fish of the same type (lean, round, white) can certainly be used, too.

2 red snapper (about 1¼ pounds each)

Fennel Stuffing

2 pounds fresh fennel
1 small onion
1 teaspoon chopped fresh chives
1½ ounces prosciutto
2½ tablespoons minced fresh parsley
2 tablespoons unsalted butter
1½ teaspoons Pernod
½ teaspoon black pepper

Preparation: Clean and bone the fish.

For the stuffing, trim and chop the fennel. Chop the onion, chives, and prosciutto. Mince the parsley.

In a large frying pan, melt the butter over medium-low heat. Add the onion and cook for 2 minutes. Stir in the fennel, chives, and prosciutto. Cover and cook for 5 minutes. Remove from the heat and stir in parsley, Pernod, and pepper. Cool.

Rub 2 large sheets of heavy-duty aluminum foil with oil. Put 1 snapper on each sheet. Fill each fish with the stuffing. Bring the edges of the foil up and fold together to seal tightly.

Cooking: Heat a covered grill. Put the fish packets on the grill and cook, covered, until the fish is just done, 20 to 25 minutes.

SERVING: Carefully unwrap the fish and flip out onto a serving platter. Pour the juices over the top of the fish.

YIELD: 4 servings

WARM ORIENTAL GRILLED TUNA OR SWORDFISH AND BEAN SALAD

Fresh tuna is delectable when kept at least somewhat rare, as in this recipe. If you cook it until uniformly gray, you might as well eat the canned variety at much lower cost.

Marinade

1½ tablespoons minced fresh ginger
⅔ cup mirin (sweet Japanese cooking wine) or plum wine

Preparation: Mince the ginger. In a nonreactive bowl, combine all the marinade ingredients. Put the fish into the marinade, turn to coat, cover, and marinate in the refrigerator for about 5 hours if possible. Wash and trim the green beans.

Cooking: Heat the grill. Drain the fish and reserve marinade. Grill the fish about 5 minutes per side. It should still be pink inside.

In a large pot of boiling salted water, cook the beans until tender with a slightly crunchy bite, 6 to 7 minutes. Drain.

In a small saucepan, simmer the marinade over medium-high heat for 3 to 4 minutes. Remove the skin from the fish and cut on the diagonal into thick slices.

SERVING: Arrange the fish slices in the center of a serving plate and surround with the beans. Pour the marinade over the beans and fish and serve hot or warm.

YIELD: 4 servings

⅔ cup soy sauce
1 tablespoon sesame oil

1 pound 1-inch-thick tuna or *swordfish steak*
1 pound green beans

CHICKEN STUFFED WITH GRAPE LEAVES

From Jerry Goldstein of California's Acacia Winery comes an unusual—and extremely easy to prepare—grilled chicken stuffed with grape leaves. If you are lucky enough to have access to grape cuttings, add them to the fire for a delicious smoky flavor.

Preparation: Cut grape stems and leaves into 2-inch pieces and rinse the bottled grape leaves. Sprinkle salt and pepper into the cavity of the chicken. Stuff the cavity with the grape stems and leaves or with the bottled grape leaves and truss.

12 to 14 grape stems and leaves or *bottled grape leaves*
Salt and black pepper
1 roasting chicken (3½ to 4 pounds)

Cooking: Heat a covered grill, using charcoal, grape cuttings, or a combination of cuttings and charcoal. For an indirect fire, spread the charcoal, grape cuttings, or grape cuttings and coals around the perimeter of the grill and put a drip pan in the center. Put the chicken, breast-side down, on the grill. Grill, turning once, until the juices run clear when the thigh is pricked with a fork, 20 to 25 minutes per side.

YIELD: 4 servings

GRILLED SALMON WITH MUSTARD AND LEEKS

This elegantly simple recipe is from Barry Wine, chef and co-owner of New York City's Quilted Giraffe. He brushes salmon steaks with a mustard sauce before grilling and serves them with lightly grilled leeks.

2 medium-sized leeks
2 1-inch-thick salmon steaks
    (8 to 10 ounces each)
    Olive oil for brushing
    Salt and black pepper
2 tablespoons sugar
2 tablespoons dry mustard

Preparation: Cut the dark green leaves from the leeks. Slice the bulbs in half lengthwise down to the base without going through it. Clean the leeks thoroughly. In a pot of boiling salted water, blanch the leeks until tender, about 1½ minutes. Drain, dip into cold water to stop the cooking, and drain thoroughly.

Cut each salmon steak in half and remove the bone. Brush the fish generously with olive oil and season with salt and pepper.

In a small bowl, mix the sugar with dry mustard and add enough warm water (about 3 tablespoons) to make the mixture the consistency of heavy cream.

Cooking: Heat the grill. Put the salmon on the grill and brush with the mustard mixture. Now cut leeks all the way in half and put them on grill. Brush the leeks with olive oil and cook until lightly browned. Sprinkle with salt and pepper and move to the cooler edges of the grill if done before the salmon.

Cook the salmon, turning once and brushing occasionally with the mustard sauce, until just done but still rare in the center, about 8 minutes.

YIELD: 4 servings

PEPPERY LEMON–ROSEMARY CHICKEN WINGLETS

Tangy lemon, pungent rosemary, and a generous amount of coarsely ground black pepper give these chicken "winglets" character. The chicken can be cooked in a 425°F oven as well as grilled.

Lemon–Rosemary Basting Sauce

2 lemons
1 clove garlic
2 tablespoons unsalted butter
2 tablespoons olive oil
1½ teaspoons coarse black pepper
2 teaspoons dried rosemary
½ teaspoon salt

2 pounds chicken wings
Salt and black pepper
Rosemary sprigs for garnish (optional)

Preparation: *For the sauce,* grate 1 tablespoon of zest from the lemons and put it in a small saucepan. Squeeze 1 tablespoon of lemon juice into the pan. Chop the garlic and add it to the pan along with the remaining sauce ingredients. Simmer for 10 minutes. Cool slightly.

Meanwhile, cut off wing tip joints of chicken wings. Cut the remaining V-shaped pieces of chicken at the joints to make "winglets." Pour the basting sauce over the winglets and toss to coat well.

Cooking: Heat the grill. Grill the winglets over moderately hot coals until the skin is golden and crisp and the juices run clear, 20 to 25 minutes. Season with salt and pepper to taste.

SERVING: Heap the winglets on plates. Garnish with rosemary sprigs if desired.

YIELD: 4 servings

GRILLED GINGER DUCK BREASTS WITH PEACHES

Duck and fruit is a familiar combination, with duck à l'orange probably the most well known example. This innovative recipe uses peaches and adds an Oriental accent with a gingery soy sauce and sherry marinade.

Marinade

1 tablespoon minced fresh ginger
2 tablespoons dry sherry
2 tablespoons soy sauce
2 tablespoons peanut oil

4 skinned and boned duck breasts
   (about 1 pound in all)
  Salt and black pepper
2 ripe but firm peaches

Preparation: Mince the ginger. Combine all the marinade ingredients in a nonreactive bowl. Season the duck breasts with salt and pepper, cover, and marinate in the refrigerator for 5 hours, if possible, or even longer, turning occasionally.

Cooking: Heat the grill. Halve and pit the peaches. Brush the peach halves with some of the marinade and put cut side down at the outer edge of the grill. Grill for 2 minutes, brush with the marinade, turn, and grill until the peaches just begin to soften, about 2 more minutes.

Meanwhile, drain the duck and put the pieces on the hotter part of the grill. Grill until medium-rare, 2 to 2½ minutes per side, brushing with the marinade before turning.

YIELD: 4 servings

GRILLED PIGEON WITH GARLIC SAUCE

This recipe comes from Alice Waters, founder of the renowned Chez Panisse in Berkeley, California. Other small birds could be used as well as pigeon.

Garlic Marinade

12 heads early-harvest garlic (about the
   diameter of a quarter) or 6 heads
   regular garlic
1 small onion
½ cup Beaumes de Venise or other
   sweet white wine
Fresh thyme branches

Preparation: *For the marinade,* if using regular garlic, separate into cloves. Slice the onion. Combine the marinade ingredients in a nonreactive bowl.

Cut along breastbone of first pigeon, then angle the knife so that the edge is against the ribs and remove the breast. Repeat for the other side. Cut off the leg sections, keeping the thigh and drumstick attached. Repeat for the remaining birds. Reserve carcasses and necks.

Cover and marinate the breasts and legs in the refrigerator for about 5 hours.

Meanwhile, heat the oven to 450°F. Put the pigeon carcasses and necks in a roasting pan and cook in the preheated oven until well browned, 20 to 30 minutes.

With a cleaver or heavy knife, chop the carcasses and necks into small pieces. Put the chopped bones and stock into a pot and bring to a boil. Simmer for 1½ hours; then strain the stock and refrigerate until ready to use.

Remove the pigeon from the marinade. Put the olive oil in a heavy pot. Transfer onion and garlic from the marinade to the pot and cook very slowly until caramelized, 30 to 40 minutes. Add the stock to the onion-garlic mixture, a little at a time, and reduce the mixture slightly after each addition. When reduced to about 1¼ cups, put the mixture through a sieve, pushing the softened garlic and onions through. Whisk in the butter, Madeira, vinegar, and salt and pepper to taste.

Cooking: Heat the grill to medium-hot using mesquite or fig wood if available. Season the pigeon breasts and legs lightly with salt and pepper. Cook on the preheated grill, mostly on the skin side, until browned and cooked rare, about 8 minutes for the breasts, slightly longer for the legs. Let rest for 5 minutes. Reheat the sauce.

SERVING: Slice the breasts and arrange with legs on warm plates. Spoon the sauce over the pigeon.

YIELD: 4 servings

4 ¾- to 1-pound pigeons
1½ quarts Chicken Stock (page 81)
2 to 3 tablespoons olive oil
4 tablespoons unsalted butter
1 tablespoon Madeira
½ teaspoon red wine vinegar
Salt and black pepper

MUSHROOM-FILLED SAUSAGES

These unusual mushroom-stuffed sausages were developed by James Moore, chef of the Mountain Home Inn in Mill Valley, California, and a connoisseur of wild mushrooms. He likes to use trumpet-of-death mushrooms, though others are also good in this recipe. Despite its name, the dramatic trumpet of death, also known as horn of plenty or black chanterelle, is a perfectly edible, delicate, and somewhat fruity-tasting mushroom.

½ pound boneless veal
⅔ pound boneless pork shoulder
⅓ pound boneless chicken breast
1 small clove garlic
1 small onion
3 tablespoons minced fresh parsley
½ ounce bacon
⅓ cup grated Parmesan cheese
1 tablespoon dry white wine, plus a dash
*   for the apples*
*   Salt and black pepper*
⅓ pound trumpet of death or other
*   mushrooms*
1 tablespoon olive oil
½ pound caul fat
3 cooking apples
3 tablespoons unsalted butter
*   Watercress for garnish*

Preparation: Put the veal, pork, and chicken through a meat grinder using a plate with medium-sized holes. Mince the garlic, onion, parsley, and bacon. Grate the cheese.

In a bowl, combine the veal, pork, chicken, garlic, onion, parsley, cheese, bacon, 1 tablespoon of the wine, about 1 teaspoon salt, and ½ teaspoon pepper. Fry a small patty of the mixture, taste, and adjust the seasoning with salt and pepper. Form 8 thin patties.

Cut the mushrooms in half lengthwise. In a frying pan, sauté the mushrooms in the oil until tender, about 2 minutes. Remove with a slotted spoon. Set aside 4 mushroom halves for garnish and dice the remaining mushrooms. Divide the diced mushrooms among 4 sausage patties and top with the remaining 4 patties. Press the edges together so that the mushrooms are sealed in. Top each patty with a reserved mushroom half. Wrap in caul fat.

Cooking: Heat the grill. Peel, quarter, and core the apples and slice thin. Sauté the slices in the butter over medium-high heat until tender, 4 to 5 minutes. Add a dash of wine and keep warm.

Grill the sausages for 4 to 5 minutes per side.

SERVING: Serve the sausages on a bed of warm sautéed apples. Garnish with watercress.

YIELD: 4 servings

VEAL SAUSAGE WITH GREENS

This green-flecked sausage is rather fragile and, therefore, best cooked within 6 hours after the mixture is prepared.

Preparation: Put the veal, pork belly, and pork through a meat grinder using a plate with large holes. Cut the fatback into chunks and add to the ground meat. Chill the mixture and grind again.

Heat the cream and soak the bread crumbs in it. Grate Parmesan if using. Combine the meat mixture with the soaked bread crumbs and Parmesan cheese and season with salt and nutmeg.

Trim and wash the arugula, chicory, or spinach. Chop ½ cup of the greens. In a frying pan, melt the butter over medium heat and heat the chopped greens until just wilted. Drain and chill.

Combine the chilled greens with the meat mixture. Fry a small patty of the mixture, taste, and adjust the seasoning. Stuff the meat mixture into hog casing or shape loosely into 3- to 4-ounce patties and wrap each in a bit of caul fat.

Cut the onion and red pepper into thick slices.

Cooking: Heat the grill. Drizzle the olive oil over the onion and pepper slices and put them on the grill. Turn once while cooking. At the same time, grill the sausages, turning once, until they just lose their pink color, about 8 minutes.

SERVING: Put the sausages on plates and garnish with the remaining greens and grilled onion and pepper slices.

YIELD: 4 servings

1 pound boneless lean veal leg
2 ounces "green" pork belly (uncured bacon) or pancetta
¼ pound boneless pork butt with about 30 percent fat content
4 ounces fatback
3 tablespoons heavy cream
3 tablespoons fresh bread crumbs
1 tablespoon grated Parmesan cheese (optional)
1½ teaspoons coarse salt
Pinch of ground nutmeg
3 cups arugula, chicory, or spinach
1½ teaspoons unsalted butter
½ pound caul fat or 1½ feet hog casing
1 large red onion
1 red bell pepper
¼ cup olive oil

GRILLED LAMB SAUSAGE WITH WATERCRESS AND WARM POTATO SALAD

Chef Alfred Portale of The Gotham Bar & Grill in New York City accompanies his herbed lamb sausage with a warm potato and bell pepper salad.

1¼ pounds boneless lamb shoulder
1 pound pork shoulder with fat
¼ teaspoon chopped fresh rosemary leaves
    or pinch of dried rosemary
¼ teaspoon chopped fresh thyme leaves or
    pinch of dried thyme
1¼ teaspoons chopped fresh sage leaves or
    pinch of dried sage
2 tablespoons chopped fresh flat-leaf
    parsley
½ small clove garlic
2½ teaspoons salt
½ teaspoon white pepper
¼ teaspoon sugar
2 feet hog casings (optional)
    Warm Potato Salad (recipe follows)
    Watercress for garnish

Preparation: Put the meats through a meat grinder using a plate with medium-sized holes. Mince the herbs and garlic and add along with the salt, pepper, and sugar.

Form a small patty and fry until it just loses its pink color. Taste and adjust the seasoning. Stuff the sausage meat into rinsed hog casings or form into patties.

Cooking: Make the potato salad. Heat the grill. Cook the patties or sausages until they just lose their pink color, turning once, about 8 minutes in all.

SERVING: Toss the watercress with some of the vinaigrette from the Warm Potato Salad. Put the sausages and potato salad on plates and garnish with the watercress.

YIELD: 4 to 6 servings

WARM POTATO SALAD

3 shallots
3 tablespoons chopped fresh flat-leaf
    parsley
1 red bell pepper
1 yellow bell pepper
8 to 12 small red potatoes
2 tablespoons red wine vinegar
    Salt and black pepper
½ cup olive oil

Preparation: Cut the shallots into very thin slices. Chop the parsley. Cut the bell peppers into fine dice.

Cooking: In a saucepan of boiling salted water, cook the potatoes until tender, 20 to 25 minutes. Drain and set aside until cool enough to handle. While the potatoes are still warm, cut into rounds and put into a large bowl. Sprinkle the potatoes with shallots, parsley, and bell peppers.

In a small bowl, whisk together the vinegar and the salt. Whisk in the oil. Pour enough vinaigrette over the potatoes to moisten them well, reserving some to dress the watercress garnish. Adjust the seasoning with salt and pepper if necessary.

YIELD: 4 to 6 servings

SKEWERED PORTUGUESE SCALLOPS

This version of a well-known dish from Portugal, *vinho d'alhos,* is typical of the cooking in the many Portuguese communities along our New England coast.

Preparation: *For the marinade,* grate the orange zest into a nonreactive bowl. Crush the garlic and add it to the bowl along with the remaining marinade ingredients. Stir well. Add the scallops, stir, and cover. Refrigerate, stirring occasionally, for about 5 hours, if possible, or longer—overnight is not too long.

Thread the scallops onto skewers, reserving the marinade.

Cooking: Heat the grill. Grill the scallops on both sides, basting frequently with marinade, until the scallops are lightly browned and just done, about 6 minutes altogether.

YIELD: 4 servings

Marinade

⅛ teaspoon grated orange zest
1 clove garlic
½ cup dry white wine
4½ teaspoons white wine vinegar
1 bay leaf
¼ teaspoon ground cumin
2 whole peppercorns
¼ teaspoon paprika
Salt
1 tablespoon olive oil

1⅓ pounds sea scallops

GRILLED SWEETBREADS WITH POTATO PANCAKES AND BOLETE BUTTER

This is an elaborate and unusual dish from Jeremiah Tower of San Francisco's Stars. Grilled sweetbreads are presented on individual potato pancakes, topped with melting wild mushroom butter, and garnished with grilled baby artichokes and red peppers. Though the preparation is time-consuming, the final cooking is brief.

Sweetbreads

2 whole sweetbreads (about 1½ to 2
    pounds in all)
1 small onion
½ rib celery
½ carrot
1 teaspoon unsalted butter
2 sprigs parsley
¼ teaspoon dried thyme
1 small bay leaf
1 cup Chicken Stock (page 81) or veal
    stock
    Salt and black pepper
2 teaspoons chopped fresh thyme leaves or
    ¼ teaspoon dried thyme
2 tablespoons olive oil

Bolete Butter

4 tablespoons unsalted butter
    Sweetbread cooking liquid from above
¼ ounce dried boletes

Artichoke and Pepper Garnish

1 lemon
6 baby artichokes
3 red bell peppers
    Vegetable oil for brushing

Potato Pancakes

2 baking potatoes (about 1 pound in all)
3 tablespoons rendered duck fat or oil
    Salt and black pepper

4 large sprigs watercress (optional)
4 small sprigs fresh thyme (optional)

Preparation: Soak the sweetbreads in cold water for 3½ hours, changing the water several times. Drain. In a saucepan, blanch the sweetbreads in boiling salted water for about 3 minutes and then drain. Trim off the membranes.

Heat the oven to 325°F. Chop the onion, celery, and carrot. In a baking pan, melt the butter. Add the onion, celery, carrot, parsley, thyme, and the bay leaf. Cook, covered, over low heat until the vegetables are softened, 6 to 8 minutes. Add the sweetbreads and stock. Bring to a simmer.

Put the pan in the preheated oven and cook until the sweetbreads are just done, 35 to 40 minutes. Cool in the cooking liquid.

Drain the sweetbreads, reserving the liquid, and season them with salt and pepper and thyme. Brush with the olive oil and set aside for at least 30 minutes.

For the Bolete Butter, bring the butter to room temperature or soften in a microwave oven.

Strain the sweetbread cooking liquid into a small saucepan. Bring to a boil and reduce to 1 cup, about 5 minutes. Remove from the heat, add the dried boletes, and let steep for about 30 minutes.

Remove the boletes from the liquid with a slotted spoon and set them aside. Strain the liquid through a double layer of cheesecloth into a clean pan. Reduce to about 2 tablespoons over high heat, about 10 minutes. Cool.

In a food processor, puree the boletes, softened butter, and reduced cooking liquid until smooth.

For the Artichoke and Pepper Garnish, cut the lemon in

half. Trim the tough outer leaves and stems from the artichokes. Rub all cut surfaces of the artichokes with the lemon. Boil the artichokes in salted water, acidulated with more lemon juice, until just tender, 5 to 10 minutes. Drain, plunge into cold water, and drain well. Cut the artichokes in half.

Peel, seed, and quarter the red peppers. String the artichoke halves and pepper pieces on skewers and brush with oil.

For the Potato Pancakes, peel and grate potatoes. Blanch for 1 minute in boiling salted water. Drain and gently squeeze dry in a towel. Toss with 2 tablespoons of the duck fat and season with salt and pepper. Pat the potato mixture into four 5-inch rounds, using about ½ cup mixture for each, and put between layers of wax paper or plastic wrap.

Cooking: Heat the grill. Heat the oven to 150°F. In a large frying pan, melt ½ tablespoon of the remaining duck fat. Cook 2 of the pancakes at a time over medium heat until golden brown on each side, about 8 minutes altogether. Remove and keep warm in the preheated oven. Repeat with the remaining ½ tablespoon duck fat to make 2 more pancakes.

Grill the sweetbreads and vegetable garnish about 4 minutes per side. Cut the sweetbreads into 4 pieces.

SERVING: Put the potato pancakes on warm plates. Put the sweetbreads on top and arrange the bell pepper pieces and artichoke halves around the edge. Top the sweetbreads with Bolete Butter and garnish with a sprig each of watercress and thyme.

YIELD: 4 servings

GRILLED LAMB ON CABBAGE LEAVES

Blanched, grilled cabbage leaves make an unusual bed for the lamb, which is steeped in a flavorful orange/coriander marinade and quickly grilled. You can begin the marinating up to three days ahead; the flavor just gets better.

Lamb Marinade

1 clove garlic
1 small onion
½ orange
1½ teaspoons ground coriander
¼ cup olive oil
⅓ cup sherry or *Madeira*
2 teaspoons salt
½ teaspoon black pepper

1 pound boneless leg of lamb
4 large leaves savoy cabbage or *other green cabbage*
2 cups Chicken Stock (page 81) or *water*
4 tablespoons unsalted butter
Salt and black pepper
1½ teaspoons minced fresh thyme leaves or ½ teaspoon dried thyme

Preparation: *For the marinade,* chop the garlic and slice the onion. Put them in a nonreactive bowl large enough to hold the lamb and squeeze the ½ orange over them. Add 1 teaspoon of the coriander and the remaining marinade ingredients.

Cut the lamb into ¼-inch-thick slices. Put the meat in the marinade, turn to coat, cover with plastic wrap, and refrigerate for at least 5 hours, turning occasionally.

Remove the tough ribs from cabbage leaves. In a saucepan, bring the stock or water to a simmer. Add the cabbage, cover, and cook over medium heat until the leaves are just tender, about 5 minutes. Remove the leaves carefully and let them cool. Reserve the cooking liquid for another dish, such as soup.

Melt the butter. Brush cabbage leaves on both sides with melted butter and season with salt and pepper.

Cooking: Heat the grill. Remove the meat from the marinade and sprinkle it with salt and pepper, the remaining ½ teaspoon coriander, and thyme. Put the meat and butter-brushed cabbage leaves on the grill and cook until the meat is medium-rare and the cabbage leaves are lightly browned, about 2 minutes per side.

SERVING: Put the cabbage leaves on plates and top with the meat.

YIELD: 4 servings

CURRIED LAMB CHOPS WITH BANANA–ALMOND CHUTNEY

The Indian influences are obvious in this dish from Cindy Pawlcyn, executive chef for Realrestaurants, who own the Fog City Diner in San Francisco, the Rio Grill in Carmel, and Mustard's Grill in Yountville, California. After marinating for several hours, the curried lamb chops are cooked to medium-rare in a few minutes.

Curry Marinade

½ cup olive oil
¼ cup curry powder
4 cloves garlic
2 tablespoons grated fresh ginger
1 bay leaf
½ teaspoon salt
½ teaspoon white pepper

12 lamb chops
  Banana–Almond Chutney
  (recipe follows)

Preparation: *For the marinade,* heat the oil in a small frying pan. Add the curry powder and cook, stirring, over low heat until fragrant. Cool. Mince the garlic. Grate the ginger. In a nonreactive bowl, combine the oil-curry mixture, garlic, ginger, bay leaf, broken in half, and the salt and pepper. Cover and marinate the lamb chops in this mixture in the refrigerator for about 5 hours. Make the chutney about an hour before serving.

Cooking: Heat the grill. Cook the lamb chops until medium-rare, about 2 minutes per side.

SERVING: Serve the lamb chops with chutney on the side.

YIELD: 4 servings

BANANA–ALMOND CHUTNEY

¼ cup almonds
1 large clove garlic
1 tablespoon grated fresh ginger
3 tablespoons minced fresh coriander leaves
2 firm ripe bananas
  Salt and white pepper
  Cayenne
¼ cup rice wine vinegar
¾ cup olive oil

Preparation: Heat the oven to 325°F. Toast the almonds until brown, 5 to 10 minutes. Chop. Mince the garlic. Grate the ginger into a nonreactive bowl. Mince the coriander. Mash the bananas in the bowl with a fork. Add coriander and all the remaining ingredients and let sit for about 1 hour.

YIELD: about 2 cups

MENUS

Mediterranean Olives

Grilled Sweetbreads with Potato Pancakes and Bolete Butter (page 164)   Rheingau Riseling *Spätlese*

Grilled Pigeon with Garlic Sauce (page 158)   California Syrah, such as Joseph Phelps

Chocolate–Kona Cake with Figs and Pistachios (page 243)

Shellfish in Dill Brine (page 20)   Bouvet Brut

Grilled Ginger Duck Breasts with Peaches (page 158)   Red burgundy, such as Nuits-St.-Georges

Hazelnut Angel Ring with Coffee Ice Cream Balls and Chocolate Sauce (page 252)

Mushroom-Filled Sausages (page 160)   Dry Chenin Blanc, such as Raymond or Dry Creek Tarragon

Tarragon Chicken and Kale Stir-Fry (page 148)   Simi Chardonnay

Golden Apricot–Carrot Soup (page 235)   Late-Harvest Gewurztraminer, such as Chateau St. Jean

CHAPTER 9

PIZZA, CALZONE, AND FOCACCIA

*Standard Yeast Dough · Quick Yeast Dough · Parsley Pizza
Tarragon Mussel Pizza · Kale and Roasted Shallot Calzoni
Sausage and Cheese Calzoni with Fresh Tomato Sauce
Chili-Filled Calzoni · Lamb, Eggplant, and Goat Cheese Pizza
Goat Cheese and Scallion Tart · Tomato and Mozzarella Tart
Focaccia · Zucchini and Yellow Squash Tart*

T hough we Americans can take the credit for some startling new toppings, Italian pizza has always meant more than tomato sauce and cheese on a round of bread. Traditional pizzas in Italy include many delicately topped versions, such as those simply brushed with olive oil and sprinkled with a handful of minced herbs, chopped shellfish, or sliced mushrooms. Possibilities from capers to squid can be found as pizza ingredients in Italian cookbooks. The crust can be delicate pastry as well as hearty bread, and the more elegant pizzas were offered as first courses long before we elevated them from the snack category to respected elements of our new freestyle cuisine.

Still, Lamb, Eggplant, and Goat Cheese Pizza is probably new. The versatility of Italian pizza was rediscovered several years ago by innovative American chefs, and they took it one step further. Instead of tomato sauce and mozzarella, the standard topping for California pizza became pumante and goat cheese. Cooks all around the country soon realized that a crispy, golden crust could be the perfect vehicle for a variety of toppings, and pizza's history paralleled that of pasta's.

The new pizza's success is due not only to the appeal of the unusual, but to pizza's practical ease and quickness. Americans love pizza so much that they've figured out how to alter it to fit into contemporary hectic schedules. With the new fast-rise doughs (see our Quick Yeast Dough recipe, page 172) and the demise of the long-simmered tomato sauce, delectable pizzas have become time-saving favorites. Most of our toppings take no longer than the time to cut up a few ingredients. Even our "pizza-tarts" with puff-pastry bases are made with quick puff pastry, and they have the added advantage over yeast-dough pizzas that they often can be assembled entirely ahead of time. You can also make any of the tart-like pizzas in this chapter with regular pie pastry rather than puff pastry.

Another Italian yeast specialty has also become popular with American diners—calzone. Calzoni are essentially pizza turnovers—a yeast dough is rolled out into a circle, filled, and folded into a half-moon. The traditional calzone stuffing is a hearty combination of cheese, meat, and tomatoes. We have included an updated version of this filling, but we've also come up with some appealing new variations, such as Kale and Roasted Shallot Calzoni. Still relatively unknown in America is focaccia, a flat yeast bread native to northern Italy, the answer to the pizza more typical of the southern regions. Perhaps the most classic focaccia is topped only with olive oil, black pepper, and coarse salt, but other variations, such as adding paper-thin slices of red onion, cubes of Provolone, or a few teaspoons of rosemary, are not amiss.

Focaccia is unquestionably at its best when hot from the oven. Calzone, on the other hand, reheats well. We leave the verdict on leftover pizza, reheated or not, to you.

The Crispest Crust

Whether partisans of the thick- or thin-crust school, most people prefer the outside of their pizza crust to be crisp. Pizza—and calzone and focaccia, too—requires a hot oven, usually at least 400°F and often more, to produce the crispest crust. For a perfect crust, we like to use an unglazed ceramic pizza stone for all three bread specialties, but when making more than one pizza at a time, this is often not practical. Lining an oven shelf with unglazed ceramic tiles is an excellent solution. When using a baking sheet, try sprinkling it with corn-meal, a good trick to increase the crispness of the baked dough.

The ingredients of the yeast dough will also affect the finished texture. The liquid used is almost always water; milk will make a softer dough. Not all doughs require oil, but its addition will help produce a crusty exterior.

Yeast Dough Made to Your Schedule: Speeding It Up and Slowing It Down

Rising times can be varied, either short-ened or lengthened, according to need. The most obvious way to rush rising is to use the new quick-rising yeast. Another ploy is to start with all the ingredients at room temperature or slightly warmer (up to 115°F). You can also add a pinch of sugar when dissolving the yeast. This "food" will speed up the yeast growth. Food processor doughs tend to rise faster because the machine's friction generates heat, and covering the bowl of dough with plastic wrap instead of a towel will trap the heat of the carbon dioxide released during rising.

The simplest way to slow down rising time is to refrigerate the dough. A full rise will take from 5 to 8 hours in the refriger-ator. The dough cannot be left totally un-attended, because after 8 hours it will overrise, but it can be punched down and allowed to rise again several times in the refrigerator. You can also gain time by adding a rising or two to unrefrigerated dough. Most dough can be punched down and allowed to rise up to four times before the yeast begins to "tire."

Fast-Rising Yeast

Just as dry yeast has more or less replaced compressed cake yeast, the new fast-rising yeast may well displace conventional dry yeast. In most cases, quick yeast reduces the rising time for a recipe by half. The new yeast works faster because it is a more active, stronger strain, previously available only to commercial bakers. The processing method for this type of yeast differs from that for the conventional dry type, incor-porating both new techniques for nurtur-ing the yeast during fermentation and a quicker dehydration method that retains more active yeast cells. In addition, the granular particles are finer, and so the yeast blends with dry ingredients and absorbs liquid more rapidly. Differences in flavor and texture between dough made with fast-rising and standard yeast do exist—standard yeast does produce a marginally superior product—but the advantage is often a very agreeable trade-off.

STANDARD YEAST DOUGH

1 package active dry yeast
¾ cup warm water
2 cups flour, plus more if needed
1 teaspoon salt
1 tablespoon olive oil

Preparation: Dissolve the yeast in ¼ cup of warm water. Mix the flour and salt together and add the remaining ½ cup of water, oil, and dissolved yeast. Stir to combine and knead the dough on a floured work surface, adding flour if necessary, until the dough is soft, silky, and resilient, 10 to 15 minutes. Transfer the dough to an oiled bowl, turn to coat with oil, and cover the bowl with plastic wrap. Let rise in a warm place until doubled in bulk, 1½ to 2 hours.

QUICK YEAST DOUGH

2 cups flour
1 package quick-rising yeast
1 teaspoon salt
¾ cup warm water

Preparation: In a food processor, combine the flour, yeast, and salt. With the machine running, add the water slowly through the feed tube. Process until a ball forms and then about 30 seconds longer to knead. Cover the processor bowl with plastic wrap and let the dough rise for about 15 minutes.

PARSLEY PIZZA

Parsley is more than just a decorative garnish, as this tasty pizza proves. You can use either curly parsley or the stronger, slightly more flavorful flat-leafed Italian variety.

1 recipe Standard Yeast Dough or
    Quick Yeast Dough (above)
6 cups loosely-packed parsley leaves
¼ cup chopped fresh basil leaves or 4
    teaspoons dried basil
3 scallions
6 ounces mozzarella cheese
3 ripe tomatoes
    Salt and black pepper
¼ cup olive oil

Preparation: Make the dough. Remove stems from the parsley. Chop the basil if using fresh. Cut the scallions, including the green tops, into pieces. Cut the cheese into chunks. Peel and seed the tomatoes and cut them into chunks. Put the parsley, basil, scallions, mozzarella, and tomatoes in a food processor. Process only until all ingredients are coarsely chopped, not pureed. Season with salt and pepper to taste. Oil 4 round pizza pans or 2 baking sheets.

Cooking: Heat the oven to 475°F. Punch down the dough and cut into 4 pieces. On a floured work surface, roll 1 section into an 8-inch round. Transfer the dough to prepared pan and, using your fingers, push the dough out into a very thin 10- to 12-inch round. Repeat with remaining dough to make 4 rounds. Brush half of the oil over the dough rounds. Top with the parsley mixture and drizzle the remaining oil over top.

Bake in the preheated oven until the crust is dark golden brown and crisp and the filling is bubbling, 5 to 7 minutes. Remove the pans from the oven and transfer the pizzas to a rack for a couple of minutes to crisp.

YIELD: 4 servings

TARRAGON MUSSEL PIZZA

The flavors of tarragon and mussels marry beautifully atop this new American version of Italian shellfish pizza.

Preparation: Make the dough. Mince the garlic and tarragon if using fresh and add them to the olive oil. Beard, shuck, and chop the mussels. Grate the cheese. Sprinkle 2 baking sheets with cornmeal.

1 recipe Standard Yeast Dough or Quick Yeast Dough (page 172)
1 clove garlic
1 tablespoon minced fresh tarragon or 1 teaspoon dried tarragon
2 tablespoons olive oil
12 mussels
1 cup grated Parmesan cheese
Cornmeal for sprinkling

Cooking: Heat the oven to 450°F. Punch down the dough and cut it in half. Roll 1 piece of the dough into a round about 9 inches in diameter. Repeat with the other half of the dough. Put the dough rounds on the prepared baking sheets, and brush with the oil mixture. Spread the mussels over the dough. Top with the cheese.

Bake in the preheated oven until the crust is golden brown, 10 to 15 minutes.

YIELD: 4 servings

KALE AND ROASTED SHALLOT CALZONI

Roasting shallots gives them a delicious flavor. For these unusual calzoni, they are combined with bacon, kale, and Monterey Jack cheese.

1 recipe Standard Yeast Dough or
  Quick Yeast Dough (page 172)
12 shallots
  Olive oil for tossing and brushing
  Salt and black pepper
2 bunches kale (about 3 pounds in all)
8 slices bacon
¾ cup Chicken Stock (page 81)
⅓ pound Monterey Jack cheese
1 egg
  Cornmeal for sprinkling

Preparation: Make the dough. Heat the oven to 350°F. In a roasting pan, toss the unpeeled shallots with the oil. Season with salt and pepper. Cook the shallots in the preheated oven until soft, about 45 minutes. Cool.

Stem, wash, and chop the kale. In a pot of boiling salted water, blanch the kale until just tender, about 6 minutes. Drain, refresh under cold running water, and drain well.

Chop the bacon. In a large frying pan, sauté the bacon until golden, about 6 minutes. Remove with a slotted spoon and drain on paper towels. Pour off all but about 1½ tablespoons of the fat.

Heat the reserved bacon fat, and add the kale and stock. Simmer over medium heat until the kale is tender and liquid has reduced to a syrup, about 10 minutes. Season with salt and pepper.

Remove the skins from the roasted shallots. Grate the cheese. Whisk the egg with 1 tablespoon of water for the egg wash. Sprinkle a baking sheet with cornmeal.

Cooking: Heat the oven to 475°F. If using a pizza stone, heat it.

Punch down the dough and divide it into 4 pieces. Roll out each piece of dough on a lightly floured work surface into a ⅛- to ¼-inch-thick oval. Sprinkle the cheese over half of each oval, leaving a ¾-inch border. Divide the kale, shallots, and bacon among calzoni. Brush the border of dough with the egg wash. Fold the dough over and press with a fork to seal. Brush the calzoni with olive oil.

Put on the prepared baking sheet and slide onto the pizza stone if using. Or put the baking sheet in the preheated oven and bake until golden brown, about 15 minutes.

YIELD: 4 servings

SAUSAGE AND CHEESE CALZONI WITH FRESH TOMATO SAUCE

Sausage and cheese is a traditional calzone filling; our version is updated with an uncooked tomato–basil sauce. If fresh basil is unavailable, use a total of ⅓ cup minced parsley for the sauce instead.

Preparation: Make the dough. *For the sauce,* peel, seed, and chop the tomatoes. Put tomatoes into strainer to drain. Mince the ⅔ cup basil and the parsley. Toss the basil and parsley together with the drained tomatoes and season with salt and pepper to taste.

Cook the sausages in a large frying pan over medium heat until browned and cooked through, about 10 minutes. Cool and cut into ½-inch-thick slices.

Grate the mozzarella and Parmesan cheeses. Chop the basil if using fresh. Whisk the egg with 1 tablespoon water for egg wash. Sprinkle a baking sheet with cornmeal.

Cooking: Heat the oven to 475°F. If using a pizza stone, heat it.

Punch down the dough and divide into 4 portions. Roll each piece into a ⅛- to ¼-inch-thick oval. Put sausage slices on half of each oval. Sprinkle the sausage with the mozzarella cheese, leaving ¾-inch borders. Mound the ricotta cheese on top of mozzarella. Sprinkle Parmesan, basil, and salt and pepper to taste on top. Brush the borders of the dough with the egg wash. Fold the dough over and press the edges with a fork to seal them. Brush the calzoni with the olive oil.

Put on the prepared baking sheet and slide onto the pizza stone or put the baking sheet in the preheated oven and bake until golden brown, about 15 minutes.

SERVING: Serve the calzoni with the Fresh Tomato Sauce alongside.

YIELD: 4 servings

1 recipe Standard Yeast Dough or
   Quick Yeast Dough (page 172)

Fresh Tomato Sauce

 6 plum tomatoes
⅔ cup minced fresh basil leaves
 2 tablespoons minced fresh parsley
   Salt and black pepper

¾ pound Italian sausages
½ pound mozzarella cheese
⅓ cup grated Parmesan cheese
 2 tablespoons chopped fresh basil leaves or
    2 teaspoons dried basil
 1 egg
   Cornmeal for sprinkling
½ cup ricotta cheese
   Salt and black pepper
   Olive oil for brushing

CHILI-FILLED CALZONI

Two ethnic favorites are paired to create a hearty Italian-Mexican dish.
The calzoni are split open before serving and garnished with sour cream,
coriander, red onions, and tomatoes.

1 recipe Standard Yeast Dough or
    Quick Yeast Dough (page 172)
1 onion
2 cloves garlic
1 mild Italian frying pepper
¾ pound boneless beef, such as chuck
3 ripe tomatoes
1 tablespoon vegetable oil
2 teaspoons ground cumin
½ teaspoon paprika
¾ teaspoon dried oregano
¼ teaspoon dried thyme
    Salt and black pepper
1 cup Chicken Stock (page 81)
    Cayenne
½ pound Monterey Jack cheese
1 egg
    Cornmeal for sprinkling
1 red onion
1 small bunch fresh coriander
    Olive oil for brushing
½ cup sour cream

Preparation: Make the dough. Chop the onion. Mince the garlic. Core, seed, and chop the frying pepper. Cut the beef into ¼-inch dice or grind coarsely. Core, peel, seed, and chop 2 of the tomatoes.

In a cast-iron or other heavy pot, heat the oil over medium heat. Add onion, cumin, paprika, oregano, thyme, and salt and pepper, and cook until the onion is soft, about 4 minutes. Stir in garlic and frying pepper. Add the beef and cook, stirring frequently, until the meat loses its red color. Add the stock and chopped tomatoes and bring to a simmer. Cook, stirring occasionally, until the beef is tender and the liquid is thick, about 1 hour. Season with cayenne and salt and pepper to taste. Cool completely.

Grate the cheese. Combine the egg with 1 tablespoon water to make an egg wash. Dust a baking sheet with cornmeal. Slice the red onion. Slice the remaining tomato and cut the slices into quarters. Mince the coriander.

Cooking: Heat the oven to 475°F. If using a pizza stone, heat it.

Punch down the dough and divide into 4 pieces. Roll each piece of dough on a lightly floured work surface into a ⅛- to ¼-inch-thick oval. Spread one quarter of the filling over half of each oval, leaving a ¾-inch border. Top the filling with the cheese. Brush the entire border of dough with the egg wash. Fold the dough over, press with a fork to seal the edges, and brush with olive oil. Put the calzoni on the prepared baking sheet and slide onto the pizza stone if using or put the baking sheet in the preheated oven and bake until golden brown, about 15 minutes. Transfer to a rack and cool for 5 minutes before serving.

SERVING: Slit the calzoni lengthwise. Spoon some sour cream into each slit. Garnish with the red onion slices, coriander leaves, and quartered tomato slices.

YIELD: 4 servings

LAMB, EGGPLANT, AND GOAT CHEESE PIZZA

Eggplant, garlic, and lamb, natural complements, are staples in Greek cooking. They can also be used for an unusual pizza topped with goat cheese. To carry out the Greek theme, you could use feta rather than chèvre.

Preparation: Make the dough. Peel and chop the eggplant. Chop the onion. Mince the garlic. Peel, seed, and chop the tomato.

Sauté the lamb in ½ tablespoon of the oil, stirring, until cooked through. Drain. Add salt and pepper to taste and remove from the heat.

Sauté the eggplant and onion in the remaining 1½ tablespoons of oil over medium-low heat until softened, about 5 minutes. Add the garlic and tomato and sauté for 2 minutes. Season with salt and pepper to taste. Add to the lamb, tossing to combine, and set aside. Sprinkle a baking sheet with cornmeal.

Cooking: Heat the oven to 500°F. Punch down the dough and divide it into 2 equal balls. Roll the dough into rounds about 8 inches in diameter. Put the rounds of dough onto the prepared baking sheet. Divide the lamb topping evenly over the dough. Crumble the cheese over all.

Bake in the preheated oven until golden brown, about 10 minutes.

YIELD: 4 servings

1 recipe Standard Yeast Dough or Quick Yeast Dough (page 172)
1 small eggplant
1 small onion
2 cloves garlic
1 tomato
¾ pound ground lamb
2 tablespoons olive oil
Salt and black pepper
Cornmeal for sprinkling
¼ pound mild goat cheese

GOAT CHEESE AND SCALLION TART

A puff pastry strip topped with overlapping rounds of fresh goat cheese and accented by savory, thyme, and scallions makes a simple and delicious tart.

½ recipe Quick Puff Pastry (page 263)
1 egg
2 teaspoons minced fresh savory leaves or
    ½ teaspoon dried savory
2 teaspoons minced fresh thyme leaves or
    ½ teaspoon dried thyme
1 clove garlic
    Salt and black pepper
5 scallions
2 teaspoons lemon juice
2½ tablespoons olive oil
⅓ cup fresh bread crumbs
½ pound log goat cheese

Preparation: Make the puff pastry. Roll the pastry into an 18- by 8-inch rectangle. Trim to even the edges. Put on a baking sheet. Brush a 1-inch border on each of the two long sides of the rectangle lightly with water. Fold a ½-inch border on each side and press gently to seal. Cut off the fold by trimming ⅟16 inch from the border. Beat the egg with 2 teaspoons of water to make a glaze. Brush the border with the egg glaze. Using the back of a paring knife, nick the entire outside edge of the tart at ¼-inch intervals. Score a design in the border if desired. Prick the bottom of the tart with a fork at ½-inch intervals. Cover with plastic wrap and refrigerate.

Bruise the herbs by rubbing them with your fingers and put them in a bowl. Mash the garlic with a little salt and add it to the bowl. Cut the scallions, including the green tops, into thin slices. Add ¼ cup of the scallions to the bowl along with lemon juice and oil.

Spread the bread crumbs over the bottom of the pastry rectangle and sprinkle the remaining sliced scallions over the bread crumbs. Cut the cheese into ⅛-inch-thick slices and arrange it over the scallions in overlapping rows. Brush the oil mixture over the top. Grind pepper over the cheese. Cover and refrigerate if not baking immediately.

Cooking: Heat the oven to 425°F. Bake the tart on the lower rack of the preheated oven for 15 minutes. Lower the oven temperature to 375°F and move the tart to the upper rack of the oven until the pastry is browned, 10 to 15 minutes more.

YIELD: 4 servings

TOMATO AND MOZZARELLA TART

This summery tart combines slices of ripe tomatoes with mozzarella that has been marinated in a flavorful mixture of fresh herbs and olive oil. In winter, choose plum tomatoes, which seem to be better year-round than regular tomatoes.

Preparation: Make the puff pastry. Roll the pastry into a very thin, 20- by 10-inch rectangle. Put on a baking sheet. Trim the edges. Brush a 1-inch border on each of the two long sides with water. Fold a ½-inch border over on each side and press gently to seal. Trim ¹⁄₁₆ inch off the border to remove the fold. Beat the egg with 2 teaspoons of water to make a glaze. Brush the border with the egg glaze. Using the back of a paring knife, nick the outside edges of the tart at ¼-inch intervals. Score a design in the border if desired. Prick the bottom of the tart with a fork at ½-inch intervals. Cover with plastic wrap and refrigerate.

Bruise the herbs by rubbing them between your fingers and put them in a bowl. Mash the garlic with a little salt and add it to the bowl. Chop the basil and add with the hot pepper, lemon juice, and oil.

Cut the mozzarella into ¹⁄₁₆-inch-thick slices and put the slices in a large dish. Pour the oil mixture over the cheese. Cut the onion in half and then into thin slices and scatter the slices over the cheese. Cover with plastic wrap and let sit at room temperature for at least 1 hour. Cut the tomatoes in half vertically and then crosswise into slices.

Sprinkle the bread crumbs over the pastry. Arrange rows of alternating tomato and cheese slices over the crumbs. Distribute the onions over the top of the tart and sprinkle with salt and pepper.

Cooking: Heat the oven to 425°F. Bake the tart on the bottom rack of the preheated oven for 15 minutes. Lower the oven temperature to 375°F and move the tart to the top rack of the oven until it is browned, 10 to 15 minutes more.

YIELD: 4 servings

½ recipe Quick Puff Pastry (page 263)
1 egg
¾ teaspoon minced fresh thyme leaves or ¼ teaspoon dried thyme
¾ teaspoon minced fresh oregano leaves or ¼ teaspoon dried oregano
¾ teaspoon minced fresh rosemary leaves or ¼ teaspoon dried rosemary
1 clove garlic
Salt and black pepper
3 tablespoons chopped fresh basil leaves
¼ teaspoon crushed dried hot red pepper
1 tablespoon lemon juice
¼ cup olive oil
½ pound mozzarella cheese
1 small onion
4 tomatoes
½ cup fresh bread crumbs

FOCACCIA

This crisp *and* chewy Italian flatbread is delicious served topped with nothing more than olive oil, coarse salt, and black pepper. If you love it as much as we do, you'll also want to try the variations, from adding roasted garlic or a sprinkling of sesame seeds to incorporating cheese or herbs into the dough—or invent your own focaccia flavors.

1 package active dry yeast
1 teaspoon sugar
1¼ cups warm water
2¾ cups bread or all-purpose flour,
    approximately
½ cup olive oil
    Salt and black pepper
    Cornmeal for sprinkling
    Coarse salt

Preparation: In a large bowl, dissolve the yeast and sugar in ¾ cup of the warm water. Beat in 1 cup of the flour, cover the bowl with plastic wrap, and let the sponge rise in a warm place until approximately tripled in volume and very bubbly, about 3 hours.

Add the remaining ½ cup warm water, 2 tablespoons of the oil, ¾ teaspoon salt, and enough of the remaining flour to form a soft but workable dough. Knead on a lightly floured work surface until smooth and elastic, about 10 minutes. Oil a bowl. Put the dough in the prepared bowl, turn to oil the top, cover with plastic wrap, and put in a warm place until doubled, about 1½ hours. Sprinkle a baking sheet lightly with cornmeal.

Cooking: Heat the oven to 475°F. If using a pizza stone, heat it. Roll or pat dough on a floured work surface into a 15-inch round. Carefully slide prepared baking pan under the dough. Drizzle the focaccia with the remaining 6 tablespoons of oil and sprinkle with pepper and about 4 teaspoons of coarse salt.

If using a stone, shake the pan to loosen the dough. Slide it from the baking sheet directly onto the stone. Be sure the dough is loosened from the baking sheet before sliding. If not using a stone, bake directly on the baking sheet on the bottom rack of the oven. Bake focaccia in the preheated oven until golden, 15 to 20 minutes.

YIELD: **4 servings**

VARIATIONS

These variations are good alone or in combination. The herbed olive oil, for instance, can be used with the red onions or with roasted shallots or garlic; fresh herbs can be stirred into dough that's topped with cheese. Mix and match according to your own taste.

Focaccia with Sesame Seeds
Sprinkle the basic focaccia with 2 tablespoons sesame seeds before baking.

Focaccia with Red Onion
Quarter 1 large red onion, cut it into paper-thin slices, and scatter the slices over dough before drizzling it with the oil and sprinkling with salt and pepper.

Focaccia with Roasted Shallots or Garlic
Toss 16 unpeeled shallots or 4 heads garlic, separated into cloves, with the olive oil, season with salt and pepper, and roast in a preheated 350°F oven until soft, about 45 minutes. Cool. Remove from their skins, halve or chop if large, and sprinkle on the dough before baking.

Focaccia with Herbed Olive Oil
Steep 4 teaspoons dried thyme, rosemary, or oregano in the ½ cup olive oil for at least 1 hour before using.

Focaccia with Fresh Herbs
Stir ¼ cup minced fresh herbs, such as parsley, basil, or sage, into the sponge after it has risen and before adding the remaining flour to form dough.

Focaccia with Cheese
Stir ⅓ cup grated Parmesan or 6 ounces Provolone, cut into ¼-inch cubes, into the sponge after it has risen and before adding the remaining flour to form the dough.

ZUCCHINI AND YELLOW SQUASH TART

Light and colorful, this is one of our favorite "elegant" pizzas.

½ recipe Quick Puff Pastry (page 263)
 1 egg

Quick Tomato Sauce

 5 plum tomatoes (about 1 pound in all)
 6 scallions
 1 clove garlic
   Salt and black pepper
 1 tablespoon chopped fresh basil leaves
 2 tablespoons olive oil
 ¾ teaspoon chopped fresh mixed herbs, such
     as oregano, thyme, and rosemary, or
     ¼ teaspoon dried herbs

 1 medium-sized yellow summer squash
 1 medium-sized zucchini
 2 cloves garlic
 1 bay leaf
 ½ cup fresh basil leaves
 ¼ cup olive oil
   Salt and black pepper
 ¼ cup grated Parmesan cheese
 ½ cup fresh bread crumbs

Preparation: Make the puff pastry. Roll the pastry into a very thin round. Using a 12½-inch cardboard circle, pot lid, or other even round as a guide, trim the edges to a perfect circle. Put on a baking sheet. Brush a ¾-inch border with water. Fold a ⅜-inch border over and press gently to seal. Beat the egg with 2 teaspoons water to make a glaze. Brush the border with egg glaze. With the back of a paring knife, nick the outside edge at ¼-inch intervals. Prick the bottom of tart with a fork at ½-inch intervals. Refrigerate.

For the sauce, chop the plum tomatoes and scallions. Mash the garlic with a pinch of salt. Chop the 1 tablespoon basil. Heat the 2 tablespoons of oil in a frying pan. Add tomatoes, scallions, the mashed garlic mixture, chopped basil, and the mixed herbs. Sauté over medium-low heat until the juices have evaporated, about 10 minutes. Season with salt and pepper and set aside.

Cut the yellow squash and zucchini into ⅛-inch-thick slices. You should have about 1 cup of each. Bring a large pot of salted water to a boil with 1 garlic clove, halved, the bay leaf, and 2 of the fresh basil leaves. Add yellow squash and zucchini, bring back to a boil, and cook for 1 minute. Drain and spread the squashes on paper towels to dry.

Put the rest of the basil leaves, 1 garlic clove, and ¼ cup olive oil in a food processor and whir until smooth. Season with salt and pepper to taste. Grate the cheese.

Sprinkle the pastry round with the bread crumbs. Spread the cooled tomato mixture evenly over bread crumbs. Cover the tomato sauce with overlapping circles of the squash, alternating zucchini and yellow squash slices.

Brush the tops of the vegetables with the herbed oil. Sprinkle the cheese over the top of the tart. Cover and refrigerate if not baking immediately. The tart can be assembled up to an hour ahead.

Cooking: Heat the oven to 425°F. Bake the tart on the bottom rack of the preheated oven for 15 minutes. Lower the oven temperature to 375°F. Transfer the tart to the top rack of the oven and bake until it is browned, 10 to 15 minutes more.

YIELD: 4 servings

MENUS

Goat Cheese and Scallion Tart *(page 178)*   Crisp Fumé Blanc, such as Iron Horse
Zucchini and Yellow Squash Tart *(page 182)*
Salad of Greens with an Herb Vinaigrette

Red Raspberry Mousse *(page 232)*   Champagne Rosé
Pistachio Butter Cookies *(page 227)*

Provençale Green Bean Salad *(page 49)*
    Muscadet
Tarragon Mussel Pizza *(page 173)*

Winter Compote with Raspberry Sauce
   (page 232)

Cabbage Pancakes *(page 19)*
    Full-bodied Chardonnay, such as Acacia or
Son of a Gun Seafood Stew *(page 87)*   Sonoma–Cutrer
Focaccia with Roasted Shallots or Garlic
   (page 181)

Fresh Pears and Roquefort   Sauternes

Skewered Portuguese Scallops *(page 163)*   Vinho Verde (Portugal)
Parsley Pizza *(page 172)*

Mascarpone with Figs *(page 236)*   Port, such as Founder's Reserve Porto
   (Sandeman)

CHAPTER 10

NEW–AGE SANDWICHES

*Cucumber and Marinated Tomato Rolls · Cajun Shrimp Sandwiches
Steak and Wilted Watercress Sandwiches · Salad Sandwiches
Crab and Tomato Sandwiches · Lobster Quesadillas
Fried Fish and Arugula Sandwiches with Balsamic Mayonnaise
Café Fanny Basil Sandwiches · Ham, Leek, and Brie Sandwiches
Black Pepper Batter Bread · Crusty White Bread · Pear Bread
Pear Picadillo Sandwiches*

T he sandwich—bread layered or filled with other ingredients—is one of the most versatile basic combinations of food. It can be served at almost any time of the day, from the plain fried-egg sandwich at breakfast to an after-theater Crab and Tomato Sandwich, and it can show up at any point in the modular menu, from hors d'oeuvre to major course. Though a sandwich can be as simple as a few slices of cheese on bread, it can also be a rococo production such as our Cucumber and Marinated Tomato Rolls, which include, besides the base of cucumbers, tomatoes, and vinaigrette, optional additions of arugula, mozzarella cheese, radish sprouts, and red onion.

While old favorites, such as BLTs and grilled cheese, will never go out of style, there have been some notable changes in the quintessentially American sandwich. We're taking this institution more seriously, using fine ingredients, such as the filet mignon in our Steak and Wilted Watercress Sandwich, and bringing imagination to bear even on longtime favorites. Grilled ham and cheese has given way to a Ham, Leek, and Brie Sandwich, fried fish to a Fried Fish and Arugula Sandwich with Balsamic Mayonnaise. Ethnic influences are evident here, too, as in the rest of the new cuisine. Stuffed pita pockets have become as American as egg salad on white, and soft tortillas are now a staple bread. Popular American regional dishes take to a bread holder, too, as in the Cajun Shrimp Sandwich. The basically simple idea of the sandwich is as useful and satisfying as ever.

Flavored Mayonnaise

Basic Mayonnaise

It's important to have all your ingredients at room temperature. Beat the other ingredients well first and then add the oil very slowly—not more than a few drops at a time until the mayonnaise thickens and then in a fine stream.

> 1 large egg yolk
> ½ teaspoon lemon juice
> ½ teaspoon white wine vinegar
> ⅛ teaspoon dry or prepared mustard
> Salt and black pepper
> 1 cup oil

Preparation: In a large bowl, whisk or beat together the egg yolk, lemon juice, vinegar, mustard, ¼ teaspoon salt, and pepper to taste. Add the oil, very slowly at first, whisking or beating with an electric mixer continuously. Adjust seasoning if necessary.

YIELD: about 1 cup

Variations

With Flavored Oil
(asparagus, artichoke, shellfish, or garlic)

Asparagus peelings, shrimp shells, or other such ingredients that are usually discarded can be steeped in oil to impart a delicious taste. Use about 1 cup artichoke or asparagus trimmings or crushed shrimp, crab, lobster, or crayfish shells per cup of oil. Combine in a saucepan and cook, covered, over very low heat for 20 minutes, stirring occasionally. Cool to room temperature and strain, pressing the solids against the strainer to extract all oil. For garlic oil, use 3 cloves lightly crushed, and cook in the same way. Use the flavored oil in place of plain in the Basic Mayonnaise recipe. A sharper garlic mayonnaise can be made by crushing a garlic clove to a paste and adding it to the Basic Mayonnaise. If you have lobster coral, mash it with a fork and add to the mayonnaise made with the lobster oil.

With Citrus Juice
(lemon or lime)

Vary the acidic ingredients in the mayonnaise by using all lemon juice rather than lemon juice and vinegar or use lime juice instead of lemon, for either half or all of the acid. Keep the basic proportions of acidic ingredients to oil the same when making the mayonnaise and then add more juice as desired for a stronger flavor.

With Herbs
(basil, parsley, chives, tarragon, etc.)

For the most intense herb flavor, steep 2 tablespoons minced fresh herbs, such as basil, parsley, chives, tarragon, or a combination, in 1 cup oil. Use the herb oil in place of plain oil in the Basic Mayonnaise recipe. Or simply fold the herbs into the completed mayonnaise.

With Spices
(mustard, cayenne, etc.)

A variety of spices can be used to make special mayonnaises as well. For example, add 2 tablespoons dry or prepared mustard or ½ teaspoon cayenne to the basic mayonnaise recipe. You can experiment with other spices to make, for instance, saffron or curried mayonnaise.

Sandwich Ideas with Flavored Mayonnaise

Homemade mayonnaise, varied by using flavored oils, by substituting different acidic ingredients, or by adding herbs or spices, makes the simplest sandwich special. Some of the following suggestions use more than one variation at once, and you could certainly vary mayonnaise in all three ways, using a flavored oil, an unusual acid, *and* herbs and spices. The following ideas will get you started.

Sliced tomatoes and red onions with basil mayonnaise

Crabmeat, sliced red onions, and romaine lettuce with crab mayonnaise

Fried smelts with mustard mayonnaise

Fried fish with lemon and shrimp mayonnaise

Roast chicken, sliced or made into salad, with asparagus mayonnaise

Poached chicken with an herb mayonnaise, such as tarragon

Grilled chicken with artichoke mayonnaise

Turkey breast, sliced or made into salad, with cayenne mayonnaise

Grilled pork tenderloin with garlic mayonnaise

Thinly sliced roast beef with garlic, parsley, and cayenne mayonnaise

CUCUMBER AND MARINATED TOMATO ROLLS

Summer's bounty in a sandwich. The tomatoes and cucumbers can be topped with any or all of the optional ingredients—arugula, mozzarella, red onion, and/or radish sprouts.

4 tomatoes
  Salt and black pepper
4 teaspoons chopped fresh parsley and/or
    marjoram leaves
¼ cup olive oil
4 teaspoons vinegar
1 small cucumber
1 red onion, optional
4 large hard rolls
1 cup arugula leaves (optional)
½ pound mozzarella, sliced thin (optional)
1 cup radish sprouts (optional)

Preparation: Cut a slice from the top of each tomato. Scoop out and discard the seeds. Cut the tomatoes into thin slices, spread them out on a plate, and season with salt and pepper. Chop the parsley and/or marjoram and sprinkle over the tomatoes. Drizzle with the oil and vinegar. Macerate for about 30 minutes.

Peel and cut the cucumber into thin slices. Cut red onion into thin slices if using.

Slice the rolls in half. Layer the tomato slices on each bottom half. Drizzle the remaining juices onto the top halves of the rolls. Top the tomatoes with cucumbers and add your choice of optional ingredients. Close the sandwiches, pressing them down gently. Weight the sandwiches with a plate and something heavy, such as a can, and let sit for about 30 minutes or up to 3 hours.

YIELD: 4 servings

CAJUN SHRIMP SANDWICHES

For this new-style Southern sandwich, shrimp are sautéed with a spicy mixture of celery, green peppers, scallions, and tomatoes and served with hot red pepper sauce.

8 slices Black Pepper Batter Bread
    (page 194) or 4 large hard rolls
½ rib celery
½ green bell pepper
4 scallions
1 tomato
¾ pound shrimp
4 tablespoons unsalted butter
½ teaspoon crushed dried hot red pepper

Preparation: Slice the rolls if using. Chop the celery, green pepper, and scallions. Peel, seed, and chop the tomato. Peel and devein the shrimp.

Cooking: Warm the rolls, if using, in a 350°F oven. In a frying pan, melt the butter. Sauté the celery, green pepper, and scallions until wilted, about 3 minutes. Stir in the tomato, hot pepper, oregano, salt and pepper, and shrimp. Cook until the shrimp are pink and cooked through, 2 to 3 minutes. Stir in the Madeira and cook over high heat for about 30 seconds. Adjust the seasonings.

½ teaspoon dried oregano
  Salt and black pepper
1 tablespoon Madeira or sherry
  Hot red pepper sauce

SERVING: Put the shrimp mixture on 4 slices of bread and top with the remaining slices or put into warm rolls. Serve with hot red pepper sauce on the side.

YIELD: 4 servings

STEAK AND WILTED WATERCRESS SANDWICHES

Made with rare filet mignon, a cream-and-brandy deglazing sauce, and wilted watercress, these elegant sandwiches take only minutes to prepare.

Preparation: Cut the bread diagonally into 8 slices. Mince the shallot. Cut tough stems from watercress and wash leaves. Press the pepper into both sides of the meat.

8 slices Crusty White Bread (page 195) or
  French bread
1 large shallot
3 cups loosely packed watercress leaves
  Salt and coarse pepper
4 ¼-pound filet mignons
4 tablespoons unsalted butter
1 tablespoon brandy
½ cup heavy cream

Cooking: Toast the bread. In a frying pan, melt the butter. Sauté the meat over medium-high heat, turning once, until medium-rare, about 5 minutes. Season with salt to taste. Remove from the pan and keep warm. Add the shallot and brandy to the pan and scrape the bottom of the pan with a wooden spoon to deglaze. Add the cream and simmer, stirring, until slightly thickened, about 2 minutes. Add all but 4 sprigs of watercress and toss until slightly wilted, about 10 seconds. Season with salt and pepper.

SERVING: Put the filets on 4 slices of the toast. Top with the cooked watercress and pan juices and then with the remaining toast. Garnish with the watercress sprigs.

YIELD: 4 servings

SALAD SANDWICHES

Provençale cooking means garlic, olive oil, tomatoes, and olives. A loaf
of crusty bread stuffed with these ingredients and topped with chèvre
makes delicious, summery sandwiches.

1 clove garlic
¼ cup olive oil
2 tomatoes
½ red onion
1 green bell pepper
½ cup Niçoise olives
*1 loaf Crusty White Bread (page 195) or
    French bread*
*¼ pound goat cheese
    Salt and black pepper*

Preparation: Crush the garlic, add to the oil, and let
sit for 30 minutes. Slice the tomatoes and onion. Seed
and slice the pepper. Remove the pits from the olives.

Slice off the top third of the loaf of bread. Scoop out
the bread from the bottom, leaving a ½-inch shell.
Brush or drizzle the bread with the garlic oil. Layer the
bread shell with the tomato, onion, and pepper slices,
and olives. Crumble the cheese over all. Season with
salt and pepper to taste. Replace the top of the bread
and weight down with 2 plates and something heavy,
such as several cans. Let sit for about 30 minutes or up
to 3 hours.

SERVING: Cut into sections.

YIELD: 4 servings

CRAB AND TOMATO SANDWICHES

A cut above the usual stuffed pitas, these are filled with a dill-scented
crab salad bound with sour cream.

2 scallions
2 tablespoons minced fresh parsley
*½ teaspoon minced fresh dill leaves or ¼
    teaspoon dried dill*
½ cup sour cream
*1 pound crabmeat
    Salt and black pepper*
2 tomatoes
*8 slices Black Pepper Batter Bread
    (page 194) or 2 large pita breads*
4 leaves romaine lettuce

Preparation: Mince the scallions, parsley, and dill if
using fresh. Combine with sour cream and crabmeat.
Season with salt and pepper to taste. Slice the tomatoes.
Halve the pitas if using.

SERVING: Fill the sandwiches or stuff each pita half with
1 leaf romaine, several slices of tomato, and one quarter
of the crabmeat mixture.

YIELD: 4 servings

LOBSTER QUESADILLAS

The flavors of several cuisines are evident in these unusual sandwiches. Fresh lobster and avocado are briefly sautéed with Oriental snow peas, wrapped in flour tortillas, and accompanied by both spicy salsa and French crème fraîche. The various flavors meld beautifully.

Preparation: Cook the lobsters in rapidly boiling water until done, about 12 minutes. Remove from the pot and cool enough to handle. Remove the meat from the tail and claws and cut into bite-sized pieces.

For the salsa, seed the jalapeño. Peel and seed the tomato. Cut the onion in half. Whir the jalapeño, tomato, garlic, onion, chile, and 4 sprigs of the coriander in a food processor briefly. Season with salt and pepper.

Cut the scallions into thin slices. Cut the snow peas into 1-inch pieces.

Cooking: Wrap the tortillas in aluminum foil and warm in a 350°F oven. Peel the avocado and cut the flesh into bite-sized chunks.

In a frying pan, melt 3 tablespoons of the butter. Sauté the scallions and snow peas over medium-high heat for 2 minutes. Add the lobster, cumin, lime juice, avocado, and salt and pepper to taste. Sauté until just warmed through, about 30 seconds. Put the filling on the tortillas and fold them over.

Wipe out the frying pan. Using ½ tablespoon of the remaining butter per batch, cook 2 quesadillas at a time over high heat, turning once, for about 40 seconds altogether.

SERVING: Put the quesadillas on plates with salsa on one side and crème fraîche on the other. Garnish with the remaining coriander sprigs.

YIELD: 4 servings

2 1- to 1½-pound lobsters

Salsa

1 jalapeño pepper
1 large tomato
1 small onion
1 clove garlic
1 canned mild green chile
8 sprigs coriander
   Salt and black pepper

4 scallions
¼ pound snow peas
8 large flour tortillas
1 avocado
4 tablespoons unsalted butter
¼ teaspoon ground cumin
1 tablespoon lime juice
   Salt and black pepper
   Crème fraîche for garnish

FRIED FISH AND ARUGULA SANDWICHES WITH BALSAMIC MAYONNAISE

Cornmeal-coated fish fillets, tangy arugula, and homemade mayonnaise put these fried fish sandwiches in a class of their own.

Balsamic Mayonnaise

1 tablespoon balsamic vinegar
1 egg yolk
½ teaspoon dry mustard
  Salt and black pepper
¾ cup olive oil

3½ cups loosely packed arugula
3 tablespoons flour
3 tablespoons yellow cornmeal
  Salt and black pepper
1 pound perch or other lean, white fish
  fillets
¼ cup oil
4 large hard rolls

Preparation: *For the mayonnaise,* whisk or beat together the vinegar, egg yolk, mustard, ¼ teaspoon salt, and pepper to taste. Add the oil, very slowly at first, whisking or beating with an electric mixer continuously. Adjust the seasoning if necessary.

Trim, wash, and dry the arugula. In a shallow dish, combine the flour, cornmeal, and salt and pepper to taste. Cut the fish into 8 pieces.

Cooking: Dip the fish into the flour mixture to coat completely; then shake off any excess. In a frying pan, heat the oil. Fry the fish over medium-high heat, turning once, until golden brown and just cooked through, about 5 minutes altogether.

SERVING: Cut the rolls in half and make a sandwich with the fish, mayonnaise, and arugula.

YIELD: 4 servings

CAFÉ FANNY BASIL SANDWICHES

This delicious vegetable sandwich from Alice Waters, of Chez Panisse and the newer Café Fanny in Berkeley, uses flavorful basil as you normally use lettuce on a sandwich.

  Anchovies (optional)
1 red or yellow bell pepper
1 clove garlic
  Olive oil for frying and tossing
1 large eggplant or 3 small Oriental
    eggplants
  Salt and black pepper

Preparation: If using anchovies, soak them in milk for 15 minutes and then rinse. Over a glass flame or under the broiler, roast the pepper until the skin is black and blistered. Peel, seed, and cut it into quarters. Mince the garlic. Toss the bell pepper with the garlic and a little oil.

Cut the eggplant into ¼-inch-thick slices. In a frying

Salmon Sauté with Corn and Sugar Snap Peas

Pork Tenderloin Sauté with Apples and Plums

Skewered Portuguese Scallops

Veal Sausage with Greens

Focaccia with Herbed Oil and Roasted Garlic

pan, heat a thin layer of oil. Add the eggplant and sauté until browned. Add salt and pepper to taste and cool.

Slice the tomatoes. Split the baguette. Cover both sides of the baguette with eggplant slices. Do not overlap. Lay the tomatoes on 1 side of the baguette, season lightly with salt, and top with the basil leaves. Lay the prosciutto slices along the other side, and top with the roasted pepper. Add anchovy fillets if desired and close the sandwich.

2 ripe tomatoes
1 long, thin loaf French bread (baguette)
1 small bunch sweet basil leaves
4 slices prosciutto

SERVING: Slice into 4 portions.

YIELD: 4 servings

HAM, LEEK, AND BRIE SANDWICHES

This elegant "grilled cheese" sandwich layers smoked ham, glazed leeks, and melting Brie.

Preparation: Halve the leeks lengthwise. Trim off the root end from each leek and all but 2 inches of the green part. Clean thoroughly under cool running water. Cut the leeks crosswise into ⅛-inch-thick slices.

In a frying pan, melt 2 tablespoons of the butter. Add the leeks and season with salt and pepper. Sauté until the leeks just begin to turn golden. Add ¾ cup water and simmer over medium heat until the leeks are tender and the water has evaporated, about 10 minutes. Remove from the heat.

Cut the Brie into thin slices. Layer 4 slices of the bread with half of the cheese; then add the ham and spread with the sautéed leeks. Top with the remaining cheese and bread slices.

3 medium-sized leeks
4 tablespoons unsalted butter
* Salt and black pepper*
½ pound Brie
8 slices Pear Bread (page 196) or whole-wheat bread
⅓ pound smoked ham, sliced thin

Cooking: Using the remaining 2 tablespoons of butter, cook the sandwiches in a frying pan over medium heat until the bread is golden brown and the cheese has melted, about 2 minutes per side.

YIELD: 4 servings

BLACK PEPPER BATTER BREAD

This is a batter bread: it's beaten rather than kneaded. We love the bite of coarse-ground pepper, but it can be omitted, or another spice or almost any herb substituted.

6 tablespoons unsalted butter
1 package active dry yeast
2½ teaspoons sugar
¼ cup warm water
2 eggs, room temperature
½ cup milk, room temperature
1 teaspoon salt
1½ teaspoons coarse pepper
2½ to 2¾ cups flour

Preparation and Cooking: Melt the butter and let it cool. In a large mixing bowl, dissolve the yeast and ½ teaspoon of the sugar in the warm water. Let stand until bubbly, 5 to 10 minutes. Blend in the butter, eggs, milk, remaining 2 teaspoons of sugar, salt, and pepper. Add 2 cups of the flour and beat for 4 minutes at medium speed with an electric mixer or 400 vigorous hand strokes. At low speed or by hand, beat in enough of the remaining flour to make a smooth, thick, and quite sticky batter. Cover the bowl with plastic wrap and let the dough rise in a warm place until doubled in bulk, 1 to 1½ hours.

Generously butter two 6-cup loaf pans. Stir down the risen batter and pour it into the pans, filling slightly less than half full. Cover with buttered plastic wrap and let rise in a warm place until doubled in bulk, about 1 hour.

Heat the oven to 375°F. Bake the breads in the center of the preheated oven until golden brown and a cake tester inserted in the center comes out clean, 30 to 35 minutes. Turn out onto a wire rack. Cool completely before attempting to slice.

YIELD: 2 loaves

CRUSTY WHITE BREAD

Misting the loaves with water before cooking gives this honest loaf a good, chewy crust.

1⅓ cups warm water
1 package active dry yeast
3 to 3½ cups bread flour
1½ teaspoons salt

Preparation and Cooking: Put the warm water in a large bowl, stir in the yeast, and let stand for 5 to 10 minutes. Beat in 1½ cups of the flour and the salt to make a smooth batter. Gradually add enough of the remaining flour to make a soft dough.

Knead dough on a lightly floured work surface until smooth and elastic, about 12 to 15 minutes. Put the dough into a buttered bowl and turn to coat the entire surface. Cover with a damp towel and let rise until doubled in bulk, about 1 to 1½ hours. Deflate the dough and let rise again until doubled in bulk, about 1 hour.

Deflate the dough and divide it into two portions. Put the dough on a floured work surface, cover with a damp towel, and let rest for 10 minutes. Butter a baking sheet.

Roll each piece of dough into a rectangle about 9-by-14 inches. Tightly roll up each rectangle lengthwise and put the dough, seam side down, on the prepared pan. Make ½-inch-deep diagonal slashes at 1-inch intervals along the length of the loaves. Cover with a damp towel and let rise until doubled in bulk, about 1 hour.

Heat the oven to 450°F. Use an atomizer to mist the loaves lightly with cold water. Bake the loaves until well browned and crusty, 25 to 30 minutes. Remove from the oven and cool on racks.

YIELD: 2 loaves

PEAR BREAD

Fresh pears, dried pears, and pear juice all contribute to the unique flavor of this bread.

1 cup dried pears
¼ cup honey
2 cups lukewarm pear juice
1 package active dry yeast
5 cups unbleached bread flour
4 tablespoons unsalted butter
2 firm ripe pears
4 teaspoons salt
2 cups whole-wheat flour
1 egg
Cornmeal for dusting

Preparation and Cooking: Soften the dried pears in boiling water to cover for 1 hour. When soft, drain and chop the pears. Put the honey in a large mixing bowl and stir in the warm pear juice. Add the yeast and 3 cups of the bread flour, 1 cup at a time, beating well after each addition. Whip 100 strokes to incorporate a lot of air. The mixture should look spongy. Cover the bowl well with a warm, damp towel or plastic wrap and set aside at slightly cool room temperature, for 45 minutes to 2 hours.

Bring the butter to room temperature or soften in a microwave. Puree the fresh pears; you should have ½ cup. Fold into the dough along with the softened butter, salt, chopped dried pears, whole-wheat flour, and all but ½ cup of the remaining bread flour. Continue folding until the dough holds together and no longer sticks to the side of the bowl. The dough will look somewhat ragged.

Transfer the dough to a floured work surface and knead, incorporating the extra flour little by little. Continue kneading until the dough becomes smooth and elastic and an indentation made with a finger vanishes rapidly.

Butter or oil a bowl and put the dough into it. Turn the dough over, making sure all surfaces are coated. Cover the bowl with a warm, damp towel or plastic wrap and set aside until doubled in size and an indentation made with a finger remains, 1½ to 2 hours.

Punch down the dough to release all air. Set aside again until doubled in volume and an indentation made with a finger remains, about 1 hour.

Punch the dough down again and remove from the bowl. Knead it a little to release all air, divide the dough in half, and set aside for 5 minutes.

Butter two 6-cup loaf pans. Shape the loaves and turn into prepared pans, seam side down. Press the dough firmly into the corners and bottoms of the pans. Cover the pans with warm, damp towels to prevent skins from forming on the loaves and set aside to rise until the center of each loaf is level with the top of the pan, 45 to 60 minutes.

Beat the egg with 1 teaspoon water to combine. Using a sharp knife or razor, slash the top of each loaf decoratively with shallow slits. Brush with the egg glaze and sprinkle lightly with cornmeal.

Heat the oven to 350°F. Bake the loaves in the preheated oven until deep golden, 35 to 40 minutes. Tapping the bottom of a loaf should produce a hollow sound. Cool on wire racks.

YIELD: 2 loaves

PEAR PICADILLO SANDWICHES

An unusual variant of the spicy beef mixture known as picadillo is used
in these Mexican-style sandwiches.

⅓ cup almonds or *pine nuts*
1 onion
1 clove garlic
1 ripe tomato
1 firm ripe pear
3 whole canned green chiles
1 tablespoon unsalted butter
1 pound lean ground chuck
1 teaspoon salt
¼ teaspoon ground cinnamon
    Pinch of ground cloves
¼ teaspoon sugar
¼ teaspoon ground cumin
⅛ teaspoon cayenne
½ teaspoon dried oregano
1 teaspoon pure chili powder
1 tablespoon red wine vinegar
¼ cup raisins
8 slices Pear Bread (page 196) or 8 flour
    tortillas

Preparation: Heat the oven to 325°F. Toast the almonds or pine nuts until golden brown, 5 to 10 minutes. Chop the almonds.

Chop the onion. Mince the garlic. Peel and core the tomato and pear. In a food processor or by hand, chop together the tomato, pear, and chiles.

Cooking: In a large frying pan, melt the butter. Sauté the onion over medium-high heat for about 3 minutes. Add the garlic and sauté for about 1 minute. Remove from the pan and set aside. In the same frying pan, cook the ground chuck until it loses its red color, about 5 minutes. Add the onion and garlic, chopped tomato, pear, and chiles, salt, cinnamon, cloves, sugar, cumin, cayenne, oregano, chili powder, vinegar, and raisins. Stir to combine well. Simmer over low heat for about 20 minutes. Adjust the seasoning if necessary.

If using tortillas, wrap in aluminum foil and warm in a 350°F oven for about 10 minutes.

SERVING: Put about ½ cup of the picadillo on 4 of the bread slices or down the center of each tortilla. Sprinkle with the nuts. Top with a second slice of bread or fold the tortillas over.

YIELD: 4 servings

MENUS

Mixed Greens with Curried Clams (page 65)

——

Ham, Leek, and Brie Sandwiches (page 193)

Alsace Riesling, such as Trimbach

Pear and Cinnamon Basil Sorbet (page 228)

Summer Seviche (page 43)

Dry white Graves, such as Château Olivier

Steak and Wilted Watercress Sandwiches (page 189)

Pomerol, such as Château Petit-Villages

Tropical Coconut–Papaya Soup (page 236)

Salad Sandwiches (page 190)

——

Pumpkin and Bean Stew (page 109)

Dolcetto d'Alba

Sliced Mangoes

Late-Harvest Riesling, such as Firestone

CHAPTER 11

BREAKFAST AND BRUNCH

Smoked Cheese and Meat Strata
Eggs and Fried Green Tomatoes with Red Tomato Sauce
Rhode Island Johnnycakes · *Apple Omelet*
Eggs with Mushrooms and Almonds · *Venison Hash*
Chicken Pot Pie · *American Breakfast Sausage*
Herbed Cheese Biscuits · *Blueberry–Corn Muffins* · *Saffron Coffeecake*
Popovers · *Maine Buckwheat Pancakes*
Honey–Oat Waffles with Raspberries and Cream

B reakfast and brunch are the most practical of meals. Because they're eaten shortly after rising, the dishes must be either prepared nearly entirely ahead of time or made quickly at the last moment. Unusual ideas like our Smoked Cheese and Meat Strata or updates like the tarragon-sparked Chicken Pot Pie can be assembled the day before and baked when ready to eat in the morning. More typical breakfast foods, especially quick breads such as biscuits, muffins, and pancakes (we include two traditional regional versions of pancakes), are whipped up and cooked in minutes. For some dishes, our Apple Omelet, for one, part of the recipe can be made in advance, in this case the apple filling. Later, the eggs themselves are cooked in just moments.

In part because the lack of time before the brunch hour dictates simplicity, it's an increasingly popular meal for entertaining. Besides being easy, traditional breakfast and brunch foods are generally inexpensive, too. Weekend guests have long been an impetus for the development of interesting breakfast dishes, and now that Sunday is the only day that many of us have time for entertaining, the brunch phenomenon has elicited even more recipes to start the day. In truth you can find appropriate recipes anywhere and needn't be restricted to typical breakfast foods. All the chapters in this book will yield ideas. Why not serve the Lobster–Grapefruit Salad (page 42) or Green and White Ravioli in Broth (page 135).

A hot soup is an ideal morning refreshment, as is a warm, sweet soup, such as the Banana–Caramel Soup or Ruby Pear Soup from the "Light Desserts" chapter. And from "Lavish Desserts," the Pastry Cornucopia filled with fruit and nuts would be ideal. The only rule is that people usually prefer to avoid quantities of strong ingredients, such as garlic or onions, first thing in the morning.

With that one rule, and practicality, in mind, you can hardly go wrong in your choices. Be sure to try our brunch drink suggestions in this chapter, too. Just the novelty of eating and drinking well early in the day sets a morning gathering off on the right track.

Brunch Drinks

Bloody Marys and screwdrivers are probably the most common brunch drinks, with mimosas (champagne and orange juice) a close third. Here are some suggestions for variations and for new libations:

Tequila with tomato juice and a tiny dice (⅛ inch) of vegetables (such as bell pepper, shallot, or a bit of jalapeño pepper)

Cranberry and orange juices with vodka or rum

Rum mixed with 1 part canned or bottled sweetened cream of coconut, 2 parts fresh berry puree (such as strawberry, raspberry, blackberry, or currant), strained if needed, and 2 parts water

Concord grape juice and dry vermouth

Pernod and sparkling water over ice

Warm cider laced with Southern Comfort

Tea and liqueur or brandy (such as Chartreuse, apple brandy, or crème de cassis) with warm milk

Coffee and liqueur, brandy, or hard liquor (such as Kahlua, bourbon, or B & B) with warm milk

Popovers

The golden, airy balloons known as popovers have been around since at least the early nineteenth century. Made simply from eggs, milk, flour, and butter, they are related to Britain's Yorkshire pudding but undeniably an American invention.

It takes only a few minutes to whip together the batter. The one essential guideline is to avoid overbeating. A whisk, rotary beater, electric mixer, or fork can be used for beating, or the batter can be made in a blender in a few seconds. (Making the batter in a food processor is likely to result in an overbeaten mixture.) The batter can be made ahead of time, and some cooks believe it is better prepared in advance.

While early cookbooks insisted that popovers be made only in cast-iron pans, heavy aluminum popover pans or individual earthenware custard cups produce results just as good. Most important is to use cups that are deeper than they are wide, and to preheat them.

Popovers "pop" because of the high proportion of liquid in the batter, which creates steam during baking. As the exterior surface of the batter sets far more quickly in the hot oven than does the interior, steam builds up rapidly and causes the muffin to puff up and pop over the edge of the pan.

SMOKED CHEESE AND MEAT STRATA

An ideal entertaining dish, the Italian strata can be prepared in advance and just popped into the oven an hour before brunch.

1/4 pound bacon
1/2 pound smoked ham
 8 slices white bread
1/4 cup minced fresh chives
1/2 pound smoked mozzarella cheese
1/4 pound Monterey Jack cheese
 4 eggs
1 1/2 cups milk
1/4 teaspoon coarse black pepper
1/2 teaspoon salt
 2 tablespoons unsalted butter

Preparation: Cut the bacon into 1/2-inch pieces. Cook until golden, about 4 minutes. Remove with a slotted spoon and set aside 3 tablespoons of the drippings. Brush a 1 1/2-quart soufflé dish or 4 8-ounce dishes with some of the reserved bacon drippings.

Cut the ham into 1/2-inch cubes; toss with bacon. Trim the crust off the bread and cut the bread into 1/2-inch cubes. Mince the chives. Grate the cheeses and toss them together. Whisk together the eggs, milk, pepper, and salt.

Layer the prepared soufflé dish(es) with one third of the bread cubes, then half of the bacon and ham, half of the chives, and top with one third of the cheese. Pour about half of the egg-milk mixture over the layers. Drizzle with some of the bacon fat. Repeat the layering again, using half of the remaining bread, the rest of the meats, half the remaining cheeses, the rest of the chives, and some bacon drippings. Pour the remaining milk mixture into dish(es). Top with the remaining bread cubes and cheese. Drizzle with the remaining bacon drippings and dot with the butter. The strata can be assembled a day before cooking, covered, and refrigerated.

Cooking: Heat the oven to 350°F. Place the dish(es) in a large pan and add 1 to 1 1/2 inches of boiling water to the pan. Bake in the preheated oven until the top is golden brown, about 1 hour for the 1 1/2-quart dish, 45 minutes for the 8-ounce dishes.

YIELD: 4 servings

EGGS AND FRIED GREEN TOMATOES WITH RED TOMATO SAUCE

Green tomatoes are sautéed and topped with a fresh red tomato sauce. Serve them with fried or scrambled eggs for a simple, satisfying brunch.

¾ cup Tomato Sauce (recipe follows)
 1 ounce prosciutto
 1 large green tomato
 1 tablespoon unsalted butter, plus more if
    necessary
 2 tablespoons flour
   Salt and black pepper
 9 eggs
¼ cup dry bread crumbs

Preparation: Make the tomato sauce. Cut the prosciutto into ½-inch squares. Core and seed the tomato and cut it into 4 slices.

In a frying pan, sauté the prosciutto in the 1 tablespoon of butter over medium heat until golden brown and crisp, about 2 minutes. Remove with a slotted spoon. Set aside the pan and drippings.

In a shallow dish, combine the flour with the salt and pepper. Beat 1 of the eggs in a small bowl. Pat the tomato slices dry with paper towels. Dredge in the flour and shake off the excess. Dip in the egg and then into the bread crumbs.

Cooking: Reheat the tomato sauce. Heat the reserved pan drippings. Sauté the tomato slices over medium heat, adding more butter if necessary, until the tomatoes are golden, about 10 minutes. Meanwhile, fry or scramble the remaining eggs in another frying pan.

SERVING: Spoon the tomato sauce over half of each plate. Top with green tomato slices and put the eggs alongside. Sprinkle tomatoes with prosciutto.

YIELD: 4 servings

TOMATO SAUCE

Preparation: Chop the onion. Peel, seed, and chop the tomatoes. Mince the basil.

In a frying pan, melt the butter. Add the onion and sauté over medium heat until it is softened, about 4 minutes. If using dried basil, add it at this point. Add the wine and cook for about 1 minute. Add the chopped tomatoes and salt and pepper to taste. Simmer over medium-low heat for about 2 minutes. Add the minced fresh basil if using and simmer until slightly thickened and reduced, about 3 minutes.

YIELD: about ¾ cup

½ small onion
½ pound ripe tomatoes
2 teaspoons minced fresh basil leaves or ½ teaspoon dried basil
1 tablespoon unsalted butter
1 tablespoon dry red or white wine
Salt and black pepper

RHODE ISLAND JOHNNYCAKES

White cornmeal is used in the authentic version of this regional dish. We confess to having made johnnycakes with yellow cornmeal and find they taste the same, but any real Rhode Islander would disdain yellow johnnycakes.

Preparation: In a large bowl, combine the cornmeal, salt, and sugar. Add the boiling water and mix well. The batter should be thick, but if you prefer thinner cakes, add more boiling water. Set aside for 30 minutes.

1 cup white cornmeal, preferably stoneground
1 teaspoon salt
1 teaspoon sugar
1½ cups boiling water

Bacon fat for frying
Unsalted butter and maple syrup for serving

Cooking: Grease a large frying pan or griddle with bacon fat and heat to medium-low. Drop the batter by tablespoons onto the pan or griddle. Cook until the bottom is golden brown, about 6 minutes. Turn and cook until second side is golden brown, about 5 minutes. Repeat with the remaining batter.

SERVING: Serve hot with butter and maple syrup.

YIELD: 4 to 6 servings

APPLE OMELET

An omelet can, in fact must, be cooked in seconds. This sweet omelet, filled with a tasty mixture of apples, lemon juice, brown sugar, applejack, and cream, and emblazoned with a crosshatch design, is elegant simplicity. We've included complete directions for making a perfect omelet. You can follow them to make any type of omelet, sweet or savory, with your own choice of filling.

Apple Filling

> 1 large apple
> ¾ to 1 teaspoon lemon juice
> 4 teaspoons unsalted butter
> 2 tablespoons dark-brown sugar
> 2 tablespoons applejack
> 2 teaspoons heavy cream
> ⅓ teaspoon grated lemon zest

Omelets

> 8 eggs
> 3 tablespoons applejack
> 3 tablespoons heavy cream
> ¼ teaspoon salt
> 4 tablespoons unsalted butter
> Confectioners' sugar for topping

Preparation: *For the filling,* peel the apple and cut it into ¼-inch-thick slices. In a bowl, toss the apple slices with ¾ teaspoon of the lemon juice.

In a frying pan, melt the butter. Add the apples and cook over medium-high heat for 1 minute, turning once. Stir in the brown sugar. Cook over medium heat until dissolved, 3 to 5 minutes.

Pour the applejack and cream into the pan and cook until the alcohol has evaporated and the sauce is reduced, 3 to 5 minutes. Add the lemon zest and taste for seasoning. Add more lemon juice if necessary.

Cooking: *For the omelets,* in a bowl, beat the eggs until frothy. Stir in the applejack, cream, and salt.

In an omelet pan, heat 1 tablespoon of the butter until foamy. Pour in one quarter of the egg mixture and stir with the flat side of a fork, shaking the pan with your free hand until the eggs form a creamy mass. Grasp the pan handle with your right hand and hit your right arm with the fist of your left hand to slide the eggs toward the edge of the pan.

Put one quarter of the apple filling in the center of the omelet. Using the back of a fork, fold the bottom half of the omelet over the filling. Grasping the pan handle from underneath with your fingers on top of handle, invert the pan toward you to turn the omelet onto a warm plate. Keep warm.

Repeat the procedure to make 3 more omelets.

SERVING: Sprinkle the omelets with confectioners' sugar. If you like, heat a skewer over a burner for a few minutes, and use it to make a crosshatch design on the top of each omelet.

YIELD: 4 omelets

EGGS WITH MUSHROOMS AND ALMONDS

Fairy-ring mushrooms, also known as scotch bonnets, *boutons de guêtre,* or *mousserons,* have a faint almond-like fragrance. James Moore of Mountain Home Inn in Mill Valley, California, developed this recipe to enhance the aroma of the mushrooms, but it makes a delicious dish with other varieties, too, including regular white or brown mushrooms.

6 tablespoons unsalted butter
1 tablespoon minced fresh parsley
Salt and black pepper
¼ pound sliced almonds
1 pound fairy-ring or other mushrooms
8 slices crusty white bread
Unsalted butter for spreading
8 eggs

Preparation: Clarify the 6 tablespoons of butter: Heat it gently in a small pan, skim off the foam on top, and pour the clear butter into a frying pan. Discard the milky liquid at the bottom. Mince the parsley. Heat the clarified butter in the frying pan with a pinch of salt.

Add the almonds and cook until browned, about 5 minutes. Remove the almonds with a slotted spoon.

Add the mushrooms to the pan and sauté over high heat until they begin to brown, 3 to 5 minutes. Season with salt and pepper, lower the heat, and cook until tender, about 5 minutes more.

Cooking: Toast and butter the bread. Reheat the mushrooms if necessary. Toss with minced parsley and almonds. Taste for seasoning. Poach, shir, bake, or scramble the eggs.

SERVING: Put the eggs in the center of warm plates, remove the mushrooms from the pan with a slotted spoon, and arrange them around the eggs. Spoon the remaining butter over the eggs and serve with toast.

YIELD: 4 servings

VENISON HASH

Hash is an underrated dish. Here venison makes it especially party worthy, but we've yet to find guests who didn't love this hash made with plain old roast beef or corned beef.

1 medium-sized onion
1 medium-sized carrot
1 small red or green bell pepper
1 rib celery
1 clove garlic
2 tablespoons minced fresh parsley
2 teaspoons minced fresh thyme leaves or
   ½ teaspoon dried thyme
1 teaspoon minced fresh rosemary leaves or
   ¼ teaspoon dried rosemary
1 pound cooked venison
2 baking potatoes (about 1 pound in all)
3 tablespoons unsalted butter
¼ cup venison or beef stock or juices from
   venison roast
⅛ teaspoon grated nutmeg
½ teaspoon hot red pepper sauce
   Salt and black pepper
2 tablespoons oil
4 poached eggs (recipe follows)

Preparation: Chop the onion, carrot, bell pepper, and celery. Mince the garlic, parsley, and thyme and rosemary if using fresh. Cut the venison into ½-inch dice. Peel the potatoes and cut them in half.

Cook potatoes in boiling salted water until tender, 10 to 12 minutes. Drain and cut into ½-inch dice.

In a heavy frying pan, sauté the onion, carrot, bell pepper, celery, and garlic in 2 tablespoons of the butter over medium heat, stirring often, until the vegetables are softened but not browned, about 5 minutes.

In a large mixing bowl, gently but thoroughly combine the sautéed mixture with the potatoes, venison, parsley, stock, nutmeg, thyme, rosemary, and ¼ teaspoon of the hot red pepper sauce. Season with salt and pepper to taste.

Cooking: In a large frying pan, heat the remaining tablespoon of butter and the oil. Add the hash and press evenly into the pan with a spatula. Cook, uncovered, over medium heat until a crust forms on the bottom, 7 to 10 minutes. Flip the hash or turn carefully with 2 spatulas. Or you can invert the hash onto a plate that has been filmed with oil and then slide it back into the pan. Continue to cook until crusty brown on second side. Meanwhile, poach the eggs.

SERVING: Cut the hash into 4 wedges and top each with a poached egg. Sprinkle each egg with a few drops of hot red pepper sauce.

YIELD: 4 servings

POACHED EGGS

Preparation: Break eggs into individual cups.

4 eggs
1½ to 2 quarts water
2 tablespoons vinegar

Cooking: In a large saucepan, bring the water to a boil and add the vinegar. Lower the heat so that the water barely simmers. With a wooden spoon, swirl the water in a circle and slide 1 egg into the vortex. Repeat with the other eggs, maintaining a low simmer. Keep the water moving slightly by shaking the handle gently, in order to prevent the eggs from sticking to the pan. Once the whites have set, the eggs will no longer be in danger of sticking. Simmer the eggs for 3 to 4 minutes.

Lift the eggs with a slotted spoon to test for doneness. The white should be opaque and firm, the yolk soft to the touch.

SERVING: Serve immediately or transfer the cooked eggs to a bowl of cold water to stop the cooking process and reheat in hot water when needed.

YIELD: 4 servings

CHICKEN POT PIE

This old favorite, updated by noted food writer Miriam Ungerer, is made even better by the addition of tarragon. Using all thigh meat avoids the problem of choosing between two negatives—overcooked light meat or undercooked dark meat. Or use all chicken breast if you prefer.

Short Crust (recipe follows)
½ ounce dried chanterelles
2 tablespoons minced fresh parsley
*1 tablespoon minced fresh tarragon
     leaves or 1 teaspoon dried tarragon*
2 shallots
6 to 8 scallions
8 large fresh mushrooms
1 cup baby carrots or 1 carrot
*9 tablespoons unsalted butter, plus
     more if necessary*
1 cup tiny green peas, fresh or frozen
*12 chicken thighs
     (about 4½ pounds in all)*
Salt and black pepper
*3 tablespoons flour, plus more for
     rolling*
3 cups Chicken Stock (page 81)
½ cup heavy cream
*1 heaping tablespoon cornstarch if
     necessary*
*1 egg yolk beaten with 1 teaspoon
     water (optional)*

Preparation: Make the crust. Reconstitute the dried mushrooms in warm water to cover. Strain the mushrooms, reserving the soaking liquid, and chop. Mince the parsley, tarragon, and shallots. Cut the scallions into ½-inch lengths. Slice the fresh mushrooms. Slice the carrot if using a large one. Cook the carrot(s), uncovered, over medium heat in 1 tablespoon of the butter and 3 tablespoons of water until tender, about 8 minutes. If using fresh peas, blanch them in boiling water for 30 seconds.

Remove the bones and skin from the chicken. Cut the thighs in half. Season the chicken with salt and pepper, roll in the flour, and shake off any excess.

In a large frying pan, sauté the chicken in the remaining 8 tablespoons of butter over medium heat until just colored, turning often, about 10 minutes. Add the shallots and fresh mushrooms and fry gently for a few minutes, stirring. Remove the mixture from the pan with a slotted spoon. Stir in the 3 tablespoons of flour, adding more butter if needed to absorb it, and cook for 3 minutes. Pour in the stock and stir over medium heat until smooth. Add the dried mushrooms, reserved soaking liquid, and cream.

Return the chicken-mushroom mixture to the sauce. Add the carrots, peas, parsley, tarragon, and scallions. If the sauce seems too thin, mix together a thick paste of cold water and cornstarch. Stir into the very center of the mixture over medium-low heat, using only enough of the paste to achieve a good consistency. Pour the chicken and vegetables into a deep pie pan or shallow soufflé dish, filling it to within ½ inch of the rim.

On a floured work surface, roll out the pastry to about a ⅛-inch thickness and center it over the pie. Flute the edges over the rim of the dish. If you want a glossy crust, brush it with the optional egg wash. Cut a few steam vents.

Cooking: Heat the oven to 400°F. Bake in the center of the preheated oven until the crust is golden brown, about 20 minutes.

YIELD: 4 servings

SHORT CRUST

Preparation: Combine the flour and salt in a bowl. Work the lard into the flour with a pastry blender or your fingers until the mixture is the consistency of meal with a few pea-size pieces of lard left. Add just enough cold water to hold the dough together, mixing with a fork. Form the dough into a ball, flatten, and wrap in plastic wrap. Refrigerate for 30 minutes or longer.

1¼ cups flour
1 teaspoon salt
6 tablespoons cold lard or shortening
3 tablespoons (approximately) cold water

YIELD: crust for 1 pot pie

AMERICAN BREAKFAST SAUSAGE

There is no comparison between commercial and homemade sausages, and these juicy, sage-flavored pork sausages, perfected by Chef Judy Rodgers, are easy to prepare. Adjust the seasoning to suit your taste. You might prefer thyme or another herb to the sage. The patties are dredged in flour before frying for a crisp, golden-brown crust.

*5 pounds boneless pork butt with about 30
    percent fat content*
2 large cloves garlic
20 large fresh sage leaves or *2 teaspoons
    dried sage*
4 teaspoons coarse salt
2 tablespoons coarse black pepper or *more
    to taste*
*2 teaspoons crushed dried hot red pepper
    or more to taste*
Flour for coating
Unsalted butter for frying

Preparation: Cut the pork into chunks. Grind using a plate with ¼- or ⅜-inch holes. Chop the garlic. Chop the sage if using fresh.

Combine the ground pork with the salt, garlic, sage, black pepper, and hot pepper. Panfry a small patty, taste, and adjust the seasoning with salt and pepper. Refrigerate for at least 30 minutes.

Cooking: Shape the mixture into small patties. Flour lightly. Over medium heat, melt enough butter in a frying pan to film the bottom of the pan and fry the patties until they just lose their pink color, about 4 minutes per side.

YIELD: about 5 pounds sausage meat

HERBED CHEESE BISCUITS

These flaky baking powder biscuits are enhanced with Monterey Jack cheese and coriander, a formula that can be varied at will. Include just the cheese or just the herb, or try another combination such as mozzarella and basil, cheddar and parsley, or chèvre and rosemary.

*1 tablespoon minced fresh coriander leaves
    or other herb*
4 ounces butter
3 ounces Montery Jack or *other cheese
    (about ½ cup grated)*
1½ cups flour

Preparation: Mince the coriander and cut the cold butter into 8 pieces. In a food processor, shred the cheese. Distribute pieces of butter around bowl of processor, and whir just to combine. Add flour, baking powder, salt, and coriander and whir just until butter is incorporated into dry ingredients and mixture resembles large crumbs. Add the milk and whir until the dough begins to clump together.

Turn the dough out onto a lightly floured surface, knead 2 or 3 times to form a ball, and pat or roll to a ¾-inch thickness. Cut the dough into rounds, using a floured 1½- or 2-inch biscuit cutter. Put on an ungreased baking sheet and refrigerate if not baking immediately.

Cooking: Heat the oven to 425°F. Bake the biscuits until golden, 12 to 15 minutes.

YIELD: about 2 dozen biscuits

1½ teaspoons baking powder
½ teaspoon salt
¼ cup milk

BLUEBERRY–CORN MUFFINS

Two traditional muffins, blueberry and corn, are combined here for double the pleasure.

Preparation and Cooking: Heat the oven to 425°F. Butter and flour 2-inch muffin tins. Melt the butter. In a mixing bowl, sift together the cornmeal, flour, sugar, baking powder, and salt. Make a well in the center.

In another bowl, beat together the eggs and milk. Pour the egg mixture and melted butter into the well and stir just enough to combine. Fold in the blueberries.

Fill the prepared muffin tins two-thirds full. Bake in the preheated oven until a toothpick inserted into the center of a muffin comes out dry, 15 to 20 minutes. Serve immediately or cool on a wire rack.

YIELD: 16 to 18 muffins

4 tablespoons unsalted butter
1 cup cornmeal, preferably stoneground
1½ cups flour
⅓ cup sugar
4 teaspoons baking powder
½ teaspoon salt
2 eggs
1½ cups milk
¾ cup blueberries, fresh or frozen

SAFFRON COFFEECAKE

Saffron adds a distinctive taste to this coffeecake, which is further enhanced by the flavor of oranges.

½ pound butter
1 cup blanched almonds
¾ teaspoon saffron threads
2 teaspoons grated orange zest
2 packages active dry yeast
½ cup milk
4½ to 5 cups flour
1¾ teaspoons salt
1 cup sugar
4 teaspoons orange-flower water
   (optional)
3 large eggs
Confectioners' sugar for sprinkling

Preparation: Bring butter to room temperature or soften it in a microwave oven. Heat the oven to 325°F. Toast the almonds until golden, 5 to 10 minutes; then chop them. Toast the saffron threads for 4 minutes and then powder them. Grate the orange zest.

Combine the yeast with ½ cup of warm water. In a saucepan, warm the milk to tepid and add the saffron powder. Remove from the heat and steep for 10 minutes.

In a large bowl, combine the flour, salt, and ⅔ cup of the sugar. Add the yeast and milk-saffron mixture. Beat for 1 minute. Add the orange-flower water, if using, and zest. Beat in the eggs 1 at a time. Add the butter and beat with a wooden spoon or with the dough hook of a heavy-duty mixer until smooth and elastic, about 5 minutes. The dough will be somewhat soft, and some pieces of butter will still be visible. Transfer to a large, buttered bowl, cover, and let rise in a warm place until almost doubled in volume, 1½ to 2 hours.

Butter a 10-cup ring mold and sprinkle it with ¼ cup of the almonds. On a floured board, roll the dough into a 12- by 14-inch rectangle. Sprinkle the remaining ⅓ cup of sugar and ¾ cup of the almonds over the dough and roll it up. Place seam-side down in the mold and pinch the two ends together to seal. Cover and allow to rise until it is light and almost fills the mold, 1 to 2 hours.

Cooking: Heat the oven to 375°F. Bake in the preheated oven until golden, 50 to 60 minutes. Turn out onto a wire rack.

SERVING: Serve warm or cooled. When ready to serve, sprinkle with confectioners' sugar.

YIELD: 12 servings

POPOVERS

Popovers are light, quickly and easily made, and a good accompaniment to a variety of breakfast and brunch dishes.

Preparation: Melt the butter. Beat all the ingredients together until just smooth, being careful not to over-beat. The batter should be the consistency of heavy cream.

1 tablespoon unsalted butter
1 cup flour
¼ teaspoon salt
1 cup milk
2 eggs

Cooking: Heat the oven to 450°F. Generously oil eight popover pans or 6-ounce custard cups and preheat them. Fill the prepared pans to one-half to two-thirds full. Bake in the preheated oven for 15 minutes. Lower the oven temperature to 350°F without opening the oven door and bake until the popovers are firm and golden brown, 15 to 20 minutes more. Remove from the oven and make a slit in the bottom of each popover to release the steam.

YIELD: 8 popovers

VARIATIONS

Bacon Popovers
Add 4 slices bacon, cooked until crisp and crumbled, to the completed batter.

Whole-Wheat Popovers
Substitute ½ cup whole-wheat flour for ½ cup of the white flour in the popover recipe. Mix the flours together and beat just until smooth with the remaining ingredients.

Sweet Popovers
Reduce the salt in the popover recipe to a pinch and add 2 tablespoons of sugar to the other ingredients.

Orange Popovers
Add 1 teaspoon minced orange zest to the completed Sweet Popover batter (above).

MAINE BUCKWHEAT PANCAKES

Buckwheat pancakes, also called ployes, are served flat, rolled, or folded. Once a Maine staple, they're still likely to show up at any meal, spread with butter and served alongside meat or baked beans, or topped with highbush cranberry jelly or maple syrup at breakfast.

1 cup buckwheat flour
½ cup all-purpose flour
½ teaspoon salt
1¼ to 1½ cups water
1 teaspoon baking powder
Butter and maple syrup for serving (optional)

Preparation and Cooking: Sift both the flours and salt into a large bowl. Beat or whisk in ¾ cup cold water to make a thick batter. Stir in ½ to ¾ cup boiling water to thin batter to a pourable consistency. Add the baking powder and stir until batter becomes slightly bubbly.

Heat an oiled griddle or cast-iron frying pan over medium-high heat. Drop about 2 tablespoons batter per pancake onto griddle or frying pan and cook until pancakes have risen slightly and are full of holes on top, about 2 minutes. Bottoms should be light brown and crisp. Flip and cook another 1 to 2 minutes.

SERVING: Serve with butter and maple syrup if desired.

YIELD: 6 servings

HONEY–OAT WAFFLES WITH RASPBERRIES AND CREAM

Terrific waffles with any topping, they are dressed up here with crushed berries and cream.

Preparation: In a small bowl, crush the berries coarsely with a fork. Squeeze the lemon juice over the berries and stir in ¼ cup of the honey. Bring the cream to room temperature.

In a small, heavy saucepan, bring 1 cup of water to a boil. Stir in the oatmeal, turn the heat to very low, and cook, stirring, until very thick, about 10 minutes. In a small bowl, whisk the eggs until well beaten.

Scrape the oatmeal into a mixing bowl. Stir in buttermilk and remaining ¼ cup of honey. Whisk in the eggs. In a bowl, combine the flour, baking powder, baking soda, and salt, mixing thoroughly.

Cooking: Heat a waffle iron and oil according to the manufacturer's directions. Stir the dry ingredients into the egg mixture until partially combined. Melt the butter and mix it in until the ingredients are just combined. Spoon ½ cup of the batter onto prepared iron and cook until the waffle is crisp and golden brown. Repeat with the remaining batter.

SERVING: Spoon the raspberry sauce over the waffles and top each waffle with a dollop of cream.

YIELD: 4 servings

3½ to 4 cups fresh raspberries
2 tablespoons lemon juice
½ cup honey
1 cup crème fraîche or *clotted cream (Devon cream)*
¼ cup steel-cut oats or *Irish oatmeal*
2 eggs
½ cup buttermilk
1 cup flour
1 teaspoon baking powder
½ teaspoon baking soda
Salt
6 tablespoons unsalted butter

MENUS

Poached Oranges with Anise (page 228)

Eggs and Fried Green Tomatoes with Red   Warm cider with Southern Comfort
   Tomato Sauce (page 204)
American Breakfast Sausage (page 212)
Popovers (page 215)

Eggs with Mushrooms and Almonds   Champagne Rosé
   (page 207)

Saffron Coffeecake (page 214)   Coffee and liqueur

CHAPTER 12

LIGHT DESSERTS

Pistachio Butter Cookies · *Pear and Cinnamon Basil Sorbet*
Poached Oranges with Anise · *Champagne–Cassis Ice*
Cold Grapefruit Soufflé · *Biscoitos de Porto*
Red Raspberry Mousse · *Winter Compote with Raspberry Sauce*
Maple–Walnut Zabaglione · *Cherry Soup with Strawberry Sherbet*
Golden Apricot–Carrot Soup · *Tropical Coconut–Papaya Soup*
Mascarpone with Figs · *Ruby Pear Soup* · *Banana–Caramel Soup*

L ight desserts match the modern meal. With the emphasis on
smaller, lighter dishes and on healthier eating habits in
general, it is only natural that such desserts have gained
popularity in contemporary cuisine. The new American
cooking highlights refreshing sorbets and ices, airy soufflés,
and new ways of presenting both familiar and unusual fruits.

It is not surprising that many of the desserts in this chapter are based
on fruit, for what could be a fresher conclusion to a meal? We have
always loved desserts made from a combination of mostly
unembellished fresh fruits in the summer. Now the idea seems
appropriate year round, especially with the wide variety of tropical and
other previously unknown fruits now on display on American
greengrocers' shelves. Papayas, mangoes, cherimoyas, and more—these
choice fruits can stand on their own or appear in innovative
combinations in the new light desserts.

If the preponderance of fruit in this chapter is not unexpected, there is
also evidence of a more surprising new development: five of our recipes
are for warm dessert soups. Cold fruit soups have appeared on menus
over the past few years, most often as a first course rather than dessert,
and we do include an unusual cold dessert soup. But how often has a

warm soup been presented for dessert? Soup for dessert is simultaneously soothing and exciting. Hot dessert soups combine freshness with the right amount of sweetness to conclude any sort of meal with good flavor and originality. Hot soup has always been appreciated as a first course, and now we find sweet, warm soups to be the perfect finale.

Exotic Fruits

Papayas, mangoes, guavas, cherimoyas, kiwi fruit, starfruit, persimmons, ugli fruit, pear apples, and fresh figs—until recently, many of these were unheard of in the United States. Yet now they are becoming more and more common, not just in gourmet stores in New York City and Los Angeles but in local supermarkets throughout the country as well. Most of these fruits are now grown in the United States, primarily in Hawaii, Florida, and California.

Peeled and attractively cut, both for the sake of presentation and to make eating them easier, the exotic fruits, as well as more common ones, can stand alone as a refreshing dessert. A selection of unusual fresh fruits makes a sophisticated dessert that is not only a natural result of the recent emphasis on fitness and health but an appropriate conclusion to any meal, robust or light.

Papaya

Grown the world over in tropical climates, the papaya is sometimes referred to as a tree melon, which gives a hint of its flavor.

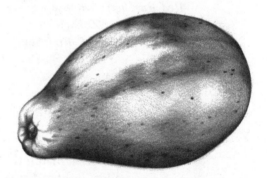

Papayas are at their prime in spring and summer. The skin of the ripe fruit is golden, and the flesh coral colored. A fully ripe papaya is slightly softer than a ripe avocado. Papayas do continue to ripen once picked, and if a soft spot develops, the fruit should be used as soon as possible. A squeeze of lime or lemon juice balances the lush sweetness of the papaya flesh.

Mango

Well-known for their role in Indian chutney, mangoes are also widely grown in Africa, Latin America, and even in Florida. Now available in the United States from mid-winter through the summer, these

tropical fruits can be difficult to eat, but the delicious flesh is worth the trouble. The skin is thin but strong, and cutting the flesh away from the pit can be a struggle. Mangoes are golden red when at their peak, with a deep-orange flesh. Firmer fruits are fine for making chutney or other cooking, but choose soft, fragrant mangoes for eating raw. Avoid any fruit with large black spots, but those with slightly speckled skin should be fine.

Guava

Guavas grow primarily in Asia and Latin America but are now grown in Florida, California, and Hawaii as well. There are several varieties, which range from green to yellow to red, with flesh of any hue from white through dark pink. Slightly underripe guavas should be used for cooking, but soft ones are best for eating raw. The relatively thin skin of the ripe fruit will

give when pressed gently. Guavas can be eaten uncooked complete with seeds, or sliced and served with cream. Be warned that they should be poached with care—overcooking will turn a guava into a creamy paste.

Cherimoya

Cherimoyas are South American natives that reach their peak of flavor when grown on tropic mountains at elevations between 3,000 and 7,000 feet (a fact that may explain their price). They have been successfully cultivated, however, in southern California. Cherimoyas must be handled carefully to avoid bruising; the fruit is so naturally creamy that the cherimoya is also called custard apple or sherbet fruit. The cherimoya tastes somewhat like a combination of the flavors of pear, pineapple, and banana, with a hint of lemon-lime. Ripe cherimoyas have yellow-green skin and yield to gentle pressure; firmer ones with a light-green color will ripen in a few days at room temperature. The skin is tender despite its leathery appearance. The smooth black seeds aren't eaten, but they are easily separated from the creamy flesh.

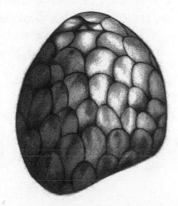

Kiwi

Almost unknown until a few years ago, the kiwi fruit has gained notoriety for its all-too-frequent appearance in nouvelle cuisine. Still, to dismiss it because of this would be unfair. The oval fruit, with furry brown skin, is bright green inside and tastes like a cross between a strawberry and a banana.

Starfruit

Starfruit, or carambola, is a waxy-skinned, yellowish-green fruit native to India and grown in Hawaii, California, and, increasingly, in Florida. The thin, oval fruit is deeply lobed so that slicing it produces star-shaped cross sections—hence its name. Starfruit ranges in taste from tart to sweet. The fruit is best purchased slightly underripe, when the skin is firm and shiny and still tinged with green, and allowed to

ripen at room temperature. Fully ripe, it is a translucent yellow; it can then be stored in plastic bags in the refrigerator for several days.

Persimmon

Excellent persimmons grow in the United States, but the Oriental persimmon is sometimes preferred as it tends to be larger and to have fewer seeds. The fruit has a shiny reddish-orange skin when ripe and is slightly soft. Persimmons bruise easily, so choose them carefully. They also are extremely astringent when underripe; a slightly firm persimmon will ripen in a few days at room temperature. Once the fruit is ripe, use it as soon as possible or store it in the refrigerator for a day or two.

Ugli Fruit

The ugli fruit, a cross between the grapefruit and the tangerine, has been around only since 1915 when it was hybridized in Jamaica. The fruit is slightly pear-shaped, with thick, bumpy skin and a mottled greenish-yellow color. It is aptly named, but the pinkish-golden flesh is juicy and somewhat sweeter than that of a grape-

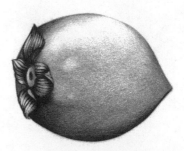

of which the most popular is the type known as Twentieth Century. Pear apples are generally yellow-green in color, and the yellower ones are the sweetest. The fruit can be kept in a cold place for up to three months. They are perhaps most delicious when raw, although they are also good when cooked with such compatible flavorings as lemon and ginger.

fruit. Ugli fruit are at their best in the spring. They have relatively few seeds and can be substituted for grapefruit in any recipe or fruit combination.

Fig

While dried figs have long been available year round in this country, fresh ones are relatively recent additions to the marketplace. Figs are grown in California as well as Asia, India, and, primarily, the Mediterranean countries, but the fact that they are extremely perishable limits their availability and increases their price. Fresh figs can be black, purple, yellow-brown, or pale green, and are found here from late spring through early fall. Ripe ones are plump and slightly soft to the touch; the flesh will be pink and juicy. Those that seem about to burst or have any hint of a fermented smell should be avoided.

Pear Apple

Pear apples, otherwise known as Asian pears or apple pears, offer an uncanny combination of the juicy sweetness of a ripe pear and the crisp crunch of an apple. Theoretically the pear apple tree will grow wherever apples thrive, but so far these fruits are relatively uncommon. Many Oriental markets feature several varieties,

Apples and Pears

The increasing popularity of more exotic fruits is unlikely to affect the market for apples and pears, long-time American favorites. If anything, the demand for a wider variety of better-quality fruits has also brought attention to these familiar fruits, and a greater selection of tastier apples and pears has become available, too.

Apples

The all-American apple is not, in fact, native to the United States, but was introduced to this country by missionaries and traders during the seventeenth century. By now, there are more than 500 varieties of apples grown here, with new strains still being developed. Apples can be divided generally into cooking and eating apples although many varieties are versatile enough to be all-purpose.

Although harvest time for all apples extends only from late summer through early winter, modern storage methods have extended the buying season. However, the apples available from spring through midsummer are likely to be mealy or to have little flavor. Apples should be stored in a cool, dry place, ideally between 32° and 40°F. Be sure the apples you have chosen are firm and unblemished, for the proverbial bad apple can indeed ruin your whole bag.

CORTLAND

The Cortland is a red-skinned apple with a slightly tart, snow-white flesh. Available beginning in the early fall, it is a good all-purpose apple, particularly as its flesh does not darken as quickly as others'.

EMPIRE

Also harvested in the early fall, the Empire apple is a new variety that is a cross between a McIntosh and a Red Delicious. It has a shiny red skin and is slightly tart, making it a good eating and general cooking apple.

DELICIOUS

The juicy Golden Delicious, available early in the fall, is one of our sweetest apples; unlike the Red Delicious, it holds its shape in cooking, making it a good general-purpose variety. The Red Delicious, also harvested in the early fall, is probably the most familiar of apples, with its bright red skin, tapered shape, and sweet yellow flesh. It is an eating apple and is the variety most likely to be available year round; still, like all apples, it will hardly be at its best in the spring and summer.

GRANNY SMITH

The green-skinned Granny Smith is an excellent, relatively new variety. Harvested in the late fall, it is a tart, firm, all-purpose apple, as good in pies as it is raw.

GRAVENSTEIN

This red-and-yellow-green-skinned apple is among the first apples to appear, showing up in markets as early as August. Tart and juicy, it is good for cooking.

IDARED

The bright red Idared is harvested in the late fall. It stores better than most other varieties, making it a fine choice for general cooking or eating raw throughout the winter.

JONATHAN

The red-skinned Jonathan, available in early fall, is a superior all-purpose apple, firm and juicy, with a tart, almost spicy, flavor.

MCINTOSH

The familiar red or reddish-green McIntosh, harvested in early fall, is a favorite eating apple. Its flesh is very juicy and sweet, but its softness makes it inappropriate for most cooking.

NEWTOWN PIPPIN

This greenish-yellow, slightly tart, firm fruit, harvested in the early fall, is worth looking for. It's as good for cooking as for eating out of hand.

NORTHERN SPY

The Northern Spy is one of the best apples for cooking, although it can be eaten raw as well. Red and green skinned, with mildly tart flesh, it is available in the late fall.

RHODE ISLAND GREENING

The bright green Rhode Island Greening, harvested in mid-fall, has a tart and juicy yellow flesh that has made it a long-time favorite for cooking.

ROME BEAUTY

The red-skinned Rome Beauty, also available in mid-fall, is a good choice for baking as it keeps its shape; its firm yellow flesh is too mild to make it desirable as an eating apple.

STAYMAN

Available in the mid-fall, the Stayman apple has a red skin and tart, flavorful yellow flesh, Related to the older Winesap, this more versatile variety can be eaten raw or cooked in pies and sauces.

WINESAP

The dark-red Winesap, less prevalent than it used to be, has a tart yellow flesh suitable for use in pies or eating raw.

YORK IMPERIAL

The popular York Imperial is an excellent cooking apple that also holds its shape when baked. Harvested in mid-fall, it has a red skin, pale yellow flesh, and a mild, almost "winy" flavor.

Pears

The cultivation of pears has been traced back to ancient times, and there are around 5,000 different varieties known today. Needless to say, in the United States our choices are rather more limited. There are three basic types of pears: eating, cooking, and perry, or cider, pears.

Harvest time for pears, also in the fall, is far shorter than that for apples. In addition, pears do not keep as well as apples, although some winter pears are available through the early spring.

Most pears are picked underripe and so must be allowed to ripen for a few days at room temperature. Unfortunately, pears that are too underripe will never develop fully, becoming mealy and tasteless rather than flavorful and juicy. Pears ripen from the inside out, and by the time a pear yields to slight pressure, it is fully ripe. Keep in mind that slightly underripe pears are best for poaching, for they contain more pectin and will firm up nicely again when cooled and chilled.

ANJOU

The Anjou is one of the firmer varieties, light green to yellowish-green in color. (Avoid dark-green Anjou pears, which will never ripen properly.) Available November through May, it has a succulent, slightly winy flavor.

BARTLETT

The bell-shaped Bartlett, the most popular of all commercial pears, is available from early August through November. It is a thin-skinned pear that becomes a rich yellow color, often with a slightly rosy blush, when fully ripe. Suitable for cooking and for eating raw, it is especially good poached. The Bartlett is known as the William pear in Europe, where it is used to create the special clear alcohol known as poire William.

BOSC

The brown, sometimes russet-skinned, Bosc pear is, like the Anjou, a firmer pear available from November through May. It is an all-purpose variety with excellent flavor and a sharply tapered shape. A favorite eating pear, the Bosc is also good poached.

COMICE

The fragrant Comice pear, which we consider the best eating pear, is usually available only from October through December. This large, round pear has light yellowish-green, speckled skin and soft, creamy, sweet, and juicy flesh.

SECKEL

The small, firm Seckel pear, wth its spicy-sweet flavor, is especially good for cooking and preserving. In fact, it is often too hard for other uses. It's generally available during September and October.

PISTACHIO BUTTER COOKIES

These rich, delicate butter cookies are enhanced by the addition of crunchy pistachio nuts. The dough can be cut into plain rounds or into any other shapes.

Preparation: Bring butter to room temperature. Mince the pistachios.

In a mixing bowl, cream the butter and sugar until light and fluffy. Add the egg and mix well, scraping the sides and bottom of the bowl often. Add the almond extract, salt, flour, and 3 tablespoons of the pistachios; mix only until thoroughly combined. Flatten into a disk. Wrap in plastic wrap and chill until the dough is firm, 30 to 45 minutes.

¼ pound unsalted butter
¼ cup unsalted minced pistachios
  (see Note)
½ cup sugar
1 egg
½ teaspoon almond extract
  Pinch of salt
1 cup flour

Cooking: Heat the oven to 350°F. Butter a baking sheet.

On a floured work surface, roll one third of the dough out to a ⅛-inch thickness. Using a cookie cutter or knife, cut any shape desired. Sprinkle with the reserved pistachios. Put the cookies on the prepared baking sheet. Repeat with the remaining dough.

Bake in the preheated oven just until the edges of the cookies begin to brown slightly, 10 to 12 minutes. Cool on a wire rack and then store in an airtight container.

YIELD: about 30 cookies

NOTE: If unsalted pistachios are unavailable, rinse salted nuts until they no longer taste salty. The dough can be refrigerated for several days or frozen. The cookies can also be frozen after baking.

PEAR AND CINNAMON BASIL SORBET

This unique and easy-to-prepare sorbet is the creation of Jimmy
Schmidt, now chef of The Rattlesnake Club in Denver, Colorado.
When he was at The London Chop House in Detroit, Schmidt was
famous for his lavish desserts; his lighter desserts are equally impressive.

8 or 9 ripe pears
6 tablespoons lemon juice
1 cup sugar
1 cup loosely packed cinnamon basil
leaves or sweet basil and a pinch
ground cinnamon
Sprigs of cinnamon basil or sweet
basil for garnish

Preparation: Peel and core the pears. In a food processor or blender, puree the pears with the lemon juice
until smooth. Transfer the pureed pears to a saucepan.
Add the sugar and ground cinnamon if using. Over
medium heat, bring just to a boil. Return the puree to
processor or blender and add the basil. Puree just 10
seconds. Cool and then strain. Freeze in an ice-cream
machine according to the manufacturer's directions.

SERVING: Garnish the servings with a sprig of cinnamon
or sweet basil.

YIELD: 4 servings

POACHED ORANGES WITH ANISE

This quickly made dessert is an original, refreshing, and delicious finish
to any meal. Developed by Jim Dodge, pastry chef at the Stanford
Court Hotel in San Francisco, it's one of our favorite light desserts.

3 large seedless oranges
1 cup water
1 cup sugar
½ cup orange juice
1 tablespoon aniseed

Preparation: With a knife, peel the oranges all the way
down to the flesh, removing all the white pith. Slice.
    In a heavy saucepan, bring the water, sugar, and or-
ange juice to a boil. Add the oranges and aniseed and
bring to a boil again. Cool.

SERVING: Serve at room temperature.

YIELD: 4 servings

CHAMPAGNE–CASSIS ICE

This easily made ice does not even require an ice-cream machine. As ices include neither egg whites nor milk, they can freeze very hard and are likely to develop large ice crystals. The alcohol in the champagne and crème de cassis in this recipe prevents such rock-hard freezing and makes for a smooth consistency. You could experiment using the same basic formula with different wines and liqueurs.

Preparation: Dissolve the sugar in the water over medium heat. Chill. When the syrup is cold, stir together all ingredients except the strawberries. Pour into a metal pan or bowl and freeze until the mixture is frozen semihard, opaque in color, yet soft in the center, 4 to 6 hours or overnight.

1 cup sugar
2 cups water
1¾ cups dry champagne, chilled
1 tablespoon crème de cassis
4 tablespoons fresh lemon juice
  Fresh strawberries for garnish
  (optional)

Spoon the mixture into a food processor and whir until fluffy and slushy, but not melted, about 10 seconds. Or whip with a wire whisk or electric beater. Return to the pan and refreeze until the mixture is frozen semihard again. Return the mixture to food processor and whir until fluffy and slushy again. Or whip again with wire whisk or electric beater. Return to the pan and refreeze.

SERVING: Scoop the ice into dishes and garnish with the strawberries.

YIELD: 4 to 6 servings

COLD GRAPEFRUIT SOUFFLÉ

Either white or pink grapefruit can be used for this unusual chilled soufflé. If you use pink, you may want to cut the sugar a bit since they're slightly sweeter. The grapefruit shells can be used as containers for the soufflé as here, or it can be put into bowls.

2 large grapefruits
1 envelope gelatin
¼ cup Cointreau or *Triple Sec*
3 eggs
½ cup plus 3 tablespoons (approximately)
    sugar
⅔ cup light cream
    Pinch of salt
    Pinch of cream of tartar
⅔ cup heavy cream
    Candied violets or *fresh mint leaves for*
    garnish (optional)

Preparation: To use the grapefruit shells as containers, cut a small slice off the top and bottom of each fruit so that the halves will stand straight. If you want a decorative edge, use a large knife to make a zigzag cut around the equator of each fruit, sticking the knife in as far as the center with each cut. Pull the two halves apart. Carefully hollow out each half, working over a bowl to catch the juice. Press the pulp through a strainer; you should have a little more than 1 cup grapefruit juice. Discard the membranes. If you do not plan to serve from the skins, simply use a standard juicer.

In a heatproof bowl, sprinkle the gelatin over the Cointreau and let sit until it is spongy. Place the bowl in a pan of simmering water until the gelatin is completely dissolved.

Separate the eggs. Lightly whisk the egg yolks with ½ cup of the sugar in a large bowl. In a heavy saucepan, heat the light cream with ⅓ cup of the grapefruit juice. Gradually whisk the hot cream into the yolk mixture. Return it to the pan and cook over medium heat, stirring with a wooden spoon, until the mixture thickens sufficiently to coat the back of the spoon, about 2 minutes; do not boil or it will curdle. Strain this mixture and whisk in the dissolved gelatin and remaining grapefruit juice.

Set the bowl over a pan of ice. Stir occasionally with a rubber spatula as the mixture chills.

Beat the heavy cream to stiff peaks. Beat the egg whites with the salt and cream of tartar. Sprinkle in the remaining 3 tablespoons of sugar as the whites thicken and continue beating until stiff peaks form.

When the grapefruit mixture is on the verge of setting, fold in most of the whipped cream, reserving about ⅓ cup for decoration. Fold in the beaten egg whites. Spoon the mixture into the hollowed-out grapefruit shells or dessert bowls and refrigerate.

SERVING: Just before serving, decorate each soufflé with a rosette of whipped cream and top with candied violets or mint leaves if you like.

YIELD: 4 servings

BISCOITOS DE PORTO

These cookies are part of the heritage of the many Portuguese-Americans in New England. They would go well alongside many of the desserts in this chapter and are also good enough to serve on their own with strong black coffee or a glass of port.

Preparation: Bring the butter to room temperature. Cream the butter with the sugar until light and fluffy. Lightly beat the egg yolks and beat them into the mixture. Grate 1 teaspoon of zest from the orange and add it along with the port and cinnamon.

Mince the almonds. Mix together the almonds, flour, salt, and baking powder. Add to the egg-butter mixture, blending well.

¼ pound butter
½ cup sugar
2 egg yolks
1 small orange
¼ cup ruby port
¼ teaspoon ground cinnamon
1 cup blanched almonds
1 cup flour
¼ teaspoon salt
¼ teaspoon baking powder

Cooking: Heat the oven to 400°F. Butter a baking sheet.

Shape the dough into 2-inch balls, put on the prepared baking sheet, and flatten to about a ¼-inch thickness with the palm of your hand.

Bake in the preheated oven until the cookies are golden, 10 to 12 minutes. Cool on a wire rack and store in an airtight container.

YIELD: about 20 cookies

RED RASPBERRY MOUSSE

Fruit mousses offer a light alternative to the more common chocolate
version. The framboise used here is an eau de vie made from raspberries.
Another clear fruit alcohol, such as kirsch, could be substituted, or you
could use cognac.

1 pint fresh raspberries or 1 10-ounce
package frozen
1½ tablespoons framboise
½ cup heavy cream
1 egg white
Pinch of salt
2 to 4 tablespoons sugar

Preparation: If using frozen berries, thaw and drain
them. If using fresh, choose 8 perfect berries for garnish
and set them aside. Puree the remaining berries in a
food processor or blender. Strain the seeds from puree.
You should have about ⅓ cup puree. Combine with the
framboise.

Whip the cream until it barely mounds. Beat the egg
white with the salt until it forms soft peaks. Beat in 2
tablespoons of the sugar if using sweetened frozen berries or 4 tablespoons for fresh, a little at a time, and
continue beating until the meringue is firm and shiny.

Fold the puree into the egg white and then fold the
mixture into the cream. Divide among stemmed glasses
and chill for at least 2 hours.

SERVING: Garnish with the reserved berries.

YIELD: 4 servings

WINTER COMPOTE WITH RASPBERRY SAUCE

For this flavorful fruit combination, fresh pineapple and grapefruit are
macerated in kirsch; a simple raspberry sauce adds sweetness and color.

1 ripe pineapple
2 grapefruits
½ cup plus 1½ tablespoons kirsch
4 tablespoons sugar
1 cup fresh or frozen raspberries
Mint sprigs for garnish (optional)

Preparation: Peel, core, and dice the pineapple. With
a knife, peel the grapefruits down to the flesh. Cut the
sections out from between the membranes.

In a bowl, combine the pineapple, grapefruits, ½ cup
of the kirsch, and 2 tablespoons of the sugar. Chill,
covered, for up to 12 hours.

Thaw the frozen berries, if using. In a blender or food processor, puree the raspberries with the remaining 2 tablespoons of sugar if using fresh or unsweetened frozen. Strain to remove the seeds and stir in the remaining 1½ tablespoons of kirsch. Chill until ready to use.

SERVING: Spoon the fruit into individual dessert dishes and top with the raspberry sauce. Garnish with mint sprigs, if desired.

YIELD: 6 to 8 servings

MAPLE–WALNUT ZABAGLIONE

In this Americanization of a quick but elegant dessert, dry white wine is substituted for the Marsala of the classic Italian version, and pure maple syrup, rather than sugar, provides the sweetness.

Preparation: Heat the oven to 375°F. Spread the walnuts on a baking sheet and toast until light brown, 6 to 8 minutes. Cool and chop the walnuts.

¼ cup broken walnut meats
4 egg yolks
⅓ cup maple syrup
6 tablespoons dry white wine

Cooking: In the top of a double boiler, whisk together the egg yolks, maple syrup, and wine. Set the top of the double boiler over simmering water and cook, whisking constantly, until thickened, frothy, and quadrupled in volume, about 5 minutes.

SERVING: Pour the custard into 4 stemmed dessert glasses and sprinkle with the nuts. Serve immediately.

YIELD: 4 servings

CHERRY SOUP WITH STRAWBERRY SHERBET

Barry Wine, owner and chef of The Quilted Giraffe in New York City, serves his unusual cold cherry soup with a scoop of strawberry sherbet, garnished with candied lime zest and diced cantaloupe. The lime zest is blanched to both retain the color and remove any bitterness.

Soup

1 pound dark sweet cherries
1 quart water
½ cup sugar
¼ cup honey
2 cups fruity red wine, such as Zinfandel
½ cinnamon stick
3 whole cloves
Zest of 1 lemon, 1 lime, and 1 orange

Strawberry Sherbet

2 pints strawberries
1 cup water
½ cup sugar
Pinch of salt
Few drops of lemon juice

Candied Lime Zest

Zest of 2 limes
¼ cup sugar

½ cantaloupe

Preparation: *For the soup,* stem the cherries and put them into a saucepan with the water, sugar, and honey. Very gently bring to a simmer, uncovered. Simmer for 10 minutes and cool.

Combine the wine, cinnamon, cloves, and citrus zests in a saucepan. Boil to reduce the liquid by half, about 10 minutes. Strain the liquid into the cherries, cover, and refrigerate.

For the sherbet, hull the strawberries. Puree all the sherbet ingredients in a food processor or blender. Push the puree through a sieve. Freeze in an ice-cream machine according to the manufacturer's instructions.

For the candied lime zest, remove the zest from the limes in strips, cut crosswise into thin shreds, and bring to a boil in enough cold water to cover. Drain and repeat the process three times, starting each time with fresh water. After the final blanching and draining, return to the pan and add the sugar and 1 cup of fresh water. Cook over low heat, partially covered, for 45 minutes. Drain the zest and cool on buttered wax paper or a buttered plate.

Dice the cantaloupe.

SERVING: Spoon cherries and their liquid into chilled bowls. Add 1 scoop of sherbet to each serving and garnish with candied lime zest and cantaloupe.

YIELD: 4 servings

GOLDEN APRICOT–CARROT SOUP

The Pistachio Butter Cookies in this chapter make a good accompaniment to this golden-orange soup.

Preparation and Cooking: Cut one of the carrots into thin rounds. In a saucepan, combine the carrot rounds with half the apricots and 3 cups of the water. Bring to a boil. Lower the heat and simmer until the carrots are very soft, about 45 minutes. Puree mixture in a food processor or blender until very smooth.

Heat the oven to 325°F. Chop the pecans and toast them until golden, 5 to 10 minutes. Cut the remaining carrot in half lengthwise and then into ⅛-inch-thick slices. Cut the remaining apricots into ⅛-inch-thick strips.

Put carrot puree in a saucepan and add remaining 2¼ cups of water, the remaining carrot, 6 tablespoons of the maple syrup, and the cream. Simmer until the carrots are just tender, 10 to 15 minutes. Whisk in the butter and nutmeg. Taste and add more maple syrup if desired.

SERVING: Reheat the soup if made ahead. Ladle into warm bowls and top with the sliced apricots and the pecans.

YIELD: 4 servings

2 small carrots
½ pound dried apricots (about 1½ cups)
5¼ cups water
¾ cup pecans
6 to 8 tablespoons maple syrup
½ cup heavy cream
1 tablespoon unsalted butter
½ teaspoon grated nutmeg

TROPICAL COCONUT–PAPAYA SOUP

The beauty of this soup, saffron-yellow flecked with vanilla seeds, is matched by its smooth, delicious flavor.

1 ripe papaya
1 vanilla bean
½ cup canned or bottled cream of coconut
1½ cups water
⅔ cup heavy cream
2 to 4 tablespoons sugar

Preparation: Peel, halve, and seed the papaya, Cut the flesh into large chunks and puree in a food processor or blender until almost smooth (a few pea-sized pieces should remain). Halve the vanilla bean lengthwise. Scrape seeds into a saucepan.

Cooking: In the saucepan, combine all the ingredients including vanilla pod. Bring to a simmer over medium heat. Add more sugar if necessary. Turn the heat to low and continue to simmer, stirring occasionally, for 5 minutes.

SERVING: Remove the vanilla pod with a slotted spoon and ladle the soup into 4 warm bowls.

YIELD: 4 servings

MASCARPONE WITH FIGS

Innovative on all counts, this warm soup uses several ingredients that, until recently, were just not found in American markets. However, it can also successfully be made with cream cheese instead of mascarpone and with roasted cashews instead of raw ones. For a variation, try red or green grapes instead of fresh figs.

2 fresh figs or 1 small bunch red and/or green grapes
⅓ cup raw cashews (see Note)
1 pound mascarpone cheese or ½ pound cream cheese
1½ cups water
¼ cup sugar

Preparation: Heat the oven to 325°F. Slice the figs into ⅛-inch-thick slices, or halve and seed the grapes. Halve the cashews lengthwise. Toast the cashews in the preheated oven until golden, 5 to 10 minutes.

Cooking: Whisk together the mascarpone or cream cheese, water, and sugar until well mixed. Warm gently over low heat, stirring constantly, about 4 minutes, being careful not to boil or the cheese will curdle.

SERVING: Ladle the soup into 4 warm bowls. Sprinkle with the cashews and top with fig slices or grapes.

YIELD: 4 servings

NOTE: If you are unable to find raw cashews, rinse roasted salted cashews in cold water until they no longer taste salty.

RUBY PEAR SOUP

Beet stock serves as the base for this unusual dessert soup. The julienned pears stand out against the deep-red color and a garnish of fresh mint adds the final touch.

Preparation: Trim, peel, and chop the beets. In a saucepan, cook the beets, water, and sugar over medium heat until the beets are very soft, about 25 minutes. Strain the beet stock and reserve the beets for another use, such as in a salad. You should have about 5 cups of stock.

12 beets
6 cups water
1/3 cup sugar, plus more if necessary
1/4 cup shredded fresh mint leaves or 1 tablespoon dried mint
2 firm ripe pears, such as Anjou or Bosc

Cooking: Return the stock to a simmer. If using dried mint, stir it in at this point. If using fresh, cut it crosswise into thin strips and set aside. Peel, core, and cut the pears into 1/4- by 1-inch julienne strips. Add the pears to the stock and just heat through. Taste and add more sugar if necessary.

SERVING: Ladle the soup into warm bowls and top with the fresh mint leaves.

YIELD: 4 servings

BANANA–CARAMEL SOUP

Slightly underripe bananas are used in the puree for this delicious warm
soup to prevent its discoloring; sliced ripe bananas, along with orange
sections and orange zest for garnish, are added just before serving.

3 small seedless oranges
½ cup sugar
2¾ cups water
4 tablespoons unsalted butter
*4 bananas (2 of them ripe, 2 slightly
    green-tipped)*
¼ cup bourbon

Preparation: Peel the zest from 1 of the oranges in
strips. Slice the strips crosswise into shreds. Blanch the
zest in boiling water for 2 minutes. Drain. Remove the
pith from the orange and reserve the whole orange. Peel
the remaining 2 oranges completely down to the flesh,
removing both pith and outside membrane. Working
over a bowl to catch the juice, cut out the sections from
the membranes. Squeeze the membranes to get all the
juice.

Cooking: In a small saucepan, bring the sugar and ¼
cup of the water to a boil, stirring constantly to dissolve
the sugar. Cook over medium heat, stirring occasionally, until the sugar just turns caramel in color, about 4
minutes. Being extremely careful because the caramel
will splatter and can cause burns, ladle in the remaining
2½ cups water. Add half of the zest. Add the butter,
return to a simmer, and continue stirring until the caramel dissolves. In a food processor, puree the 2 slightly
green-tipped bananas with the reserved whole orange
until very smooth. Whisk the puree and the juice from
the sectioned oranges into the simmering liquid. Add
the bourbon. Cut the 2 ripe bananas into ¼-inch-thick
diagonal slices. Remove the soup from the heat and add
the sliced bananas and orange sections.

SERVING: Ladle the soup into warm bowls and garnish
with the remaining orange zest.

YIELD: 4 servings

MENUS

Onion and Fennel Frittata (page 103)   Pinot Blanc, such as Buehler or Jekel

Grilled Lamb on Cabbage Leaves (page 166)   Saint-Emilion, such as Château Pavie or Latour-Figeac

Cold Grapefruit Soufflé (page 230)

Herb Pâté (page 25)   Medium–bodied Italian white, such as Tocai Friulano

Pasta with Squid and Basil (page 136)   Full-bodied Italian white, such as Gavi La
Focaccia with Red Onion (page 181)   Scolca

Ruby Pear Soup (page 237)

CHAPTER 13
LAVISH DESSERTS

Chocolate–Kona Cake with Figs and Pistachios
Ancho Chocolate Soufflé · Raspberry–Pistachio Bombe
Praline and Chocolate–Espresso Bombe · Pinwheel Cake
Hazelnut Angel Ring with Coffee Ice Cream Balls and Chocolate Sauce
Pastry Cornucopia · Chocolate Meringue Cake
Strawberry–Rhubarb Mille Feuille · Chocolate–Mint Pastries
Papaya–Rum Babas · Chocolate–Cherry Bavarian Pie
Chocolate Soufflé Cake

S pecial occasions require special desserts, and even quickly
prepared meals can be lifted to the realm of the extraordinary
by the addition of a lavish dessert.
    For many people, a lavish dessert is by definition one made
of chocolate, and over half the desserts in this chapter include
it. The taste and texture of various types of chocolates differ
considerably (see page 242). Semisweet, or bittersweet, is generally
considered the best all-round choice for cooking and you'll find it in
most of our recipes from the gorgeous Chocolate–Cherry Bavarian Pie
to the unusual Ancho Chocolate Soufflé, an inventive combination of
French and Mexican cuisines that proves chiles and chocolate a
startlingly appropriate duo.
    One lavish, old-time specialty, the frozen bombe, has become popular
again. The classic dessert is composed of layers of ice cream or fruit ices,
often filled with frozen mousses. The new, simple-to-operate ice-cream
freezers and the availability of good-quality, ready-made ice creams,
make a once-daunting project seem easy. We offer several varieties here,
and the possible combinations really are limitless. The *Larousse
Gastronomique* lists 26 *bombes glacées,* from Bombe Aida (tangerine ice
filled with vanilla mousse flavored with kirsch) to Bombe Véronique
(pistachio ice cream filled with chocolate mousse studded with candied
orange peel steeped in champagne brandy). Bombes are especially
effective when made with layers of contrasting colors or textures; for

example, our tri-colored Raspberry–Pistachio Bombe, with its raspberry sherbet and vanilla and pistachio ice creams, or the Praline and Chocolate–Espresso Bombe, with its crunchy praline ice cream and center of unctuous chocolate-espresso mousse. Our Pinwheel Cake is a variation on the classic bombe, with its outer layer of ice cream cake spirals enclosing orange sherbet and chocolate-orange ice cream.

All of the bombes can, in fact must, be made in advance. One of the beauties of the most lavish desserts is that they are completed well ahead of time and wait in readiness to end a meal with a flourish.

Bombes

A bombe can be nothing more complicated than several different flavors of ice cream layered into a mold, or it can be an elaborate combination of fruit ice, ice cream, and frozen mousse. Bombes can be made in the traditional fluted melon or conical molds, in square bombe molds, in stainless-steel mixing bowls, or in almost any kind of metal container or mold. Metal is best because it reacts rapidly to temperature change, making freezing and unmolding easy, for the best results, start with a mold that has been thoroughly chilled in the freezer.

It is important to use soft ice cream for a bombe. The consistency of a homemade mixture just out of the ice-cream freezer is ideal. If you use commercial ice cream, let it soften in the refrigerator before using.

Bombes are constructed in stages. First, press ice cream or sherbet onto the sides and bottom of the prepared mold to form the outside layer. Then freeze until firm before adding the next layer. Work quickly so that the frozen mixture does not melt, and spread each addition carefully to avoid disturbing the layers underneath. You'll find that although the various freezings make for a lengthy process, the actual work time for so impressive a dessert is short.

Chocolate

All chocolate comes from cocoa trees, which grow only in tropical countries. The cocoa beans are harvested and allowed to ferment to develop flavor before they are dried. After roasting, they are broken into small pieces, the shells removed, and the "nibs," or meat of the beans, ground and refined. The refining process liquefies the nibs, creating a substance called chocolate liquor, which contains from 50 to 58 percent cocoa fat, depending on the type of bean. This liquor is partially defatted before it is made into blocks to be sold as *pure, bitter, unsweetened, or baking chocolate* (interchangeable terms), or further processed into other types of chocolate. According to U.S. government classifications, substances labeled real chocolate can contain either no fat other than cocoa butter or cocoa butter with a maximum of 5 percent dairy butter.

Cocoa powder is made from dried, pulverized chocolate liquor with much of the cocoa butter pressed out, leaving a fat content of only 14 to 25 percent. The preferred Dutch-process cocoa is made using a technique that reduces the chocolate's natural acidity, deepens its color, and makes the cocoa combine more easily with milk.

Semisweet, or bittersweet, chocolate consists of pure chocolate liquor with some sugar added. It is fuller and richer in flavor than cocoa because it contains vanilla or vanillin and far more cocoa butter. U.S. regulations require chocolate sold as semisweet to contain 35 percent chocolate liquor and 27 percent cocoa butter (in addition to that contained in the chocolate liquor). *European extra-bittersweet chocolate* contains more chocolate liquor and slightly more cocoa butter. For *milk chocolate,* powdered milk is added to sweetened chocolate.

White chocolate, which cannot be classified as chocolate, because it contains no chocolate liquor, is nothing more than the cocoa butter left over after processing the liquor, mixed with milk solids, sugar, vanilla or vanillin, and lecithin, and cooked into a thick paste.

Storing Chocolate

If chocolate is stored properly, it will keep for up to two years. For best results, store chocolate well-wrapped in an airtight container at cool room temperature (60° to 70°F) and at less than 50 percent humidity. Do not refrigerate it, for chilled chocolate "sweats" when brought to room temperature and lumps when melted. Chocolate that has been exposed to too much air or heat will develop a grayish "bloom" as a result of cocoa butter rising to the surface; it doesn't affect flavor and will disappear on melting.

Melting Chocolate

Melting chocolate over low heat is crucial, for heating it beyond 120°F results in a loss of flavor, gloss, and texture. An ideal method is to let the chocolate melt in a gas oven with no heat other than that of the pilot light, but this does take half an hour or so. Grating the chocolate first or breaking it into small pieces will speed up any melting technique. Chocolate is often melted in a quantity of liquid, but very small amounts, even a drop of water, can cause melting chocolate to "tighten" into an unworkable mass. Never cover chocolate as it melts, or the condensation that forms on the lid could ruin it. Melting chocolate in a microwave oven requires care because the chocolate retains its shape when melted—a fact that tempts cooks to leave the chocolate in the oven too long. To be safe, remove it before it is completely melted; residual heat will finish the job.

CHOCOLATE–KONA CAKE WITH FIGS AND PISTACHIOS

Chef John Elkay of Café in the Barn in Seekonk, Massachusetts, prefers to use exotic Hawaiian Kona coffee in this extravagant cake, but another strong coffee can be substituted. The dense, moist cake contains only 2 teaspoons of flour.

Preparation and Cooking: Cover the base and sides of an 8-inch springform pan with aluminum foil. Heat the oven to 350°F.

In a saucepan, melt the butter over low heat. Add the sugar and coffee and remove from the heat. Whisk the eggs. While coffee mixture is still warm, add the chocolates, honey, and eggs.

Remove the stems from the figs and cut the figs into ½-inch pieces. Chop the pistachios. In a bowl, mix the figs, pistachios, and flour. Fold into the chocolate mixture.

Pour the batter into the prepared springform pan. Bake in the preheated oven until set, 40 to 45 minutes. Cool and then chill in the refrigerator. Whip the cream.

SERVING: Run a knife around the sides of the cake to remove it from the pan. Either use a pastry bag fitted with a star tip to pipe rosettes of whipped cream along edges of the cake and then garnish with raspberries and mint sprigs, or serve each slice of cake with a dollop of whipped cream.

YIELD: 4 to 6 servings

NOTE: If you cannot find unsalted pistachios, rinse salted pistachios until they no longer taste salty.

½ pound unsalted butter
⅓ cup sugar
3 ounces double-strength Hawaiian Kona
  or other coffee
4 eggs
6 ounces bittersweet chocolate
2 ounces unsweetened chocolate
2 tablespoons honey
4 ounces dried figs
¾ cup unsalted pistachios (see Note)
2 teaspoons flour
1 cup heavy cream
1 pint raspberries for garnish (optional)
  Mint sprigs for garnish (optional)

ANCHO CHOCOLATE SOUFFLÉ

When Amy Ferguson was chef of Charley's 517 in Houston, Texas, she made unusual use of local ancho peppers in this soufflé. You'll be surprised how good a touch of pepper is in a sweet chocolate dish. Use cayenne if ancho peppers aren't available.

6 ancho peppers or a pinch of cayenne
2 teaspoons instant coffee
3 ounces extra bittersweet chocolate
1½ tablespoons milk
1½ tablespoons heavy cream
¼ teaspoon ground cinnamon
3 egg yolks
5 egg whites
Pinch of salt
¼ cup sugar
Crème Anglaise (recipe follows)

Preparation: If using ancho peppers, toast them in a 400°F oven for 3 to 4 minutes and then soak them in very hot water to cover for 30 minutes. Drain, remove the seeds, and puree the peppers in food processor. Dissolve the instant coffee in 2 tablespoons hot water.

Butter a 1½-quart soufflé dish or six 8-ounce soufflé dishes and dust them with sugar. Discard any excess sugar.

Cooking: Heat the oven to 350°F. In a small saucepan over low heat, melt the chocolate in the milk, cream, and coffee. Stir in chili paste or cayenne, and cinnamon. Remove from the heat. Whisk the egg yolks, one at a time, into the chocolate mixture.

In a mixing bowl, beat the egg whites with the salt. When the egg whites form soft peaks, start adding the sugar slowly. Continue to beat until the peaks are stiff and glossy. Gently fold the egg whites into the chocolate mixture in 3 batches. Spoon the mixture into the prepared soufflé dish.

Bake in the preheated oven until the soufflé has risen above the edge of the dish and is set but still wobbly in the center, 20 to 25 minutes for the large soufflé or 15 to 20 minutes for the individual ones.

SERVING: Serve immediately with cold Crème Anglaise.

YIELD: 4 to 6 servings

CRÈME ANGLAISE

Preparation: In a large bowl, beat the sugar and egg yolks together until they turn pale and thick.

In a saucepan, heat the milk to the boiling point. Slowly whisk the hot milk into the yolk mixture and then return to the saucepan. Stir constantly with a wooden spoon over very low heat until the custard thickens just enough to coat the back of a spoon lightly, or reaches 160°F on a thermometer. Do not allow it to boil. Strain into a clean bowl, add the vanilla, cover, and chill.

YIELD: about 1¾ cups

3 tablespoons sugar
4 egg yolks
1½ cups milk
1 teaspoon vanilla extract

RASPBERRY–PISTACHIO BOMBE

This red, white, and green ice-cream bombe is simple and stunning. Time must be allowed for the freezing of the layers, but actual preparation time is minimal.

1 quart vanilla ice cream
1 quart pistachio ice cream
1 pint raspberry sherbet
½ cup unsalted pistachio nuts (see Note*)*
   Raspberry Sauce (recipe follows)

Preparation: Put a 3-quart bombe mold or metal bowl in the freezer for at least 30 minutes.

Put the vanilla ice cream in the refrigerator until it is soft but not melted. Using a spatula, line the frozen mold or bowl evenly with a layer of vanilla ice cream, working rapidly. Immediately return the mold to the freezer.

Put the pistachio ice cream in the refrigerator until it is soft but not melted. Evenly line the firm vanilla ice cream layer with the pistachio ice cream and immediately return to the freezer.

Put the raspberry sherbet in the refrigerator until soft but not melted. When the mold is firm, fill the center of the mold with raspberry sherbet and return to freezer for at least 3 hours.

Crush the pistachio nuts. To unmold the bombe, dip mold or bowl in hot water for a few seconds just to loosen. Quickly turn the bombe out onto a frozen serving platter. Sprinkle with pistachios and immediately return to the freezer until ready to serve.

SERVING: Cut the bombe into wedges with a hot knife and serve with the Raspberry Sauce.

YIELD: 12 servings

NOTE: If you can't find unsalted pistachios, rinse salted pistachios until they no longer taste salty.

Raspberry Sauce

Preparation: If using frozen raspberries, thaw. In a food processor, puree the raspberries, with the sugar if using fresh or unsweetened frozen. Strain to remove the seeds and stir in the framboise or kirsch. Refrigerate until ready to use.

3 pints fresh or about 30 ounces frozen raspberries
¼ cup sugar
⅓ cup framboise or kirsch

YIELD: about 2½ cups

PRALINE AND CHOCOLATE–ESPRESSO BOMBE

The center of this frozen bombe is a rich, coffee-flavored chocolate mousse; the outside is vanilla ice cream enriched with crushed praline. The combination is reminiscent of the best chocolate-covered English toffee.

Praline Ice Cream

  1 cup pecans
  ½ cup sugar
  3 tablespoons water
  ¼ teaspoon lemon juice
  2 pints vanilla ice cream

Chocolate–Espresso Mousse

  ⅓ cup sugar
  ¼ cup water
  3 egg yolks
  1 teaspoon instant espresso coffee powder
  2 ounces semisweet chocolate
  1 cup heavy cream
  1 teaspoon vanilla extract
  Semisweet chocolate to make curls for
    garnish (optional)

Preparation: Put a 2-quart bombe mold or metal bowl in the freezer. Butter a baking sheet.

For the ice cream, combine the pecans, sugar, water, and lemon juice in a small, heavy saucepan. Cook over low heat, shaking the pan occasionally, until the sugar has dissolved, about 5 minutes. Turn the heat to medium and cook, stirring often, until the syrup becomes a golden caramel color, about 5 minutes more. Spread the caramelized nuts in a thin layer on the prepared baking sheet and cool completely.

Put the ice cream in the refrigerator until it is soft but not melted. In a food processor, pulverize the cooled caramelized nuts. With a wooden spoon, fold the ground nuts into the softened ice cream. Press the ice cream onto bottom and sides of the chilled mold to form a thick layer. If the ice cream is too soft to work with, return it to the freezer to harden slightly before continuing. Freeze the mold until firm.

For the mousse, combine the sugar and ¼ cup of water in a small saucepan, stirring constantly until the sugar has dissolved. Raise the heat and cook the syrup undisturbed, until it registers 232°F on a candy thermometer.

While the syrup is cooking, beat the egg yolks in a large bowl. Slowly pour the hot syrup over the yolks and beat continuously until the mousse is pale-yellow, thickened, and tripled in volume. Cool for 5 to 10 minutes.

Meanwhile, mix the espresso with ½ teaspoon of cold water. Melt the 2 ounces of semisweet chocolate and then cool it slightly. Whip the cream until it barely holds soft peaks. Beat the espresso, vanilla, and cooled chocolate into the egg yolk mixture. Fold in the soft whipped cream as gently as possible.

Pile the mousse into the frozen praline-lined mold, smoothing the top with a metal palette knife. Freeze until firm, several hours.

Make the chocolate curls for garnish by scraping a block of chocolate with the pointed end of a vegetable peeler. To unmold the bombe, dip the mold into hot water for a few seconds to loosen it. Turn the bombe out onto a chilled platter and return it to the freezer.

SERVING: Sprinkle the top of the bombe with chocolate curls. Cut bombe into wedges with a hot knife.

YIELD: 8 servings

PINWHEEL CAKE

In this impressive dessert, slices of an ice-cream roll made with a Grand Marnier-flavored cake and filled with chocolate-orange ice cream form the outside shell of the dessert. A layer of orange sherbet and a center of the chocolate ice cream complete the filling. The unmolded dessert is glazed with apricot preserves.

Sponge Cake

¼ cup almonds
    Grated zest of 1 orange
¾ cup cake flour
4 eggs
½ cup sugar
1 tablespoon Grand Marnier or orange juice

1½ quarts chocolate ice cream
1½ cups orange marmalade
1 pint orange sherbet
1 cup apricot preserves

Preparation and Cooking: *For the cake,* heat the oven to 325°F. Toast the almonds until browned, 5 to 10 minutes, and then pulverize them. Raise the oven temperature to 350°F. Line a 10½- by 15½-inch jelly roll pan with parchment paper or aluminum foil. Grate the orange zest. Sift the flour.

Separate the eggs. In a mixing bowl, beat the egg yolks with all but 1 tablespoon of the sugar until thick and light colored and the mixture forms a ribbon when trailed from a spoon or whisk. Stir in the Grand Marnier or orange juice, toasted almonds, and orange zest.

In another bowl, beat the egg whites until soft peaks form. Add the remaining tablespoon of sugar and continue beating for 30 seconds. Add one third of the egg whites to the yolk mixture. Sift one third of the flour into the batter and fold to incorporate. Repeat until all the whites and flour are mixed in.

Spread the batter in the prepared pan. Bake in the preheated oven until the cake pulls away from the sides of the pan, 12 to 15 minutes.

Remove from the oven and put a damp dishtowel over the cake. Hold the towel securely at both ends and invert the cake onto a work surface. Peel off the parchment paper or foil. Roll the cake and towel together into a loose cylinder. Cool at room temperature about 1 hour; then refrigerate the cooled cake for at least 1 hour.

Put the ice cream in the refrigerator until soft but not melted. Stir the marmalade into the softened ice cream and return it to the freezer briefly.

Unroll the cake onto a sheet of foil. Spread with

about 2 cups of the softened ice cream. Roll the cake up and cover with foil. Freeze completely, at least 2 hours.

Thoroughly chill a 2-quart round-bottomed bowl in the freezer. Put the sherbet in the refrigerator until soft but not melted. Cut the cake into ½-inch-thick slices and line the bottom and sides of the chilled bowl with the slices. Spread the orange sherbet over the cake roll slices. Freeze until firm.

Let the remaining ice cream-marmalade mixture soften in the refrigerator. Fill the center of the mold with the mixture and freeze completely, at least 2 hours.

SERVING: Strain the apricot preserves. In a small saucepan, melt the preserves over low heat. Cool this glaze slightly.

Remove the mold from the freezer, dip it into hot water for a few seconds, and unmold onto a serving plate. Brush the glaze over the cake. Cut into wedges with a hot knife.

YIELD: 8 servings

HAZELNUT ANGEL RING WITH COFFEE ICE CREAM BALLS AND CHOCOLATE SAUCE

The real secret of a sky-high angel food cake is to avoid overbeating, which makes the fluffy whites unstable. This hazelnut-flavored angel ring, developed by food writer Jean Anderson, is filled with balls of coffee ice cream and drizzled with chocolate sauce. Included here is a coffee ice cream recipe that can be frozen either in the freezer section of your refrigerator or in an ice-cream machine, or you can use good-quality store-bought ice cream.

Coffee Ice Cream

1½ cups half and half
¾ cup sugar
½ cup very strong coffee
6 extra-large egg yolks
2 teaspoons vanilla extract
1 pint heavy cream

Cake

¾ cup shelled hazelnuts
1 cup sifted cake flour
1¼ cups egg whites
   (8 to 9 extra-large eggs)
¾ teaspoon cream of tartar
⅛ teaspoon salt
1½ cups sugar
1 teaspoon vanilla extract
1 teaspoon lemon juice

Chocolate Sauce

2 tablespoons cocoa, preferably Dutch-process
⅔ cup sugar
¼ cup light corn syrup
½ cup water
1 tablespoon unsalted butter
1 teaspoon vanilla extract

Preparation and Cooking: *For the ice cream,* combine the half and half, sugar, and coffee in a heavy saucepan and bring to a simmer over medium heat. Beat the egg yolks until lightened in color. Whisk the coffee mixture into the egg yolks and then pour back into the saucepan. Turn the heat to very low, and cook, stirring constantly with a wooden spoon, until the mixture thickens just enough to coat the back of a spoon lightly, about 10 minutes. Do not boil. Stir in the vanilla and chill. You can hasten cooling by quick-chilling in an ice-water bath. Whip the cream to stiff peaks. When the custard is cool, fold in the whipped cream. Pour into a 9- by 13-inch pan and freeze until firm, about 4 hours. Or process in an ice-cream maker according to the manufacturer's instructions.

For the cake, butter a 12-cup ring mold and coat it with a thin, even layer of sugar. Be sure that the central tube is well sugared.

Heat the oven to 275°F. Toast the hazelnuts in the preheated oven until the skins are dark, about 45 minutes. Cool to room temperature and then bundle a few at a time, in a towel. Rub briskly to remove most of the skins. Put the toasted nuts into a food processor and grind very fine but be careful not to overprocess to a paste. Combine ⅓ cup of the flour with ground hazelnuts. Raise the oven temperature to 300°F.

Put the egg whites into a large mixing bowl. Beat the egg whites with the cream of tartar and salt to very soft peaks. When the bowl is tilted, the whites should just flow, not slide out of the bowl in a cohesive mass. Gently fold in 2 tablespoons of the sugar. Repeat until all the sugar is added, using as light a touch as possible. Sift 1 tablespoon of the remaining flour over the whites and fold it in gently. Repeat until all the flour is incorporated. Sprinkle the vanilla and lemon juice over the batter and fold in gently. Add the dredged hazelnut-flour mixture all at once, and fold in gently but thoroughly.

Pour the batter into prepared ring mold and smooth the surface. Rap the mold sharply once or twice on a countertop to remove the large air bubbles. Bake in the preheated oven until the top is lightly browned and feels springy to the touch, about 1 hour.

Invert the pan immediately onto a large, round platter. Cool upside-down in the pan for 1 hour. If the cake does not drop out of the pan when it is cool, loosen gently around the edges and around the central tube with a thin-bladed spatula and turn out onto the platter.

For the sauce, combine the cocoa and sugar in a small, heavy saucepan, pressing out any lumps. Mix in the corn syrup and water and bring to a simmer over medium heat. Turn the heat to very low and cook, stirring occasionally, for about 10 minutes. Remove from the heat and stir in the butter and vanilla. Set sauce aside to cool.

SERVING: Shape the ice cream into balls and mound in the center of the ring. Drizzle the room-temperature chocolate sauce over all and pass any remaining sauce.

YIELD: 10 to 12 servings

PASTRY CORNUCOPIA

This full-sized pastry cornucopia, filled to overflowing with any combination of nuts and fresh and dried fruits, is a beautiful edible centerpiece. For dessert, encourage your guests to select fruit and nuts and then break off portions of the pastry, a Rabelaisian climax to a memorable meal.

3½ cups all-purpose flour
¾ cup cake flour
¾ teaspoon salt
4½ tablespoons sugar
14 ounces unsalted butter
2 eggs
½ teaspoon almond extract
1 egg white
Fresh and dried fruit and nuts to fill the cornucopia

Preparation and Cooking: For the pastry dough, combine the flours, salt, and 2½ tablespoons of the sugar in a large mixing bowl. Using the pastry blender or your fingertips, work the butter into the flour mixture until the pieces are the size of large peas.

In a measuring cup, beat 1 egg lightly. Add the almond extract and enough cold water to measure 1¼ cups. Sprinkle over the flour-butter mixture and toss together. Gather up the dough and form into 3 flattened balls. Wrap in plastic wrap and refrigerate for at least 1 hour.

To make the mold, loosely crumple 8 to 10 9-inch squares of heavy-duty aluminum foil and form into the approximate shape of a cornucopia. Tear off a sheet of regular-weight foil about 20 inches long and loosely wrap it around the crumpled foil to form a smooth cornucopia shape. The mold should be about 12 to 14 inches long and about 5 inches high in front. Coat with vegetable oil.

Lightly flour 3 baking sheets or cover with parchment paper. Transfer 1 ball of dough from the refrigerator to a lightly floured work surface and roll the dough out no more than a ¼-inch thickness. Put the pastry on one prepared baking sheet. Place the foil form on the pastry and cut out a base for the cornucopia, making it ½ inch larger than the bottom of the foil form all around. Reserve the pastry scraps. Chill the pastry base and foil form.

On a lightly floured work surface, roll 1 of remaining balls of dough into a 10- by 14-inch rectangle about ⅛ inch thick. Using a fluted pastry wheel or a small knife, cut 1-inch-wide strips of pastry and put them on a prepared baking sheet. Repeat with the remaining ball of dough. Loosely cover all the strips with plastic wrap and refrigerate.

Lightly beat the remaining egg with 2 teaspoons of water for the egg wash. Remove the pastry strips and cornucopia form from the refrigerator. Brush the edge of a pastry strip with the egg wash. Wrap the tip of the cornucopia by winding dough onto the form in a spiral, overlapping ¼ inch and sticking the egg-washed edge to the dough above.

When the tip has been completely covered, brush the top edge of the pastry base with the egg wash. Cut pastry strips about 2 inches longer than necessary to go around the form and touch the base at each side. Brush the edges of the strips with egg wash. Lay the strips across the top of the form, overlapping each egg-washed edge over the previous dough strip by about ¼ inch. Gently press the bottom of the strips to the base to seal and trim even with the base with a small, sharp knife. Continue laying strips in the same manner until the strips come to within 1 inch of the front of the cornucopia.

Brush 2 dough strips with the egg wash, fold each in half lengthwise, and press gently to seal. Loosely wind the 2 strips together to make a braid. Brush the braid and front edge of the cornucopia with the egg wash and lay the braid across the top of the cornucopia, pressing gently to seal. Using a small knife, flare the front edge of the horn upward to make a lip. Add a foil arch or crumpled strips of foil under the front of the form for additional support if necessary. Make 2 more long braids. Brush the edge of the base with egg wash and lay the braids along the sides, making a decorative spiral at the back if desired. Refrigerate the cornucopia.

For the optional grapevine decoration, roll a strip of dough between the palms of your hands to make a single smooth rope of dough. Make small balls of dough for grapes and cut out several grape leaves from the remaining dough strips. Score the leaves with the back of a small knife to create veins.

Remove the cornucopia from the refrigerator and arrange the decorations on it to get a rough idea of desired design. Remove the decorations, brush them with egg wash, and reapply, pressing gently. Refrigerate for at least 1 hour. The cornucopia can be refrigerated for up to 2 days or wrapped well and frozen for 3 to 4 weeks before baking.

Heat the oven to 425°F. Bake the cornucopia in the preheated oven for 10 minutes. Lower the oven temperature to 350°F and bake until the pastry is set but not browned, about 10 minutes more.

Beat the egg white with 1 teaspoon of water for glaze. Remove the cornucopia from the oven. Brush with the egg white glaze and sprinkle with the remaining 2 tablespoons of sugar. Return to the 350°F oven and bake until golden, 12 to 15 minutes. Cover the tip and front of the cornucopia with foil if they are over-browning.

Cool the cornucopia on the baking sheet for 5 minutes. Using a long, wide spatula, carefully lift the cornucopia onto a rack and cool for at least 40 minutes.

Reach into the cornucopia and carefully pull out the crumpled foil. Use a small pair of scissors, if necessary, to cut the foil free. It is not necessary to remove the foil from the tail. Gently peel the mold's foil covering from inside the cornucopia. Wrap the cornucopia loosely and store in a cool, dry place (not in the refrigerator) until ready to use. The cornucopia can be baked a day before serving.

SERVING: Fill the cornucopia to overflowing with an assortment of nuts and fresh and dried fruit.

YIELD: 1 cornucopia

Chicken Pot Pie

Rhode Island Johnnycakes

Golden Apricot–Carrot Soup;
Mascarpone with Figs;
Ruby Pear Soup

Chocolate Meringue Cake

Raspberry–Pistachio Bombe

Pastry Cornucopia

CHOCOLATE MERINGUE CAKE

Crisp chocolate meringue and rich chocolate puff pastry are layered together with a creamy chocolate ganache. Developed by renowned pastry chef Albert Kumin, this elegant creation is our hands-down favorite chocolate cake.

Preparation and Cooking: *For the Chocolate Meringue,* heat the oven to 225°F. Line 2 large baking sheets with parchment paper. Draw two 8-inch circles on the paper. Fold the circles in quarters to mark the center.

Combine the egg whites and 2 tablespoons of the sugar in a bowl and set aside. In the top of a double boiler over hot water, melt the chocolate to lukewarm, about 100°F, and set aside. Or melt it in a microwave oven on medium or medium-low power, stirring occasionally. Combine the remaining 1 cup plus 2 tablespoons sugar and water in a small saucepan and bring to a boil, brushing any hardened sugar down the side of the pan with a pastry brush moistened with water.

While the syrup is boiling, beat the reserved egg whites to soft peaks. Cook syrup mixture to soft-ball stage (233°F). Add the sugar syrup to the egg whites in a slow stream, beating constantly, and continue to beat slowly until the bowl is cool to the touch. Fold the melted chocolate into meringue.

Fill a pastry bag, fitted with a plain ½-inch tip, with meringue. On parchment paper marked with circles, pipe out the meringue in a spiral, starting in the center, and making as even an 8-inch circle as possible.

To make the strips of meringue edging, use a flat pastry tip with a jagged edge and an opening that is ⅞ inch by ¼ inch. Pipe out thin strips of the remaining meringue that length of the prepared baking sheet. At least 6 feet of strips are needed to complete the cake.

Put the meringue in the preheated oven and bake until it starts to dry, about 1½ hours. The strips should dry out first. Leave in the turned-off oven overnight to dry thoroughly. Carefully peel off the parchment paper. If meringue cracks, it can be put together with

Chocolate Meringue

6 egg whites
1¼ cups granulated sugar
¼ pound unsweetened chocolate
⅓ cup water

Chocolate Pastry

¼ pound semisweet chocolate
½ pound unsalted butter
1¾ cups flour (½ pound)
¼ teaspoon salt
5 tablespoons cold water

Ganache

10 ounces semisweet chocolate
⅔ cup heavy cream
4 teaspoons butter
4 teaspoons granulated sugar

1 pound semisweet chocolate
½ pound bar semisweet chocolate for curls (optional)
Confectioners' sugar for dusting

ganache during cake assembly. Store the meringue in an airtight container until ready to use.

For the Chocolate Pastry, in the top of a double boiler over hot water, melt chocolate to 100°F. Or melt in a microwave oven on medium or medium-low power, stirring occasionally.

Using a pastry blender or your fingers, work the cold butter into the flour until the pieces are the size of hazelnuts. Make a well in the center of the mixture and add the salt and water. Gently mix until distributed. Incorporate the chocolate into the flour mixture with your hands until the mixture is crumbly and just forms a ball when lightly pressed together. Set aside to rest for 5 minutes.

Roll the dough out to about a ¼-inch thickness on a floured work surface. Fold into thirds and refrigerate for 10 minutes. Repeat this folding, rolling, and chilling procedure three times. Divide the dough in quarters and let rest, refrigerated and covered, for 20 minutes.

On a cool, floured work surface, roll out each quarter of the dough into a round about 9 inches in diameter. Put the rounds on unlined baking sheets and chill for 10 minutes. Prick the surface of the dough thoroughly (every ½ inch or so) with a fork.

Heat the oven to 400°F. Bake the pastry in the preheated oven for 8 minutes. Lower the oven temperature to 350°F and bake until just crisp, about 5 minutes.

Carefully remove with a spatula and put on a rack to cool to room temperature. While still warm, trim into 8-inch rounds.

For the ganache, chop the chocolate into ½-inch pieces. Combine the cream, butter, and sugar in a saucepan and bring just to a boil. Remove from the heat and add the chocolate all at once. Stir until the chocolate has completely melted and the mixture is smooth and well blended. Set aside at room temperature.

Melt 1 pound of semisweet chocolate in the top of a double boiler over hot water over very low heat or in a microwave oven on medium or medium-low power, stirring occasionally. It should be just lukewarm (100°F).

To assemble the cake, carefully coat each layer of Chocolate Pastry with the melted chocolate. Let the chocolate set; then turn the layers and coat the other sides with chocolate. Let the chocolate set.

Put the first layer of Chocolate Pastry on cake plate. Cover with ganache, add a meringue layer, and then spread it with ganache. Repeat layering, ending with a pastry layer. Trim any uneven layers carefully with a serrated knife. Cover the top and sides with the remaining ganache. Carefully cut the meringue strips into even lengths the height of cake, using a serrated knife. Press the meringue strips into place vertically around the outside of cake, completely covering the sides.

For the chocolate curls, warm ½-pound chocolate bar by rubbing the top with your hand. Using a long, thin knife held at a slight angle, scrape off chocolate curls. (If the chocolate is too warm or too cold, it will not form curls.) Place the chocolate curls side-by-side in rows on top of the cake, cutting uneven ends with a knife heated in boiling water.

Cut five ½-inch-wide strips of parchment or other paper, put them diagonally across the top of the cake and dust lightly with confectioners' sugar. Carefully remove the paper strips. Allow the cake to set for 1 to 4 hours at room temperature before serving.

SERVING: Cut carefully with a serrated knife.

YIELD: 1 8-inch cake

STRAWBERRY–RHUBARB MILLE FEUILLE

The name mille feuille, a thousand leaves, describes the flaky, many-layered pastry of the classic French dessert, here updated with a springtime filling of strawberries and rhubarb.

1 recipe Quick Puff Pastry (page 263)

Strawberry–Rhubarb Filling

1 pound fresh or *frozen rhubarb*
1 pint fresh or *frozen strawberries*
1 to 2 oranges
½ cup water
½ cup sugar

Sweetened Whipped Cream

2 cups heavy cream
⅓ cup sugar
2 tablespoons orange liqueur, kirsch,
  or light rum (optional)
½ teaspoon vanilla extract

Confectioners' sugar for dusting

Preparation: If using frozen rhubarb and strawberries, defrost. Make the pastry. Cut the dough in half. On a lightly floured surface, roll each half into an ⅛-inch-thick, 12- by 18-inch rectangle. Dust the surface of the dough with flour to prevent sticking. Line two 11- by 17-inch jelly roll pans with parchment paper. Put one rectangle into each prepared pan and chill for 30 minutes.

Heat the oven to 375°F. Pierce the pastry at ½-inch intervals with a fork. Cover each rectangle with parchment paper and then set another pan on top to weight the entire piece of pastry.

Bake in the preheated oven for 15 minutes. Remove the top pans and paper. Bake the pastries until browned and cooked through, about 10 minutes more. Transfer the pastries from the pans to cutting surface.

Using a 10-inch cardboard circle or bottom of a cake pan as a template, cut each rectangle into 1 whole circle and 1 half-circle. Cool the circles and scraps.

For the filling, remove all the leaves and strings from the rhubarb. Cut the rhubarb into ½-inch pieces. You should have about 3 cups rhubarb.

Grate 1 tablespoon of zest from the oranges. Squeeze ½ cup juice and strain.

In a saucepan, bring the orange juice, water, and sugar to a simmer. Add the rhubarb and turn off heat. Cool the rhubarb in the syrup. Drain.

Rinse and hull the strawberries. Slice the strawberries into the rhubarb. Add the orange zest and fold together gently. Set aside to drain thoroughly.

For the whipped cream, combine the cream, sugar, optional orange liqueur, kirsch, or rum, and vanilla in a mixing bowl. Beat to stiff peaks.

ASSEMBLY: Up to 1 hour before serving, spread 1 pastry circle with one quarter of the whipped cream. Using a ½-inch plain tip, pipe a border of whipped cream around the edge of the layer to act as a dike for the filling. Spread half of the filling over the layer. Top with 2 half-circles and then repeat the layering of one quarter of the cream, piping a border, and spreading the remaining filling. Top with the remaining pastry circle. Press down gently just so layers adhere. Spread the whipped cream that flows from between the layers around sides of mille feuille. Crush the pastry scraps and press into the cream. Dust the top with confectioners' sugar.

SERVING: Cut the mille feuille in half and then into wedges using a sharp, serrated knife in a gentle sawing motion.

YIELD: 10 to 12 servings

CHOCOLATE–MINT PASTRIES

These delicious cream pastries are made with time-saving Quick Puff Pastry and filled with the all-time favorite end-of-meal flavor combination—chocolate and mint.

½ recipe Quick Puff Pastry
    (recipe follows)
    Sugar for coating

Chocolate–Mint Filling

¾ pound semisweet chocolate
1¼ cups heavy cream
3 tablespoons white crème de menthe
    Mint sprigs for garnish (optional)

Preparation: Make the pastry. Line an 11- by 17-inch jelly roll pan with parchment paper. On a lightly floured work surface, roll the dough into a 1-inch-thick, 8- by 24-inch rectangle. Dust the dough and surface with additional flour as needed to prevent the dough from sticking to the rolling pin or surface. Cut the dough into eight 1- by 24-inch strips. With a brush dipped into water, moisten the long edge of one of the strips. Start with the moistened edge at the top facing down toward the tube and wind the strip, without stretching it, around a 5-inch-long cannoli tube mold, and as you wind, overlap the moistened edge of dough onto the dough already on the mold. Repeat with the remaining dough strips, winding each around a separate mold. Put pastries onto the prepared pan so that the end of each rolled strip is underneath. Chill for 1 hour.

Heat the oven to 375°F. Quickly roll the chilled horns in sugar and shake off any excess. Return to the pan, end of strip down.

Bake in the preheated oven until golden, 20 to 25 minutes. Carefully remove from the forms and cool on a wire rack.

For the filling, chop the chocolate into small pieces. In a heavy saucepan, heat ½ cup of the cream to a simmer. Remove from the heat and add the chocolate. Let stand for 1 minute and then whisk until smooth and chocolate has melted. Strain into a large bowl and cool to room temperature. Stir in crème de menthe.

In another bowl, whip the remaining ¾ cup cream until firm. Fold into the chocolate mixture.

ASSEMBLY: Up to an hour before serving, put the filling into a pastry bag fitted with a medium star tube and pipe into the cooled pastries.

SERVING: Garnish ends with mint sprigs if desired.

YIELD: 8 5-inch horns

QUICK PUFF PASTRY

1¼ cups all-purpose flour
⅓ cup cake flour
½ pound unsalted butter
½ teaspoon salt
2 teaspoons lemon juice
Cold water

Preparation: Sift the flours into a bowl. Rub 2 tablespoons of the cold butter into the flour until it disappears. Cut the remaining butter into ½-inch cubes. Add the butter cubes to the flour mixture and toss just to separate and distribute the butter.

Dissolve the salt in the lemon juice in a 1-cup measure. Add cold water to make ½ cup and add to the flour-butter mixture. Toss gently. Add a few drops of water if necessary to make the dough hold together. Press the dough together into a rectangle.

Turn the dough out onto a well-floured surface. Flour the top of dough. Using the palm of your hand, press down the dough to flatten into a rough 4- by 9-inch rectangle. Roll out to 9- by 18-inch rectangle. Sprinkle lightly with additional flour as needed to prevent sticking. Keep the corners as square as possible.

Fold both short ends into the center and then fold in half to make 4 layers. The folded package will resemble a 4½- by 9-inch book.

Position the package of dough so that the "spine" of the book is on the left. Dust the surface of the dough with flour and repeat the rolling and folding as before.

Roll and fold dough a third time. If the dough is very soft, chill for 15 to 20 minutes before completing the third rolling and folding.

Wrap the dough in plastic wrap. Chill for 1 hour before using to relax elasticity.

YIELD: about 1¼ pounds pastry

PAPAYA–RUM BABAS

Diced papayas are incorporated into traditional baba dough to create an unusual French/Caribbean dessert.

Babas

¼ pound dried papaya
2 cups water
¼ cup milk
4 tablespoons unsalted butter
3 tablespoons sugar
1 package active dry yeast
1 egg
1 egg yolk
¼ teaspoon grated lemon zest
⅛ teaspoon salt
2¼ cups flour

Rum Syrup

Reserved papaya poaching liquid
1 cup sugar
1 slice lemon
1 slice orange
¾ cup dark rum

½ cup heavy cream

Preparation and Cooking: *For the babas,* simmer the papaya with the 2 cups water over low heat until the papaya is softened, about 15 minutes. Drain and reserve the liquid. Chop the papaya into ¼-inch dice.

In another saucepan, heat the milk with the butter and sugar until the butter has melted. Cool to lukewarm.

In a small bowl, sprinkle the yeast over ¼ cup of warm water and stir to dissolve. In another small bowl, lightly beat the egg and extra egg yolk. Add the lemon zest and salt.

Put the flour in bowl and make a well in the center. Add the milk, yeast, and egg mixtures and beat with a wooden spoon until well mixed. Knead by hand, by picking up pieces of dough and slapping them against the side of the bowl, or knead in a mixer until the dough is elastic enough to stretch 8 to 10 inches without breaking, about 5 minutes. Form the dough into a ball, put in a buttered bowl, turn to butter all sides, cover, and put in a warm place until doubled in bulk, 1 to 2 hours.

Butter 8 baba molds. Punch down the dough and add the papaya. Flour your hands and tear off golf-ball-sized pieces of dough. Put the dough in prepared molds, filling the molds no more than halfway. Set aside, uncovered, until the dough has risen to the tops of the molds, about 45 minutes.

Heat the oven to 375°F. Bake in the preheated oven until the babas are browned and shrink slightly from the sides of the molds, 20 to 25 minutes. Remove from the molds.

For the syrup, add enough water to the poaching liquid to make 1½ cups. Combine with the sugar, lemon slice, and orange slice in a saucepan. Bring to a boil, stirring. Turn the heat to low and simmer for 5 minutes. Remove from the heat and add the rum.

Put the warm babas in a roasting pan or other large container and spoon the warm syrup over them. Baste frequently until the babas absorb as much as they can without falling apart. This may take 30 to 45 minutes. The babas may be refrigerated until serving time and then brought back to room temperature. Whip the cream.

SERVING: Serve the babas topped with the whipped cream.

YIELD: 8 babas

CHOCOLATE–CHERRY BAVARIAN PIE

This beautiful pie combines several chocolate textures—a crunchy cookie crust, creamy Bavarois filling, and a firm glaze made from heavy cream and chocolate.

Cherries

1 1-pound can Morello or Bing cherries in syrup
½ cup water
¼ cup sugar
¼ cup kirsch or brandy

Chocolate Cookie Crust

12 ounces chocolate wafers
3 ounces semisweet chocolate
1 tablespoon water

Chocolate Bavarois

2 ounces extra-bittersweet chocolate
3 egg yolks
½ cup sugar
2 teaspoons unflavored gelatin
1 cup milk
¼ teaspoon vanilla
⅔ cup heavy cream
4 teaspoons kirsch or brandy

Glaze

7 ounces semisweet chocolate
½ cup plus 2 tablespoons heavy cream
Corn syrup for glazing the cherries

Preparation: *For the cherries,* at least 12 hours ahead, drain the cherries, reserving ½ cup of the syrup. In a saucepan, combine the syrup, water, and sugar and bring to a boil, stirring. Add the cherries and simmer, covered, for 1 minute. Remove from the heat and add the kirsch or brandy. Cover and let stand for 12 to 24 hours. At this point, cherries can be refrigerated indefinitely.

For the pie, remove the cherries from the liquid and drain thoroughly on paper towels.

For the crust, melt the chocolate in the top of a double boiler over hot water. Whir the cookies in a food processor to fine crumbs and incorporate the chocolate. Add the water and whir for a few seconds. Line a 10-inch pie pan with aluminum foil, allowing the foil to extend slightly over the edges for easy removal. Press the crumbs into the pan, making the bottom as thin as possible and building up the sides. Put all but 6 drained cherries into the shell and refrigerate until the filling is prepared.

For the Chocolate Bavarois, grate the chocolate into a bowl. In another mixing bowl, combine the egg yolks with ¼ cup of the sugar and the gelatin. Beat until doubled in volume. In a saucepan, bring the milk and remaining ¼ cup of sugar to a boil. Gradually add the hot milk to the egg yolks, whisking constantly. Return the mixture to the pan and heat, stirring constantly with a wooden spoon, until it thickens just enough to coat the back of a spoon lightly (160°F). Do not boil. Remove immediately from the heat and strain into the grated chocolate, stirring until the chocolate is completely melted. Add the vanilla.

Whip the cream. Set the bowl of chocolate mixture in a larger bowl or pan of ice water and whisk until it starts to set around the edges and mound slightly but is still very liquid. Whisk in the kirsch or brandy and one quarter of the whipped cream. Fold in the remaining whipped cream. Remove from the ice water and pour the Bavarois over the cherries in the pie shell. Cover with plastic wrap and refrigerate until set, about 1 hour.

For the glaze, grate the chocolate. Bring the cream almost to a boil and add about 6 ounces of the chocolate, stirring gently until it is fully melted and the mixture is smooth. If necessary, heat slightly, being careful not to incorporate any air bubbles. Cool just until tepid. Pour about half of the glaze onto the pie. Using a long, metal spatula, smooth evenly onto the surface. Refrigerate until set, at least 1 hour, before decorating.

Lift the pie out of the pan, peel off the foil, and put on a serving platter. Melt the remaining chocolate over hot water and stir into the remaining glaze. Set the bowl of glaze over ice and stir gently until the glaze is thick enough for piping. Do not beat the glaze or it will lighten in color.

To decorate the pie, put the glaze in a pastry bag fitted with a ¼-inch star tip. Pipe a border around the edge of the crust. Brush the reserved cherries lightly with corn syrup and arrange on top of the pie. Pipe the decorative leaves for the cherries. Refrigerate for at least 1 hour to set.

SERVING: Cut the pie with a sharp knife that has been dipped in hot water and dried. Support the rim of the pie with one hand while cutting.

YIELD: 8 servings

CHOCOLATE SOUFFLÉ CAKE

This flourless chocolate cake is essentially a soufflé baked in a flat pan.
It's frosted with ganache, a simple mixture of cream and chocolate that
is a basic component of French pastry making, and decorated with
meringue sticks.

Chocolate Meringue Sticks

⅔ cup confectioners' sugar
1 tablespoon cocoa
3 egg whites
¼ cup plus 3 tablespoons granulated sugar

Whipped Ganache

8 ounces semisweet chocolate
2 cups heavy cream

Chocolate Soufflé Cake

5 ounces semisweet chocolate
7 eggs
¾ cup plus 2 tablespoons granulated sugar

Preparation and Cooking: *For the meringue,* line a
large ungreased baking sheet with parchment paper or
aluminum foil. Heat the oven to 200°F.

Sift together the confectioners' sugar and cocoa. Beat
the egg whites until frothy. Gradually add 2 tablespoons of the granulated sugar, beating until soft peaks
form. Add another tablespoon of sugar and continue
beating until stiff peaks form. Gradually beat in the
remaining ¼ cup of sugar, beating until the mixture is
stiff and shiny. Fold the sugar-cocoa mixture into the
meringue. Fit a pastry bag with a ½-inch plain tip and
fill with the meringue. Pipe the meringue in long lines
about ⅜ inch apart onto the prepared baking sheet.
Bake in the preheated oven until dry, about 50 minutes.
If the center is just a bit sticky, it will dry out after
removal from the oven. Remove carefully from the
baking sheet and cut or break into uneven lengths rang-
ing from 2 to 4 inches. Store, tightly covered, at room
temperature.

For the ganache, whir the chocolate in a food processor
until it is in very fine particles. In a saucepan, heat the
cream to the boiling point. With the processor running,
pour the hot cream through the feed tube in a steady
stream. Pour the mixture into a large mixing bowl and
refrigerate just until cool to the touch, about 1½ hours.
(If mixture gets too cold it will start to thicken before
you begin to whip in air, and so it will need to be
warmed slightly. If not cold enough, it will not whip.)
Beat just until the mixture thickens and mounds. (It
should not begin to form even soft peaks, or it will
become grainy instead of velvety. If this should happen,
you can melt, chill, and then beat the ganache again.)
Set aside at room temperature.

For the cake, melt the chocolate in the top of a double boiler over hot water. Set aside to cool.

Put an oven rack one-third up from the bottom and heat the oven to 350°F. Oil a 10- by 15-inch jelly roll pan and line it with parchment paper or wax paper, allowing the paper to extend slightly over the short edges of the pan for easy removal. Butter and flour the paper.

Separate the eggs. Beat ¾ cup of the sugar with the egg yolks until fluffy and pale yellow, about 5 minutes. Beat in the melted chocolate.

In a large mixing bowl, beat egg whites until soft peaks form. Gradually add the remaining 2 tablespoons of sugar, beating almost to stiff peaks. Stir about one quarter of the egg whites into the chocolate mixture to lighten it. Gently fold in the remaining egg whites. Pour into the prepared pan, spreading evenly with a spatula. Bake until the cake puffs and loses its shine but is not yet springy to the touch, about 20 minutes.

Remove the cake from the oven, cover with a towel, and cool to room temperature. Uncover and, using a cardboard oval template measuring 9¾ by 7 inches, cut two ovals from the cake.

To assemble the cake, spread about one third of the ganache (a ½-inch layer) onto a cake oval and top with second cake oval. Spread the remaining ganache over the top and sides of the cake. The cake will be about 1½ inches high. Surround the cake with meringue sticks, pressing the flat sides of the sticks against the ganache. This can be done up to 2 days ahead. Refrigerate uncovered.

SERVING: Up to 1 hour ahead, insert the remaining meringue sticks into cake so that they reach base. All flat ends should face the same direction. Allow cake to sit at room temperature for 1 hour before serving.

YIELD: 10 servings

Ham-and-Cheese-Stuffed Mushrooms   Sancerre Rosé
    (page 17)

Risotto with Artichokes (page 102)   Meursault
Grill-Poached Snapper Stuffed with Fennel
    (page 154)

Praline and Chocolate–Espresso Bombe   Quady Elysium Black Muscat
    (page 248)

Peppery Lemon–Rosemary Chicken Winglets   Robert Mondavi Fumé Blanc
    (page 157)

Bulgur Garden Salad (page 36)

Grilled Ginger Duck Breasts with Peaches   Rutherford Hill Merlot
    (page 158)

Chocolate Soufflé Cake (page 268)

RECIPE CREDITS

Some of the recipes in this book have on-page attribution. Additional recipe credits are given below.

Arugula Salad *Susan Herrmann Loomis*
Biscoitos de Porto *Elene Margot Kolb*
Blueberry–Corn Muffins *Anne Byrn*
Cabbage Pancakes *Carol Cutler*
Cabbage Pie *Carol Cutler*
Chicken Leg Sauté with Mushrooms and Lovage *Sheryl Julian*
Chicken and Vegetable Salad *Nancy Barr*
Chocolate–Cherry Bavarian Pie *Rose Levy Beranbaum*
Chocolate–Mint Pastries *Nicholas Malgieri*
Chocolate Soufflé Cake *Rose Levy Beranbaum*
Cold Cream of Brown Rice Soup with Sorrel *Michael McLaughlin*
Cold Grapefruit Soufflé *Steven Raichlen*
Cornbread with Ham and Maple Butter *Susy Davidson*
Cornmeal Pasta with Ham and Pepper Sauce *Anne Byrn*
Country Terrine *Merle Ellis*
Cucumber and Marinated Tomato Rolls *Elizabeth Wheeler*
Cured Pork Sausage with Rice *Judy Rodgers*
Eggplant Rollatini Stuffed with Prosciutto and Sun-Dried Tomatoes *Steven Raichlen*
Eggplant and Smoked Cheese Pie *Steven Raichlen*
Feta–Vegetable Pie with Herbed Crust *Roberta Dehman Hershon*
Fried Cheese *Harriet Reilly*
Fried Chicken Salad *Anne Byrn*
Goat Cheese and Scallion Tart *Adrienne Welch*

Green Bean and Roasted Red Pepper Frittata *Kathy Gunst*
Green and White Ravioli in Broth *Nancy Barr*
Grill-Poached Snapper Stuffed with Fennel *Phillip Schulz*
Grits, Greens, and Garlic Soufflé *Anne Byrn*
Ham-and-Cheese-Stuffed Mushrooms *Susan Goloboy and Dale Whitesell*
Herb Pâté *Merle Ellis*
Herbed Cheese Biscuits *Anne Byrn*
Honey–Oat Waffles with Raspberries and Cream *Michael McLaughlin*
Jalapeño Pasta with Lobster and Cucumber *Barbara Sause*
Lobster–Grapefruit Salad Jean-Pierre Capelle *Steven Raichlen*
Noodles with Celery Cabbage *Carol Cutler*
Parsley Pizza *Carol Cutler*
Pinwheel Cake *Susy Davidson*
Piquant Beef Salad *Nancy Barr*
Pistachio Butter Cookies *Jane Stacey*
Popovers *Judith Sutton*
Pork Tenderloin Sauté with Summer Apples and Plums *Sheryl Julian*
Praline and Chocolate–Espresso Bombe *Sheryl Julian*
Provençale Green Bean Salad *Kathy Gunst*
Raspberry–Pistachio Bombe *Jane Butel*
Red Raspberry Mousse *Carol E. Smaglinski*
Rhode Island Johnnycakes *Joan Nathan*
Risotto with Artichokes *Pat Opler*
Saffron Coffeecake *Sandra Gluck*

Salad Sandwiches *Susy Davidson*

Salmon–Butter Triangles with Caviar and Dill *Susy Davidson*

Salmon Sauté with Corn and Sugar Snap Peas *Sheryl Julian*

Sauté of Chicken Breasts, Summer Squash, and Yellow Pepper *Sheryl Julian*

Seafood and Barley Salad with Lemon and Basil *Michael McLaughlin*

Shellfish in Dill Brine *Jon Rowley*

Smoked Duck Salad *Richard Sax*

Stir-Fried Chinese String Beans with Sausage and Oyster Sauce *Kathy Gunst*

Stir-Fried Napa Cabbage and Smoked Pork *Carol Cutler*

Strawberry–Rhubarb Mille Feuille *Nicholas Malgieri*

Sugar Snap, Red Cabbage, and Ham Salad with Walnut Vinaigrette *Sarah Belk*

Summer Seviche *Michael McLaughlin*

Tomato and Mozzarella Tart *Adrienne Welch*

Tortellini Salad with Red Wine–Herb Vinaigrette *Michael McLaughlin*

Veal Sausage with Greens *Judy Rodgers*

Venison Hash *Cynthia Jubera*

Venison Soup with Dill Dumplings *Richard Sax*

Warm Oriental Grilled Tuna or Swordfish and Bean Salad *Kathy Gunst*

Zucchini "Pasta" with Tomato–Clam Sauce *Elizabeth Wheeler*

Zucchini and Yellow Squash Tart *Adrienne Welch*

Index

PHOTO CREDITS

RICHARD FELBER:
Cabbage Pie
Chocolate Meringue Cake
Focaccia with Herbed Oil and Roasted Garlic
Lobster–Grapefruit Salad Jean-Pierre Capelle
Olive Pasta
Pastry Cornucopia

VINCENT LEE:
Chicken Pot Pie
Chilled Sorrel Soup
Fried Chicken Salad
Miniature Scallion Crêpes with Salmon Caviar
   and Sour Cream
Raspberry–Pistachio Bombe
Rhode Island Johnnycakes

Skewered Portuguese Scallops
Smoked Chicken Salad
Smoked Duck Salad
Venison Soup with Dill Dumplings
Summer Seviche

NANCY McFARLAND:
Feta–Vegetable Pie with Herbed Crust
Golden Apricot–Carrot Soup/Mascarpone
   with Figs/Ruby Pear Soup
Pork Tenderloin Sauté with Apples and Plums
Salmon Sauté with Corn and Sugar Snap Peas
Veal Sausage with Greens

JERRY SIMPSON:
Smoked Catfish–Egg Roll Salad